A Cross-Cultural Conceptual Study of the Emotion of קצף in the Hebrew Bible and the Folk Theory of the Emotion of *Ngoò* in the Kĩkamba Language

George Mbithi Mutuku

© 2023 George Mbithi Mutuku

Published 2023 by Langham Monographs
An imprint of Langham Publishing
www.langhampublishing.org

Langham Publishing and its imprints are a ministry of Langham Partnership

Langham Partnership
PO Box 296, Carlisle, Cumbria, CA3 9WZ, UK
www.langham.org

ISBNs:
978-1-83973-238-6 Print
978-1-83973-810-4 ePub
978-1-83973-811-1 Mobi
978-1-83973-812-8 PDF

George MbithiMutuku has asserted his right under the Copyright, Designs and Patents Act, 1988 to be identified as the Author of this work.

All rights reserved. No part of this publication may be reproduced, stored in a retrieval system or transmitted, in any form or by any means, electronic, mechanical, photocopying, recording or otherwise, without the prior written permission of the publisher or the Copyright Licensing Agency.

Requests to reuse content from Langham Publishing are processed through PLSclear. Please visit www.plsclear.com to complete your request.

All Scripture translations in this work, unless otherwise indicated, are the author's own.

Scripture quotations marked (NIV) are taken from the Holy Bible, New International Version®, NIV®. Copyright © 1973, 1978, 1984, 2011 by Biblica, Inc.™ Used by permission of Zondervan.

Scripture quotations marked (NRSV) are from the New Revised Standard Version Bible, copyright © 1989 National Council of the Churches of Christ in the United States of America. Used by permission. All rights reserved.

British Library Cataloguing-in-Publication Data
A catalogue record for this book is available from the British Library

ISBN: 978-1-83973-238-6

Cover & Book Design: projectluz.com

Langham Partnership actively supports theological dialogue and an author's right to publish but does not necessarily endorse the views and opinions set forth here or in works referenced within this publication, nor can we guarantee technical and grammatical correctness. Langham Partnership does not accept any responsibility or liability to persons or property as a consequence of the reading, use or interpretation of its published content.

Dr. George Mbithi Mutuku's comprehensive study about how קָצַף (anger) was understood and expressed in the ancient Hebrew culture is very informative. His observation that some aspects of קָצַף as conveyed in the Hebrew Bible are lacking in the Kĩkamba Bible, such as nonexistence of the word *ngoò* that expresses intense anger, is incontestable. His 5-point logic on how קָצַף is perceived and dealt with, either by retribution or by "swallowing" it, helps the reader concerning development of the vital virtue of anger management. Thus, the research has demonstrated systematically and carefully the importance of cross-cultural communication in preaching, teaching and Bible translation. I therefore recommend the book to students in institutions of higher learning who are doing biblical and translation studies, and other serious scholars, teachers and preachers of the word of God.

Nathan Nzyoka Joshua, PhD
Lecturer and Head of Department for Biblical Studies,
Africa International University, Kenya

George Mbithi Mutuku has had extensive graduate level education in biblical Hebrew exegesis and has an intimate knowledge of both the Kĩkamba language and Akamba culture. In this monograph Dr. Mutuku has clearly demonstrated that the biblical Hebrew concept קָצַף would be best rendered in the Kĩkamba Bible by *ngoò*, a word that hitherto has been unused in the Kĩkamba Old Testament. This work is highly recommended for graduate level biblical Hebrew exegesis classes, Old Testament exegetes, and Bible translators.

Mark Mercer, ThD
Senior Lecturer (retired),
Africa International University, Kenya

Contents

Abstract ix
List of Abbreviations xi
Chapter 1 1
Introduction
    1.1 Unexplored Field: Motivation for This Study 3
    1.2 A Summary of the Lexical Meaning of קצף in the BHS 4
    1.3 A Summary of *Ngoò* in the Kĩkamba Language 5
    1.4 The Research Questions 6
    1.5 Previous Scholarship (in Addition to the Lexical Meaning)
        on קצף in the Hebrew Bible 6
        1.5.1 The Same Contextual Use of חמה and קצף 6
        1.5.2 Zacharias Kotzé: Humoral Theory as Motivation for
            Anger Metaphors in the Hebrew Bible 7
        1.5.3 Terence Collins: The Physiology of Tears in the
            Old Testament 9
    1.6 Limitation of Previous Studies on קצף 10
        1.6.1 Polysemous 11
        1.6.2 Emphatic, Stylistic, Metonymic and Distinctive
            Nature of a Word: Author's Choice 11
        1.6.3 Conceptual Study of קצף 12
    1.7 Thesis Statement 12
    1.8 Contribution to Biblical Scholarship 12
    1.9 Synopsis of the Chapters 13
Chapter 2 15
Methodology
    2.1 Charles Fillmore's Frame Semantics 15
        2.1.1 Development of the Term "Frame" as Used in Frame
            Semantics 17
        2.1.2 Frame, Base, and Domain: Overlapping Terminology 21
        2.1.3 Components of the Frame Semantics Theory 23
        2.1.4 The Value of Frame Semantics 24
    2.2 Richard Shweder and Jonathan Haidt's Symbolic Approach 31
    2.3 Daniel M. T. Fessler's "Logic" 33
    2.4 Qualitative Field Research 34
    2.5 Proposed Complementary Approach 35

Chapter 3 37
The קצף *Frame*
   3.1 The קצף Frame 39
      3.1.1 The Core Frame Elements of קצף: Investigation of
         קצף in the BHS 39
      3.1.2 Peripheral Frame Elements 90
      3.1.3 Extrathematic Frame Elements: Parallelism in Poetry 92
   3.2 Distinctiveness of קצף Frame 120
      3.2.1 The קצף Frame 120
      3.2.2 The Noun Forms of קֶצֶף: God (Deity) Is the Ego
         (Superior to Subordinate) 121
      3.2.3 The Noun Forms of קֶצֶף: Human Is the Ego 132
      3.2.4 The Verbal Form of קָצַף: God Is the Ego 137
      3.2.5 The Verbal Form of קָצַף: Human Is the Ego 156
   3.3 The Homonym of קצף 180

Chapter 4 183
The Akamba Folk Theory of Ngoò *"Anger"*
   4.1 The Akamba Origin 183
   4.2 The Kīkamba Language 184
   4.3 The Akamba Emotional Category 188
   4.4 The Akamba Folk Theory of *Ngoò* "Anger" 192
      4.4.1 Analysis of the *Ngoò* "Anger" Scenario 192
      4.4.2 *Ngoò* "Anger": The Source 198
      4.4.3 Event and State 199
      4.4.4 Somatic Phenomenology 201
      4.4.5 Antecedent Conditions 202
      4.4.6 Affective Phenomenon of *Ngoò* "Anger" 203
      4.4.7 Self-appraisal 203
      4.4.8 Social Appraisal 204
      4.4.9 *Ngoò* "Anger" as an Inferred Emotion 204
   4.5 Classification of Kīkamba Anger Words 206
   4.6 The BHS Lexical Equivalent of *Ngoò* "Anger" 208
   4.7 *Ngoò* Frame: Relationship-retribution 209
   4.8 Distinctiveness of *Ngoò* 210
      4.8.1 *Ngoò* Is an Abstract Object 210
      4.8.2 The Usage of *Ngoò* Presupposes Intended Retribution 211
      4.8.3 *Ngoò* Is Associated with Leaders 213

Chapter 5 217
Frames of קצף and Ngoò: The Differences, Similarities and How Some Facets of the קצף Frame are Represented in the Kĩkamba Bible
    5.1 A Brief History of the Kĩkamba Bible..217
    5.2 Differences of the קצף and *Ngoò* Frames.....................................220
    5.3 Similarities of the קצף and *Ngoò* Frames....................................221
        5.3.1 Both קצף and *Ngoò* Are Abstract Objects 221
        5.3.2 Both *Ngoò* and קצף Have Intended Retribution................222
        5.3.3 Both *Ngoò* and קצף Are Associated with People in Authority or Who Have Specific Roles...222
    5.4 The קצף Frame Representation in the Kĩkamba Bible.................223
        5.4.1 The Translation of קָצַף Verbal Forms in the Kĩkamba Bible..223
        5.4.2 The Translation of קֶצֶף Noun Forms in the Kĩkamba Bible 229
        5.4.3 The קצף Frame Is Partially Imported into the Kĩkamba Bible..235
    5.5 Extra Words for Anger in Kĩkamba..244
    5.6 The Value of Cross-Cultural Study in Biblical Studies 245

Chapter 6 247
Conclusion and Recommendations
    6.1 Conclusion 247
    6.2 Recommendations..249
        6.2.1 Cross-Cultural Study of Scripture 249
        6.2.2 Consistency in the Kĩkamba Translation 249
        6.2.3 Improvement of Kĩkamba Orthography 250
        6.2.4 Development of Kĩkamba Lexicography..............................250

Bibliography...251

Abstract

This dissertation is a cross-cultural conceptual study of the emotion of קצף in the Hebrew Bible and the folk theory of the emotion of *ngoò* in the Kīkamba language. The central argument advanced is that a cross-cultural conceptual study of the emotion of קצף reveals how קצף was conceptualized in the ancient Hebrew culture, and its comparative study with the folk theory of the emotion of *ngoò* shows that concept of *ngoò* would have been the best rendering for the Hebrew concept קצף in the Kīkamba Bible. In advancing this argument, three goals are met: First, this research explains the conceptualization of קצף in the ancient Hebrew culture. In particular, this research demonstrates how קצף functions within the קצף frame which will be explained in detail in chapter 3. This frame is supported by the use of קֶצֶף as subject accompanied by the הָיָה, יָצָא and בּוֹא verbs. Second, it employs a cross-cultural study of קצף and *ngoò*, and demonstrates the variance in their conceptual facets, and third, it demonstrates the value of cross-cultural study in biblical studies.

The author has used a variety of methods to analyze the collected data but the main method used is frame semantics by Charles Fillmore. This method is appropriate since it demonstrates that the meaning of words is anchored in the "frames" of those words. Therefore, a student is encouraged to, first, avoid heavy reliance on dictionaries to determine the meaning and usage of words. Instead, the student should make every effort to study the contexts of the words or phrases and their historical setting. Second, the student of Scripture or of any literature is warned not to assume that the words of a particular language carry a universal meaning. It is, therefore, prudent to engage in cross-cultural study and ensure that the meaning of the parent language is transferred into the receptor language.

List of Abbreviations

AB	The Anchor Bible
ASP	Aspect
BDB	*Brown-Driver-Briggs Hebrew and English Lexicon*
BHS	*Biblia Hebraica Stuttgartensia*
DCH	The Dictionary of Classical Hebrew
DEM	Demonstrative
FOC	Focus
FUT_a	Immediate Future
FUT_b	Distant Future
FUT_c	Remote Future
FV	Final Vowel
HAB	Habitual
HALOT	*The Hebrew and Aramaic Lexicon of the Old Testament*
BHS	Hebrew Bible
ICC	International Critical Commentary
IMPER	Imperative
INF	Infinitive
NABRE	New American Bible Revised Edition
NAC	New American Commentary
NASB	New American Standard Bible
NEG	Negation
NKJV	New King James Version
NIDOTTE	*New International Dictionary of Old Testament Theology & Exegesis*
NIV	New International Version, 2011 Edition by Biblica, Inc.

NRSV	New Revised Standard Version
OTL	Old Testament Library
PASS	Passive
PERF	Perfect
PROG	Progressive
PRT	Present Tense
PST$_a$	Immediate Past
PST$_b$	Near Past
PST$_c$	Distant Past
PST$_d$	Remote Past
QUE	Question Marker
WBC	Word Biblical Commentary

CHAPTER 1

Introduction

This research is a cross-cultural conceptual study of the emotion of קצף in the Hebrew Bible, hereafter BHS,[1] and the folk theory of the emotion of *ngoò* in the Kĩkamba language. The motivation for such a study stems from the need to communicate between one language and cultural community and another while acknowledging that there are significant differences. Biblical authors wrote from a particular cultural viewpoint and Bible translators translated that message to other languages of different cultures. It is prudent to underscore that for effective communication to occur, the differences and similarities in the conceptualization of different lexical items have to be factored in, in this case קצף and *ngoò*.

The value of a conceptual analysis of lexical items is noted by Zoltán Kövecses who, while studying the English word "anger," said that "the English word 'anger' and its counterparts in diverse languages of the world are based on concepts of anger that have a great deal of complexity."[2] Thus, for communication (proper understanding between the speaker and receptor) to occur, the complexities of these concepts should be examined. The understanding and use of words by different people groups is embedded in their minds as a concept that is rooted in their culture.[3] Therefore, "widely different cultures should produce widely different conceptualizations."[4] Usually the entry point to a people's culture is through their language and practices. The Hebrew

---

1. The Hebrew Bible used in this research is *Biblia Hebraica Stuttgartensia*.
2. Kövecses, "Concept of Anger," 159
3. The word "culture" is used here to mean people's guiding principles for life and belief.
4. Kövecses, "Anger: Its Language, Conceptualization," 183–84.

language is particularly useful in the study and understanding of the biblical culture since it (the language) is readily available to us. Benjamin Whorf claims that for communication to occur, there is need to "dissect nature along lines laid down by our native languages . . . the world is presented in a kaleidoscopic flux of impressions which has to be organized by our minds – and this means largely by the linguistic systems in our minds."[5] The way to understand how a concept is understood and used by a specific group of people is to examine their language – terminologies, synonyms and idioms among other linguistic cues that point to the concept under study. A study of קצף and *ngoò* should therefore illustrate some of the cultural underpinnings of both the Jewish people in antiquity, and those of the Akamba of today.

Catherine Lutz has highlighted the need for considering the cultural setting of the speakers whose emotional categories are under study. She notes, "Emotional meaning is fundamentally structured by particular cultural systems and particular social and material environment."[6] She further adds, "Emotion can more profitably be viewed as serving complex communicative, moral, and cultural purposes rather than simply as labels for internal states whose nature or essence is presumed to be universal."[7] The sentiments shared by Lutz are echoed by Matthew Schlimm who says, "There is a danger in relying solely on the lexical meaning of terms found in dictionaries and lexicons. Attention needs to be given to the broader encyclopedic range of meanings, associations, and cultural values that surround terms and ideas. This is particularly true when one considers anger in the Hebrew Bible."[8] An example that demonstrates the value of considering the cultural setting is illustrated by the work of Anna Wiezbicka who noted that there are significant differences between "the English emotion, the German *Gefuhl*, the Polish *uczue*, the French *émotion*, the Italian *emozione*, and the Spanish *emocion*."[9] Concerning the written text, since the researcher is limited in accessing the cultural setting of the first audience, the context of the utterances gives a useful hint to their cultural practices. Reconstructing the concept of the first audience is

---

5. Whorf, *Language, Thought, and Reality*, 213.
6. Lutz, *Unnatural Emotions*, 5.
7. Lutz, 5.
8. Schlimm, "From Fratricide to Forgiveness," 34.
9. Wierzbicka, "Everyday Conceptions of Emotion," 20.

an effort worth the investment. According to Lutz, a reader has the innate ability to mentally construct models of any information contained in a text.[10] The context which bears the קצף utterances, in both noun and verb forms, is carefully examined later in this research. While this section (introduction) has explained the need for a cross-cultural study, the following section on the motivation for this study further illustrates this need.

1.1 Unexplored Field: Motivation for This Study

Some of the scholars who have underscored the need for the study of emotions include Paul Krüger who said, "The subject of emotions in the Hebrew Bible is a most neglected theme and deserves an extensive treatment."[11] Kruger's study is on the emotions in the Hebrew Bible using the conceptual metaphor theory and he noted the need for more research. Another scholar is Matthew Schlimm who highlighted the need for the study of emotions generally, and said, "The feelings that individuals experience and the beliefs ascribed to them constitute a fascinating field of study."[12] He further singled out the study of emotions in the Hebrew Bible and said, "It is clear that analyses of emotion are becoming an important area of research among interpreters of the Hebrew Bible."[13] While the two scholars mentioned above have done their studies on the emotion of anger in the Hebrew Bible, others working in different fields have noted the need for an interdisciplinary research and a study on emotions.

One of these scholars is Robert Fuller who draws attention to the fact that "the study of religion has failed to keep abreast of recent scholarship in the natural and social sciences."[14] This, unfortunately, has led to "a regrettable paucity of truly interdisciplinary understandings of religious thought and feeling."[15] The reference to what he calls "religious thought and feeling" is centered on the study of emotions. Another scholar, Ronald Kotesky, says: "Strange enough, emotion has been outside the mainstream of both

---

10. Lutz, *Unnatural Emotions*, 332.
11. Kruger, "Cognitive Interpretation," 181.
12. Schlimm, "From Fratricide to Forgiveness," 1.
13. Schlimm, 2.
14. Fuller, "Spirituality in the Flesh," 46.
15. Fuller, 46.

psychology and Christianity."[16] Therefore, since emotions have not been adequately treated (or have been neglected) in the field of religious studies, this research will take a closer look at the emotion of anger through an examination of קצף in the BHS and *ngoò* among the Akamba.

1.2 A Summary of the Lexical Meaning of קצף in the BHS

The word קצף[17] is one of the eleven non-cognate lexical items (אף or אנף, זעם, זעף, חמה, חרה, כעס, עבר, קנא, רגז and רוח)[18] with a sense of anger in the BHS. The verbal form, קָצַף, occurs in the BHS thirty-four times and in seventeen times of these occurrences, God is the subject, in the qal stems.[19] According to the lexicons, in its qal verbal form, קָצַף means "to be angry or to be furious."[20] In its hiphil verbal form, קָצַף means to "provoke or cause to be angry"[21] and in its hithpael form, it means to be "emaciated or enraged."[22] In the noun forms, the root קצף has three distinctive usages. First, קֶצֶף I has the emotional sense of "anger, wrath, judgment, punishment, frustration and perhaps sorrow."[23] Second, קֶצֶף II has the sense of "splinter or chip"[24] and third, קֶצֶף III has the sense of foam.[25] Both קֶצֶף II and קֶצֶף III are applied in Hosea 10:7 and two different interpretations are possible. In this case, קֶצֶף I, II and III are homonyms. The focus in this research is the use of קֶצֶף I, which has the sense of anger. As a noun, קֶצֶף occurs twenty-eight times (Num 1:53; 16:46[17:11]; 18:5; Deut 29:28; Josh 9:20; 22:20; 2 Kgs 3:27; 1 Chr 27:24; 2 Chr 19:2, 10; 24:18; 29:8; 32:25–26; Esth 1:18; Pss 38:1; 102:10; Eccl 5:17; Isa 34:2; 54:8; 60:10; Jer 10:10; 21:5; 32:37; 50:13; Zech 1:2, 15; 7:12). Out of

---

16. Koteskey, "Christian Psychology: Emotion," 303.

17. This form is pointed either as a noun or as a verb depending on the discussion of the particular section. However, in some sections it is left unpointed if in such sections the meaning of both the noun and the verb forms is being communicated.

18. The lexical meaning of each of these words is discussed in detail in chapter 3.

19. Reiterer, "קצף," *TDOT*, 13:89–96.

20. Koehler and Walter, "קצף," *HALOT*, 2:1124–25.

21. Clines, "קצף," *DCH*, 7:283–84.

22. Clines. 7:283–84

23. Clines. 7:283–84

24. Clines. 7:283–84

25. Clines. 7:283–84

these, קֶצֶף was experienced by God twenty-six times and by a human being twice (Esth 1:18 and Eccl 5:17).[26]

As we will see later, the root קֶצֶף I has a number of different interpretations which will show that it is polysemous. In its verbal form, קָצַף occurs twelve times in the Pentateuch, six times in the historical books, two times in the poetic books and fourteen times in the prophetic books.[27] It is widely spread in different passages that have different genres, and occurs in both preexilic and postexilic literature.

1.3 A Summary of *Ngoò* in the Kĩkamba Language

The Akamba have several words in their language which refer to "anger." These words carry different nuances. For example, *ũthatu* (description of anger in the sense of bulging), *ũthilĩku* (anger which sometimes involves cursing and physical violence), *ngoo* (heart, anger, nausea, desire),[28] *woo* (pain, anger), and *nzika* (anger, doubt). The Akamba have many other words and figures of speech which in themselves do not directly mean "anger," but suggest it. These include *kũng'athia* (an expression of giving in to anger after resisting it), *ũũ* (bitter), *ũlalako* (irritation, a hot feeling that people get when they eat pepper), *ũkaatu* (unpalatable taste), *kũtangwa* (to be choked), and *kwĩw'a makindi* (to feel as if there are internal lumps that are making Ego bulge). The Kĩkamba lexical item *ngoò* (which is an intonation of *ngoo*) most closely approximates the Hebrew קֶצֶף.

The motivation for pursuing this research is twofold: one, the study of emotions in the BHS is not fully explored to the fullest, and two, the conceptual substrate of קֶצֶף is close to that of *ngoò*. However, the comparison of these two lexical items does not mean that they are the same; they have areas of difference but their similarities and the way their frames complement each other is sufficient for a comparative study.

---

26. Latvus, *God, Anger and Ideology*, 25–26.

27. Struthers, "קצף," *NIDOTTE*, 2:962–63.

28. These nuances are differentiated by the different intonations of *ngoo*. The specific intonation for *ngoo* with the nuance of anger is that of a raised tone *ngoò*.

1.4 The Research Questions

The research questions guiding this research are the following: Do קצף occurrences have any pattern? Do all the lexical items associated with קצף fit within the קצף pattern, if any? Is the קצף usage in the Aramaic texts different or similar to the קצף usage in the BHS? Does קצף have distinctive features?

Similarly, the same questions are asked about *ngoò*. That is, do *ngoò* occurrences have any pattern? Do all the lexical items associated with *ngoò* fit within the *ngoò* pattern, if any? Is the *ngoò* usage in the Kīkamba language[29] different or similar to the קצף usage in the BHS? Does *ngoò* have distinctive features? These questions are considered carefully and their answers stated.

1.5 Previous Scholarship (in Addition to the Lexical Meaning) on קצף in the Hebrew Bible

Since this research focuses on a conceptual study of קצף in the BHS, this section is limited to the review of the scholarly works that have studied קצף as an emotion. The definitions and descriptions of קצף in lexicons and Bible dictionaries are not reviewed in this section since they have been mentioned earlier under the summary section for קצף.

1.5.1 The Same Contextual Use of חמה and קצף

A number of other studies show a close relation between חמה and קצף. For example, Eliezer Segal, who wrote "Human Anger and Divine Intervention in Esther," notes that "anger is indicated in Esther chiefly by means of two Hebrew words: *hemah* and *qatsaf*."[30] The argument that supports his thesis is that חמה and קצף feature in similar contexts and are used interchangeably. Another scholar, Gale Struthers, makes a similar conclusion in her study of קצף. In her work, she notes that "the nom. *qeṣep* occurs 17x with the preposition '*al*, on, on account of.' The senses of this word are close to *hēmâ*, wrath."[31] These two scholars, from their surveys, have reached the conclusion that קצף

---

29. Since *ngoò* is not in the Kīkamba Bible, its comparison with קצף is based on the *ngoò* usage in the Kīkamba language.

30. Segal, "Human Anger," 248.

31. Struthers, "קצף," *NIDOTTE*, 2:963.

is close in meaning to חמה. In this research, however, the data explains that the conceptual substrate for קצף is distinct and not shared.

1.5.2 Zacharias Kotzé: Humoral Theory as Motivation for Anger Metaphors in the Hebrew Bible

In his article on the role of "Humoral Theory as Motivation for Anger Metaphors in the Hebrew Bible," Zacharias Kotzé argues that, "Classical Hebrew words and expressions for anger can be brought in direct relation with the ancient Israelite beliefs regarding the humours."[32] He has pinpointed three Hebrew words: קצף, חמה and זעם, which according to him have a close relation in the way they are conceptualized and used. For example, חמה is thought to be a close equivalent to Akkadian *imtu*, which means "venom," "saliva" or "foam."[33] This definition has been adopted by Kotzé, who, while using the humoral theory, notes that the foam flowing from the mouth or nose of an angry person was thought to be poisonous foam rising from the gallbladder.[34] This foam was physically evident in the face of an angry person who appeared to have an epileptic attack out of the experience of anger. Therefore, a person who experienced חמה (heat, poison, anger) physically acted like an epileptic person. Such a person would have קצף and/or זעם (foam) coming out of his mouth or the nose, אַף.[35] This study by Kotzé demonstrates that חמה was the internal experience of anger and when it increased, got out of control, the person experienced חמה which came out like foam from the mouth or nose. The Hebrew words used for "foam" are קצף and זעם, which Kotzé translates to mean "to foam." Kotzé concludes that these three terms are standing in parallel, which indicates that they can be considered synonyms.[36]

The other source of evidence that Kotzé uses to associate קצף with foaming from the mouth is the Akkadian reference to Hosea 10:7, which talks about the king of Samaria. The issue in this verse is the translation of כְּקֶצֶף since it is regarded as either "twig" or "foam."[37] In BHS, this verse reads as follows, נִדְמֶה שֹׁמְרוֹן מַלְכָּהּ כְּקֶצֶף עַל־פְּנֵי־מָיִם "the king of Samaria is cut off like a twig

---

32. Kotzé, "Humoral Theory as Motivation," 205.
33. Koehler and Baumgartner, "חמה," *HALOT*, 2:326.
34. Kotzé, "Humoral Theory as Motivation," 205–9.
35. Kotzé, "Conceptualisation of Anger," 110.
36. Kotzé, "Humoral Theory as Motivation," 206.
37. Clines, "קצף," *DCH*, 7:283–84.

on the surface of water." Kotzé argues that an ancient Akkadian text (Era IV: 67–68) – that is contextually related to the Hosea 10:7 passage – says, "you broke the population in its midst like a reed; you brought their din to an end like foam on the surface of the water."[38] Kotzé notes that the simile "like foam on the surface of the water" in an Akkadian text dating from some time between the eleventh and the ninth centuries BC clearly demostrates that Hosea 10:7 could be translated as above [meaning 'foam']."[39] He also notes that besides the Akkadian, the Aramaic has the root *rth* which denotes both anger and foam. This root occurs in the Targum translation in Hosea 10:7.[40] While Cohen appreciates the controversy surrounding the translation of כְּקֶצֶף in Hosea 10:7, he prefers the "foam" translation and concludes by saying that the translators who prefer foam over chip of wood "appear to be vindicated."[41]

Kotzé's assumption that anger is fluid is anchored in his use of the metaphor "anger is a fluid in a container."[42] In such cases, he argues that anger words are used with the verb מלא (to be full).[43] The example that he gives to support this position is from Esther 3:5 which says

וַיַּרְא הָמָן כִּי־אֵין מָרְדֳּכַי כֹּרֵעַ וּמִשְׁתַּחֲוֶה לוֹ וַיִּמָּלֵא הָמָן חֵמָה׃

"When Haman observed that Mordecai would not kneel and bow down to him, he was filled with anger" (NAB).

Although the verb מלא, "to be full," is not used in conjunction with קֶצֶף in the BHS, the two lexical items do occur together in the Qumran scrolls, 4QJub[f] 37:12, in the form מלא קצפוי meaning "full of anger." However, an examination of how מלא is used in other passages sheds light on how the construct above should be understood. For example, מלא is used in its construct form in Jeremiah 6:11 which says:

> Therefore I am full of the fury of the LORD.
> I am weary of holding *it* in.
> "I will pour it out on the children outside,
> And on the assembly of young men together;

---

38. Kotzé, "Conceptualisation of Anger," 105.
39. Kotzé, "Conceptualisation of Anger," 105.
40. Cohen, *Biblical Hapax Legomena*, 25.
41. Cohen, 25.
42. Kotzé, "Conceptualisation of Anger," 126.
43. Kotzé, 127.

For even the husband shall be taken with the wife,
The aged with *him who is* full of days (NKJV).

The phrase translated as "the aged with him who is full of days" is זָקֵן עִם־מְלֵא יָמִים which literally means "elder with full of days."⁴⁴ This passage clearly means an elder who has lived many days but not an elder being a container with many days. This understanding, therefore, has guided the interpretation of construct form מלא קצפוי "full of anger" to mean "a lot of anger" and not "anger in a container."

A further argument by Kotzé on "anger is a fluid in a container" is that, when it is heated it spills over. In support of this argument, he identifies verbs that imply anger as a kind of liquid that could flow. These verbs are שפך (to spill), נתך (to pour out) and עבר (to overflow).⁴⁵ However, the data employed in this research reaches a different conclusion from the above findings. It is explained later in this research that none of the aforementioned verbal forms – שפך (to spill), נתך (to pour out), and עבר (to overflow) – is used with קֶצֶף in the BHS. Kotzé also adds that when פחז (to be reckless) is used as an adjective in the BHS to describe violent people, it also supports the conceptualization of anger as an epileptic seizure, which is accompanied by foaming in the mouth.⁴⁶

Kotzé's finding that associates חמה with the humor of gall is closely linked with Terence Collins' study on "the physiology of tears in the Old Testament."

1.5.3 Terence Collins: The Physiology of Tears in the Old Testament

According to Collins, the Jewish people conceptualized tears as "the breaking down of the inner organs which turn to water and emerge as tears."⁴⁷ This explanation is affirmed by their assumption that "the heart loses its firm substance under the stress (heat) of emotional reaction and is said to 'melt,' i.e., to turn to a fluid state which causes the outflow of tears."⁴⁸ One of the psalms that Collins evaluated is Psalm 22:14–15b, which says, "as waters I

---

44. Clines, "מלא," *DCH*, 5:276–82.
45. Kotzé, "Conceptualisation of Anger," 128.
46. Kotzé, 113.
47. Collins, "Physiology of Tears," 193.
48. Collins, 193.

have been poured out, and (waters have) separated themselves from all my bones, my heart has been like wax, it is melted in the midst of my bowels. Dried up as an earthen vessel is my power, and my tongue is cleaving to my jaws." In this passage, the psalmist describes his troubles using the imagery of water, which has been poured from his body. The loss of such water has left the psalmist so dry that his tongue cleaves to his jaws symbolizing inability to speak because of going through unbearable pain.[49] A similar imagery can be found in Psalm 69:1–2 where the psalmist feels overwhelmed by danger which is described as a flood, hence his cry to God for help. This kind of weeping and the description of danger in the form of a flood is what Collins describes as a "perfect example of poetic ambiguity as a consciously artistic effect . . . the poet has cleverly interwoven the two ideas of external danger and internal emotional reaction into the one image of rising flood water."[50]

The Hebrew conceptualization of tears further helps us to understand the concept of חמה which is sometimes associated with destructive water. We find an example in Ezekiel 13, which is a condemnation against false prophets. In verse 13b, God declares: "In my wrath I will unleash a violent wind, and in my anger hailstones and torrents of rain will fall with destructive fury (חמה)" (NIV). Here the speaker is relating an external danger of water with an internal experience of fluids. Collins' study, therefore, is a strong basis for understanding why Kotzé argues for the release of חמה from the gall-bladder as a fluid which comes out of the mouth or nose as foam. This study by the various scholars, however, has several limitations.

1.6 Limitation of Previous Studies on קצף

The work done by previous scholars on קצף is commendable because it diverges from the definition in lexicons and Bible dictionaries, and enlarges a rather narrow scope of קצף. However, the existing studies are limited in three main areas as described below.

---

49. Collins, 193.
50. Collins, 195.

1.6.1 Polysemous

Kotzé argues that קצף, זעם and חמה are synonymous and mean "foam." Unfortunately, this view obscures the polysemous and figurative nature of all three lexical items. This research, on the other hand, shows that קצף can also mean "frustration" – a quite different and non-figurative sense of קצף. The lexical item, זעם, is also polysemous as demonstrated in different passages. For instance, זעם is rendered as "denounce" or "accursed" in the following passage: Proverbs 24:24 partly reads "peoples will curse him and nations denounce (יִזְעָמוּהוּ whose root is זעם) him" (NIV); in the last phrase of Micah 6:10, we read: "ill-gotten treasures, . . . and the short ephah, which is accursed (זְעוּמָה whose root is זעם)?" (NIV). The definition given by Kotzé that זעם means "foam" would not fit in the contexts above. The last lexical item, חמה, is also translated as "anger," "poison" or "irritation" among other usages as explained in chapter 3. The polysemous and figurative usage of each of the three lexical items קצף, זעם and חמה demonstrates that each has its own distinctiveness, which is worthy of examination.

1.6.2 Emphatic, Stylistic, Metonymic and Distinctive Nature of a Word: Author's Choice

The biblical text demonstrates that different Hebrew words having the meaning of "anger" are sometimes placed in close proximity to each other within the same context, or occur in parallel phrases. At other times, those same lexical items are used separately in different passages. From the contextual observations, four possibilities suffice to explain this phenomenon. First, when words with the sense of anger are used together in the same context, they serve the purpose of intensifying the intended meaning, especially when they are nouns in apposition. Second, they are used stylistically at the discretion of the author with the intention of conveying the message in different words, especially in poetry. Third, when those same words are used separately, they are sometimes used metonymically to infer "anger." Lastly, the author employs other grammatical terminologies to display the unique characteristics of the specific word in focus. For example, there are numerous passages in the BHS where each of these words – זעם, קצף and חמה – occur independently from the other (Gen 40:2; Lev 10:6; Num 1:53; Deut 1:34; Josh 9:20; 1 Sam 9:24; 2 Kgs 3:27, among others). Presuming that the occurrence and distribution of these words independently in the Hebrew biblical text is not random, then there must have been factor(s) that guided the author in the choice of one word over the other. These unspecified factors legitimize the need for this research.

1.6.3 Conceptual Study of קצף

The understanding generated from the literature review above on קצף in the BHS shows that, first, research on the conceptualization of קצף "in terms of the experience-based schematizations"[51] of the ancient Hebrew culture's world has not been done. The term "experience-based schematizations" is a term used to explain the description and/or understanding of a concept by a local people based on their own experience of the world around them. Second, the קצף concept in the BHS has not yet been analyzed with a keen focus on its conceptual subparts. It is because of these limitations that this research examines קצף.

1.7 Thesis Statement

The central argument in this dissertation can be stated as follows: A cross-cultural conceptual study of the emotion of קצף reveals how it was conceptualized in the ancient Hebrew culture, and its comparative study with the folk theory of the emotion of *ngoò* shows that the concept of *ngoò* would have been the best rendering for the Hebrew concept קצף in the Kīkamba Bible.

1.8 Contribution to Biblical Scholarship

In advancing the argument stated in section 1.7, three goals are met: First, this research explains the conceptualization of קצף in the ancient Hebrew culture. In particular, this research demonstrates how קצף functions within the קצף frame which will be explained in detail in chapter 3. This frame is supported by the use of קֶצֶף as subject accompanied by the הָיָה, יָצָא and בּוֹא verbs. Second, it employs a cross-cultural study of קצף and *ngoò*, and demonstrates the variance in their conceptual facets, and third, it demonstrates the value of cross-cultural study in biblical studies.

---

51. Petruck, "Frame Semantics and the Lexicon," 279.

1.9 Synopsis of the Chapters

The flow of the remaining part of this research is as follows. In chapter 2, this study explains the different theories that are useful in this research. At the end, a proposed complementary approach is stated. This chapter acknowledges the limitations of one theory in addressing all the questions raised in this research, hence the need for several theories. In chapter 3, this research analyzes the biblical data, explains the conceptualization of קצף in the BHS, and brings to light its unique conceptual substrate. In this chapter, there is also an exegesis of passages where קצף occurs in light of that understanding. In chapter 4, the author investigates the usage of the folk theory of *ngoò* "anger" among the Akamba people and determines the subparts that form the entire *ngoò* process. In chapter 5, this research offers a comparative study of קצף and *ngoò*, and demonstrates the variance in their conceptual facets. It also explains how the different facets of קצף have been overlooked in the 1974 Kīkamba Bible edition. In chapter 6, the author concludes his findings and gives recommendations that arise from this research.

CHAPTER 2

Methodology

This chapter examines in detail the theories that are used in this research. Since there is no single theory that can answer all the research questions raised, a complementary approach of several theories is proposed at the end of this chapter and it demonstrates how the different theories are used. The theories used are Charles Fillmore's frame semantics, Richard Shweder and Jonathan Haidt's symbolic approach, and Daniel M. T. Fessler's logic and qualitative field research. These theories are reviewed below in the order they are stated above, beginning with Charles Fillmore's frame semantics.

2.1 Charles Fillmore's Frame Semantics

Charles Fillmore, the scholar credited for the development of frame semantics, describes it as a study which identifies a framework within which concepts are communicated and understood.[1] An utterance by a speaker evokes broader information in the mind of the hearer, and both the utterance and the information evoked become crucial for the understanding of what the speaker says. The evoking of information as stated by Fillmore can occur at both verbal and written levels. On the written level, Fillmore specifically notes the role of frame semantics as "the study of how linguistic forms evoke or activate frame knowledge, and how the frames thus activated can be integrated into an understanding of the passages that contain these forms."[2] Miriam Petruck elaborates on the frame knowledge that Fillmore mentions

---

1. Fillmore, "Frame Semantics," 111.
2. Fillmore and Baker, "Frames Approach," 313–39.

and defines frame as "any system of concepts related in such a way that to understand any one concept it is necessary to understand the entire system."[3] This information is naturally processed in the brain of people, as a mental process, and therefore cannot be ignored in the study of information processing. Petruck's definition of frame semantics is in tandem with what Fillmore says. She notes, "Frame semantics is a research in empirical semantics which emphasizes the continuities between language and experience, and provides a framework for presenting the results of the research."[4] The core of frame semantics is that words signify a category of experience. Frame semantics is thus the "experience-based schematizations of the speaker's world – i.e. frames."[5] The research in frame semantics is therefore an endeavor to understand the category and the reasons for its creation, since on it is the meaning of the word anchored.[6]

Since frames are experience-related, the pressing question is "From where do we get frames?" Fillmore explains:

> As humans we have access to some of these frames by virtue of living on the earth, subject to its daily and annual cycles and the entities that we perceive; other frames we owe to just being human, with bodies that respond to gravity and to our biological and emotional needs, and with the perceptual faculties that our bodies possess; others we have by being members of a particular culture, where we consciously or unconsciously respond to its institutions, symbols, artifacts, and values; and, importantly still others we have by virtue of being a part of the specific speech community that supports and is supported by the culture.[7]

This description means our lives and interactions in this world form frames, which then exist in our minds. These frames make communication possible. When the hearer or reader cannot make a cultural association with a certain concept or word, communication fails. This has been the case especially with jokes. A joke in one culture fails to amuse members of another culture because

---

3. Petruck, "Frame Semantics," 1.
4. Petruck, 1.
5. Petruck, "Frame Semantics and the Lexicon," 279.
6. Petruck, "Frame Semantics," 1.
7. Fillmore and Baker, "Frames Approach," 314.

the particular frame does not exist in that particular culture. With these introductory remarks, and with a preliminary definition of frame semantics, in the following section we will explore the development of this theory.

2.1.1 Development of the Term "Frame" as Used in Frame Semantics

Since the purpose of this section is to shed light on the development of the term "frame" within the frame semantics field, which is Fillmore's idea, its development is traced within the confines of his usage. Fillmore says, "I use the word frame for any system of linguistic choices – the easiest cases being collections of words, but also including choices of grammatical rules or linguistic categories – that can get associated with prototypical instances of scenes."[8] According to this definition, Fillmore's use of the term "frame" is in reference to the choice of the lexical items used in communication. In the definition above, he uses another term "scene," which is important for understanding his use of the term "frame." Concerning "scene," he said, "I use the term scene in a maximally general sense, including not only visual scenes but also familiar kinds of interpretational transactions, standard scenarios defined by the culture, institutional structures, enactive experiences, body frame, and, in general, any kind of coherent segment of human beliefs, actions, experiences or imagings."[9] His usage of the term "scene" refers to the background knowledge that is evoked by certain lexical items. Thus, Fillmore uses the term "scene" to refer to the background information of "frames," frames being the elements of a word, phrase or a sentence which evoke a scene.[10] The background information, scene, is characterized by prototypes. Fillmore describes prototypes by saying:

> The prototype idea is roughly this. Instead of the meaning of a linguistic form being represented in terms of a checklist of conditions that have to be satisfied in order for the form to be appropriately or truthfully used, it is held that the understanding of meaning requires, at least for a great many cases, an appeal to an exemplar or prototype – this prototype being possibly

---

8. Fillmore, "Checklist Theories of Meaning," 124.
9. Fillmore, "Checklist Theories of Meaning," 124.
10. Fillmore, 122–26.

something which is innately available to the human mind, possibly something which, instead of being analyzed, needs to be presented or demonstrated or manipulated.[11]

The argument by Fillmore is that a prototype does not need to have conditions that must be available in the sense of "check list of conditions" for communication to occur between the speaker and the listener. Instead, the prototype is the general background information shared between the utterance and recipient. Since a prototype is not a fixed set of conditions, it can be presented, demonstrated or manipulated depending on the speaker's and the recipient's context.

Petruck, who is a proponent of Fillmore's theory, defines prototype as "the surrounding culture [background information] against which the meaning of a word is defined and understood."[12] In light of these definitions, the prototype forms the contextual foregrounded information for the frame elements. This foregrounded information is what Fillmore calls "scene" and it has the characteristics of a prototype. Comparatively, Fillmore's "scene" is similar to what Marvin Minsky, one of his contemporaries, called "frame."

Minsky[13] used the term "frame" before Fillmore adopted and redefined it. Minsky's use of the term "frame" arose out of the development of a theory that he describes as a "framework for representing knowledge" in artificial intelligence,[14] and he uses the term "frame" to mean "a data-structure representing a stereotyped situation."[15] In brief, Minsky proposes that any concept or lexical item evokes a framework, which represents the knowledge for the said concept. This framework is the background information, data-structure and the stereotypical situation. Therefore, the "framework for representing knowledge" proposes that instead of separate fragments of knowledge there exists a framework of networks whose frames are "fixed, and represent things that are always true about the supposed situation."[16] This negated the presentation of knowledge as separate fragments. Minsky further argues that

---

11. Fillmore, 123.
12. Petruck, "Frame Semantics," 2.
13. Minsky, "Framework for Representing Knowledge," 211–77.
14. Artificial knowledge refers to computer programs that are configured to perform specific tasks.
15. Minsky, "Framework for Representing Knowledge," 212.
16. Minsky.

this fixed frame has terminals, which are filled with specific information. Depending on how these terminals are filled with information by individuals in different cultures and geographical areas, the change of this frame is a result of the view from different perspectives. This means the frame does not change; only the perspectives do. The same way the frame is fixed, so the terminals are fixed as well. This framework of knowledge has two levels: nodes and relations. Nodes are those elements of the frame that are fixed and always true concerning a situation. Relations are those elements of a frame, which specify a given situation.[17]

The similarity between Fillmore's "scene" and Minsky's "frame" is that a scene is a term referring to the background information which is characterized by prototypes, and frame is a term referring to the background information which is characterized by stereotyped situations. To demonstrate the similarity of Minsky's use of "frame" and Fillmore's "scene," the example of the use of the term "breakfast" is given below.

The word "breakfast" can be understood in (at least) one of three ways: it can be understood as the first meal of the day, or the meal taken between 6:00 a.m. and 10:00 a.m. or the word can refer to the content of the meal regardless of the time it is taken. In the first scenario, if an individual stays awake all night and takes a meal after midnight, he will have had breakfast. This is true of an individual who sleeps throughout the night and wakes up in the morning to have a meal – breakfast. Similarly, an individual who sleeps all through the night and the entire morning of the following day, waking up in the afternoon, will refer to that first meal as breakfast. In this scenario, breakfast does not mean the time of the meal but makes reference to the practice of "breakfast" being the first meal of the day. In the second scenario, breakfast is the meal taken in the morning between 6:00 a.m. and 10:00 a.m. In this scenario, an individual who stays up late and takes a meal past midnight will not say he is having breakfast since that is not the time for it. Likewise, an individual who sleeps all night and wakes up in the afternoon of the following day will probably call his meal lunch since he missed breakfast during his sleep. In the third scenario, breakfast describes the contents of the meal regardless of the time it is taken. My son, Solomon, demonstrated this category to me. When he was five years old, his use of the term breakfast

---

17. Minsky.

meant the contents of the meal. Usually, we had tea and bread in the house and that is what he called breakfast. At 4:00 p.m., he would come to the house for his 4 o'clock snack and ask for breakfast – tea and bread. Sometimes after dinner and after playing in the house, before he went to bed, he would ask for breakfast – tea and bread. For him, therefore, he had "breakfast" three or four times a day because his conceptual understanding of "breakfast" was linked to the contents of the meal regardless of the time of the day.

According to Fillmore, the three scenarios detailed above share the same frame – the lexical item "breakfast" – but have different scenes. The "scene" here is referring to the backgrounded information (the common shared knowledge between the speaker and the listener). The word "breakfast" evokes beverage(s) and accompaniments that are usually different from those of the other meals of the day. However, the larger context of defining breakfast as either the first meal of the day, the meal of the day taken between 6:00 a.m. and 10:00 a.m., and breakfast as contents of the meal regardless of the time of day are the different scenes.

According to Minsky's use of the term "frame": the term "breakfast" would represent a framework of knowledge which is fixed and stereotyped differently within different cultures. In the breakfast example, breakfast is a fixed element, or node, in that it is a meal. The details on what time of the day it is taken and what contents are part of the meal are the "relations" which can differ from one situation to another. Minsky uses "stereotype" as the integral part of "frame" and similarly Fillmore uses "prototype" as the integral part of the "scene." In this example, the application of Fillmore's theory on breakfast as the background information, scene, is the same as Minsky's use of "frame" when applied to the breakfast concept.

So far, this section has explained that Fillmore's "scene" was similar to Minsky's "frame." In Fillmore's later writings, he replaces the term "scene" with "frame." In addition to the replacing of terms, his use of "frame" is not in reference to prototypical or stereotypical situations; instead, he uses it to mean shared cultural and conceptual knowledge between the speaker and the hearer.[18] Therefore, although the term "frame" was in use before Fillmore adopted it; he redefined it beyond stereotyped situations. The term "frame" in frame semantics, therefore evolved from "scene" in Fillmore's writings.

---

18. Fillmore, "Frame Semantics," 111.

However, he is not the first scholar to use it but he adopted it and used it in a different manner as explained above. It is in this current understanding, shared background information between the speaker and the hearer, that scholars use it in frame semantics. Its current usage, however, makes it similar to other terminologies within cognitive science.

2.1.2 Frame, Base, and Domain: Overlapping Terminology

Frame semantics is a subfield within cognitive science. There are, therefore, terms that have a close meaning to frame as used in cognitive science. Two such terms, which scholars use, and which may be synonymous with "frame," are base and domain. John Taylor defines base as the "conceptual content that is inherently, intrinsically and obligatorily invoked by the expression."[19] In closely related terms, Croft and Cruse define base as "that knowledge or conceptual structure that is presupposed by the profiled concept"[20] Taylor gives an example, using the diagram below, of the term "hypotenuse" to illustrate the meaning of base.

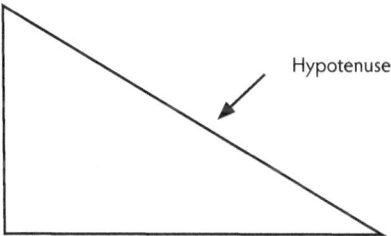

The argument by Taylor concerning the diagram above is that there is no way an individual can conceptualize the term "hypotenuse" without the background knowledge of the right triangle. Without the concept of the right triangle, the "hypotenuse" is simply a line. The background knowledge of the right triangle is therefore the conceptual content that Taylor claims "must be invoked" by the "hypotenuse" expression. This background knowledge is what Croft and Cruse call the "conceptual structure" in their definition for base as mentioned above.

---

19. Taylor, *Cognitive Grammar*, 195.
20. Croft and Cruse, *Cognitive Linguistics*, 15.

Taylor further defines domain as the "generalized background knowledge configuration against which conceptualization is achieved."[21] Applying the "hypotenuse" concept again, the background knowledge evoked is more than that of a right triangle. He notes that the evoked concepts include a triangle, a right angle and a straight line, which are in turn understood against the knowledge of geometry. Even the geometric figures have a wider background in the geometric field against which triangles are understood. The properties of this wider background are what constitute a domain. In essence, both base and domain are background information of a concept and so is a frame.

Croft and Cruse define "a frame" as "any coherent body of knowledge presupposed by a word concept."[22] In complex conceptual structures, scholars use frame and domain differently for clarity purposes. An example is that of the term "niece." The mention of niece evokes kinship relations within a family tree.[23] In this case, the entire kinship tree is the frame, which has specific relations like maternal uncle, maternal aunt, paternal uncle and paternal aunt. In this example, the specific relations are the domains within the kinship frame. This example is helpful in understanding John Taylor's definition of frame as "the knowledge network linking the multiple domains associated with a given linguistic form."[24] In this example, the evoked information is not a single entity but several. However, in the general usage, frame, base and domain are all background information of a concept.

The section above explains that Fillmore's use of the term "frame" within the field of frame semantics is not different from the way the terms "base" and "domain"[25] are used within cognitive science – and this illustrates how frame semantics is a subfield within cognitive science. Having ascertained the larger category in which frame semantics belongs, the following section sheds more light on the components of the theory.

---

21. Taylor, *Cognitive Grammar*, 195.
22. Croft and Cruse, *Cognitive Linguistics*, 17.
23. Wardlaw, *Conceptualizing Words for "God,"* 30.
24. Taylor, *Linguistic Categorization*, 87.
25. In addition to base and domain, other terms that are synonyms of frame are script, schema and scenario.

2.1.3 Components of the Frame Semantics Theory

Frame semantics has three main components: core frame elements, peripheral frame elements and extrathematic frame elements. The author of this research examines in detail each of these components in the following section, beginning with core frame elements.

2.1.3.1 The Core Frame Elements

Core frame elements are the necessary and sufficient elements that are always present in the main conceptual structure of any concept. Fillmore and Collins define "core frame elements" as "those entities or properties which may or must be present in any assistance of a given frame."[26] An example that illustrates this is a commercial frame. Consider the saying "Moses bought a shirt" or "John sold a shirt." The mention of either the buyer or seller depends on the speaker's focus in the conversation. In the commercial frame, the core frame elements that are present include a buyer, a seller and goods.[27] These are key frame elements of the commercial frame since it is hard to imagine any transaction without the three. Although the speaker may not mention all the three in a phrase, the utterance evokes the whole frame.

2.1.3.2 The Peripheral Frame Elements

The peripheral frame elements are those elements that do not form part of the core frame elements. For example, let us consider the sentence, "Moses bought a shirt on Monday at 10 o'clock along Tom Mboya Street after bargaining for twenty minutes." The mention of Monday at 10 o'clock (time), Tom Mboya Street (place) and the twenty minutes of bargaining (manner) are evoked peripheral frame elements. They form what Fillmore calls "the trio 'time, place and manner' [which] usually covers what grammarians mean by peripheral adjuncts rather than core arguments, but each of these semantic types can have core status in some lexical contexts."[28] Fillmore and Collin's "trio" are indicators of what peripheral frame elements are although they may be core in other concepts.

---

26. Fillmore and Baker, "Frames Approach," 324.

27. The amount of money used is not part of the core frame elements since its mention would evoke another frame of profit and loss.

28. Fillmore and Baker, "Frames Approach," 325.

2.1.3.3 The Extrathematic Frame Elements

The extrathematic frame elements are the additional sentences that "introduce information that is not a necessary part of the description of the central frame. In many cases such phrases introduce a new frame and in a sense attribute that frame to the rest of the sentence."[29] For example, in the sentence "Moses bought a shirt for a wedding," the inclusion of "for a wedding" is not part of the core frame element; instead it introduces a new frame – marriage ceremony.

These three categories: the core frame elements, the peripheral frame elements and the extrathematic frame elements are therefore important in the study of lexical units of utterances or texts. In summary of the cognitive linguistic key terms reviewed above, the term "frame" refers to the background information which is basic and necessary for understanding the utterance, while "frame elements" are the components of the frame that are explicitly stated and evoke the frame – which is the primary component. The table below illustrates the similarities of all these terms as used in cognitive linguistics.

Table 1

Frame	Frame element
Circle[30]	Arc
Circle, Line, Center, Diameter	Radius
Kinship Relations	Daughter
Arm	Hand, Elbow, Wrist, Fingers

Frame semantics is a useful theory in this research. This following section discusses the value of frame semantics.

2.1.4 The Value of Frame Semantics

Frame semantics is useful in this research in three main areas: in interpretation of written texts or verbal utterances, in the development of lexicology and lexicography, and in language acquisition. First, in this research, frame semantics is very useful for interpretation of the biblical texts as explained in

---

29. Fillmore and Baker, 326.
30. Wardlaw, *Conceptualizing Words for "God,"* 29.

chapters three and five. Second, some of the major differences noted in chapter 5 in the comparative data of the BHS and Kĩkamba, are a result of lack of an updated Kĩkamba lexicon. Thus, one of the recommendations in chapter 6 is for a development of an up-to-date Kĩkamba lexicon using a frame semantics model. Third, since the Kĩkamba language is taught in primary schools in the rural areas of Ũkambanĩ, the school children would be greatly helped if teaching materials could be developed using frame semantics, since such materials have been proven to aid learning both for children and for students of foreign languages. The three categories in which frame semantics is useful are worth examining in detail, starting with its usefulness in interpretation.

2.1.4.1 Frame Semantics Is Useful for Interpretation

The first step in interpretation using frame semantics is to identify a pattern – frame, that is useful for understanding a lexical unit from the perspective of the speaker's world. Through a careful study of the lexical unit and other related materials, the interpreter is able to identify the fitting frame. Once this pattern is identified, "the interpreter of a text invokes a frame when assigning an interpretation to a piece of text by placing its content in a pattern known independently of the text."[31] By way of illustrating how frame semantics is useful in interpreting a text, I consider the English label for a revenge frame. In this frame, the core frame elements are as follows: individual X has offended individual Y. Because of that offence, individual Z acts to punish individual X. This basic scenario offers what is evoked in an individual's mind once revenge is mentioned and more frame elements are added into this frame depending on the complexity of the scene.

Therefore, the revenge frame is useful in interpreting texts that deal with revenge. For example, Moses in Deuteronomy 19 urged the Israelites to set apart cities of refuge once they conquered the promised land. These cities were for people to take refuge in if they unintentionally killed another. In Deuteronomy 19:6 Moses said, "otherwise, the redeemer of blood may pursue him in his anger (when his heart is hot), overtake him if the distance is long, and kill him even though he is not being judged of death, since he did not hate him [the victim] from the past."[32] Although there is no mention of key

---
31. Petruck, "Frame Semantics," 3.
32. This is my own translation.

words like revenge, retaliate or avenge in the above verse, the mention of "the redeemer of blood" evokes a revenge frame. It is not surprising, therefore, that the phrase "the redeemer of blood" is translated as "avenger of blood" in NIV, NRSV and NASB among other major translations. In the Deuteronomy reference given above, the exegete will have to factor in the revenge frame to determine why the avenger – redeemer – is described as "the avenger of blood." If the avenger is any neighbor or a specific neighbor, what does the term "neighbor" mean? Why is the neighbor justified to retaliate? What did the idiom "his heart is hot" mean in the Jewish culture within a revenge frame?

Using frames is not just for the interpretation of biblical texts alone, but for any piece of information, whether verbal or written. Petruck gives the example of the sentence: "Julia will open her presents after blowing out her candles and eating some cake."[33] This sentence as a whole evokes the frame of a birthday party although the term "birthday party" is not mentioned. This frame, however, is conceptualized if the interpreters share the same background in which presents, candles and cake are needed for a birthday party celebration.

These two examples exemplify the relevance and usefulness of frame semantics in everyday life when either seeking to understand written texts or verbal utterances – especially by people who have different cultures and contexts. In essence, we always apply frame semantics in our daily conversations and interaction with written texts. In addition to the usefulness of frame semantics in interpretation, it is also useful for lexicology and lexicography.

2.1.4.2 Frame Semantics Is Useful in Lexicology and Lexicography

Frame semantics gives a better understanding of a particular word than the dictionary view. Limiting ourselves to encyclopedic knowledge is largely to confine ourselves to a small subset of our conceptual knowledge, which is presented as the linguistic meaning in the encyclopedia.[34] Croft and Cruse state, "the dictionary view fails because it generally describes only the concept profile, or at best a very simplified version of the concept frame implicit in a concept profile."[35] The dictionary limitations form the basis for the need

---

33. Petruck, "Frame Semantics," 3.
34. Croft and Cruse, *Cognitive Linguistic*, 30.
35. Croft and Cruse, 30.

of a frame semantics dictionary. The value of a dictionary whose entries are based on frame semantics is well highlighted by Atkins. He says, "Frame semantics is holistic in its approach to lexical meaning. In a frame semantics dictionary, there is one single underlying schematization, untrammeled by discrete dictionary senses. Individual aspects of word use cannot be isolated from the undifferentiable whole, the frame."[36] In the following paragraphs, the usefulness of frame semantics in lexicography is explained further.

One of the published monographs that demonstrate the usefulness of frame semantics in lexicology is the schematization of the body frame by Petruck.[37] She underscores the importance of frame semantics by saying, "in a frame-based organization of the lexicon, it is the frame which provides the conceptual underpinnings of related senses of a single word and semantically related words."[38] She demonstrates this claim in her study of lexical items in the BHS using the body frame. Her thesis is: "certain kinds of nouns and verbs in Hebrew [are] based on body terms . . . These lexical items are part of the body frame as well because it is experience of and knowledge about the body that provides the conceptual underpinnings for their formation."[39] The extract given below illustrates the above claim. She says,

> The clearest illustration of this is *har-* "mountain" where a schematization of the human body has been applied to a mountain to name its parts. Thus, we find *ros ha-har* (head of the mountain) – "(the) summit," *gav ha-har-* "back of the mountain," *katef ha-har-* "shoulder of the mountain," which is a military/topographic term, and *ragley ha-har* feet of the mountain – "foot of the mountain." Note that this schematization assumes the canonical upright and forward-facing orientation of the human body. Note also that *har* – "mountain," which has no inherent front/back orientation, has been schematized as facing the speaker, as evidenced by the use of *gav* – back for the distant part. Thus, knowledge of the way the body is carried and

---

36. Atkins, "Role of the Example," 27.
37. Petruck, "Frame Semantics and the Lexicon," 279.
38. Petruck, 279.
39. Petruck, 280.

oriented also figures into the way entities structured in terms of the human body are named.⁴⁰

From the above example and many others that Petruck gives, she demonstrates that using the body frame is the most reliable way of analyzing the Hebrew lexical items in the example, since the referential domain, the body, demonstrates how the masses understood the world around them. Hence, her approach offers an "approach to the study of meaning – word meaning, word structure, and semantic structure in the lexicon."⁴¹ Her monograph demonstrates how frame semantics is useful in lexicology and lexicography development. This is an invaluable input into the development of lexicon based on frame semantics.

Fillmore and Atkins used frame semantics in their analysis of "the semantics of risk and its neighbors" to show how practical frame semantics is in lexicography.⁴² They confirmed the limitations of a print dictionary in their study of the lexical item, risk. Their findings led to their conclusion that "the classical printed dictionary format is too restricted, in both length and dimension, to present an intelligible and truthful statement of the way the word RISK is used."⁴³ Since this study on "the semantics of risk and its neighbors" ascertained the need, they proposed a consideration of an online dictionary.

In their research, they offer what is likely to be the future of dictionaries – an online dictionary – which has words and their related polysemous words linked within a semantic frame. Once a word is entered for search, a window displays the meaning of the lexical item with other related lexical items within the same frame. The value for this online dictionary is that "the necessary links to the background frames are generally not made available in print dictionaries . . . [and] the lexicon inevitably uncovers much more information about words than standard dictionaries have room for."⁴⁴ With the advancement in technology and as the need becomes more apparent, Fillmore and Atkins' proposal may some day become a reality.

---

40. Petruck, 285.
41. Petruck, "Frame Semantics," 4.
42. Fillmore and Atkins, "Towards a Frame-Based Organization," 75–102.
43. Atkins and Fillmore, "Challenges of Corpus Lexicography," 350.
44. Fillmore and Atkins, "Towards a Frame-Based Organization," 76.

Atkins' article on "seeing" is an additional demonstration of the benefit of frame semantics to lexicography.[45] While the entry by Fillmore and Atkins above demonstrates broadening of the existing lexical items, Atkins in her article on seeing demonstrated that some of the existing lexical entries are erroneously entered while some of the key ones are omitted. She used the "perception frame" to analyze seeing. The elements of this frame include the one experiencing – one seeing or looking,[46] and the percept – what is being seen. Some of the verbs that occur with this frame are those that express senses of touch, hearing, taste and smell. She noted that the word "see" has synonyms of the verbs like

> *behold, note, notice, espy, descry, observe, contemplate, survey, view, perceive, discern, remark, scan, skim;* Webster's New Dictionary of Synonyms (1984: Merriam-Webster Inc.) offers the same list without *scan* and *skim;* the verbs examined in this paper add *glimpse, spot, spy and catch sight of;* Collins Dictionary and Thesaurus (1987) adds *distinguish, heed, identify, look, make out, mark, recognize, regard* and *witness*. In compiling a usage note, or an entry in a dictionary of synonyms, there are certain aspects of meaning to which one would wish to give priority. The first is the modality of perception. Synonyms of *see* in its core sense should belong exclusively to the visual modality. This requirement removes from the list above the following verbs: *note, notice, perceive, discern, remark, distinguish, heed, identify, make out, mark* and *recognize*.[47]

In this category, Atkins separates the visual sense of see from the "see" which has a sense of mental activity likened to thinking. These two senses of "see" do not belong to the same frame. Other than the visual sense of see, Atkins notes that the second in priority is the type of experience, active or passive. In frame semantics terms, 'see' has a passive experience[48] and

---

45. Atkins, "Analysing the Verbs," 42–56.
46. Atkins refers to him as "experiencer."
47. Atkins, "Analysing the Verbs," 53.
48. The experience is passive in the sense that there is no mental energy (thinking) required in the action of seeing. For example, you can see a bird flying and there is no mental energy required, by the one seeing, to make the bird fly.

this would exclude from the list those verbs where the experience "is active, namely: contemplate, look, observe, regard, scan, skim, survey and view."[49] The application of the perception frame weeds out words that Atkins has established that do not belong to the perception frame, and which, should be entered under a different category.

2.1.4.3 Frame Semantics Is Useful for Language Acquisition

Frame semantics is useful for language acquisition and foreign language learning/teaching. Fillmore gives an example of a child who is using a pencil. First, the child will associate the pencil with a specific place of sitting and the simple drawings that he draws. Later, the child will be able to differentiate the pencil from different drawings and the drawing materials. As the learning process continues, the child will tell the difference between draw, write, print and sketch, and will be able to identify and differentiate different writing tools: crayon, chalk as well as the writing materials on which to write: chalk board, paper among others.[50] In this example, the child has built knowledge from the basic scene of associating a pencil with a specific place of sitting. The description above fits within Fillmore's summary that in "language-learning the child first learns labels for whole situations, and only later learns labels for individual objects."[51]

Frame semantics is useful for foreign language learning and teaching. Fillmore notes this by stating that "in meaning acquisition, first one has labels for whole scenes or experiences, then one has labels for isolable parts of these, and finally one has a repertory of labels for schematic or abstract scenes and a repertory of labels for entities perceived independently of the scenes in which they were first encountered."[52] For example, if an individual would want to learn the word *ndũnyũ* in Kĩkamba, he will have to learn two frames of *ndũnyũ*: one is the shopping center frame and second is the commercial frame. In the first example, the frame element *ndũnyũ* evokes the shopping center frame in which there are many retail and wholesale shops, hotels, motels, dispensaries, dairies, pharmacies, among others. In the second usage, the

---

49. Atkins, "Analysing the Verbs," 53.
50. Fillmore, "Alternative to Checklist Theories," 127.
51. Fillmore, "Scenes-and-Frames Semantics," 62.
52. Fillmore, 62.

frame element *ndũnyũ* evokes the commercial day of active business frame. This is the day when people bring all sorts of things to sell. During this day, items for sale are relatively cheap compared to the other days. Apparently, *ndũnyũ* frame for commercial active business is well known (easy to infer) than *ndũnyũ* frame for shopping center. The understanding of *ndũnyũ* for active market days will also ensure the foreigner understands why people prefer to go to the market on a particular day than other days.

Thus far, this chapter has largely focused on the theory of frame semantics which is the main theory applied in this research but complemented by other theories reviewed below. The remainder of this chapter will focus on the symbolic approach proposed by Richard Shweder and Jonathan Haidt, the logic theory proposed by Daniel Fessler, the qualitative research method and the proposed complementary approach, which is the integration of these theories, in this research.

2.2 Richard Shweder and Jonathan Haidt's Symbolic Approach

The symbolic approach is part of the field of cultural psychology, which in turn is part of cognitive anthropology. The focus of cultural psychology is twofold: understanding of culture and finding the meaning of concepts from the indigenous peoples' point of view. Cultural psychology is summarized as "consisting of meanings, conceptions, and interpretive schemes that are activated, constructed, or brought online through participation in normative social institutions and routine practices."[53] The task of the researcher is to interpret concepts factoring in the different schemes that are activated. The use of the term "schema" in cultural psychology is not different from the use of the term "frame" by Fillmore. The symbolic approach is specifically applied to the study of emotions within cultures in that it "explores a cultural/symbolic/meaning-centered approach to the study of the emotions."[54] While the word "culture" has a wide variety of definitions across different disciplines, Shweder and Haidt define it as "ideas about what are true, good, beautiful, and efficient that are made manifest in the speech, laws, and customary practices

---

53. Shweder and Haidt, "Cultural Psychology of Emotions," 136.
54. Shweder and Haidt, 134.

of a self-regulating group."[55] According to this methodology, the meaning of a specific emotion is "systematically related to the kind of ethic (autonomy, community, or divinity) prevalent in a cultural community."[56] The hallmark of this method is that an "'emotion' is not something separable from the conditions that justify it, from the somatic and affective events that are ways of feeling or being touched by it, or from the actions it demands."[57] Shweder argues that an emotion is like a complete story, which is broken down into its subparts that are part of the whole emotion experience process, for the purposes of research and translation into another language. He has proposed specific questions that are essential for this symbolic approach in the study of emotions. They are as follows:

> Are they alike or different in their somatic experiences . . . ? . . . Are they alike or different in their affective experiences . . . ? . . . Are they alike or different in their antecedent conditions of those somatic and affective experiences . . . ? . . . Are they alike or different in the perceived implications of those antecedent conditions for self-esteem . . . ? . . . Are they alike or different in the extent to which showing or displaying that state of consciousness has been socially baptized as a vice or virtue or as a sign of sickness or health? . . . Are they alike or different in the plans for the self-management of self-esteem that are activated as part of the emotion script . . . ? . . . Are they alike or different in the iconic and symbolic vehicles used for giving expression to the whole package deal?[58]

When Shweder questions the somatic experiences, he is referring to those experiences that are physically felt. These experiences would include muscle tension, being nauseated, dizziness, fatigue and loss of breath among others. The enquiry about the affective feelings is geared toward examining psychological feelings like agitation or emptiness. The antecedent conditions are those events that provoke the experience of a certain emotion. Examples of antecedent conditions are like job loss which may provoke the feeling

---

55. Shweder and Haidt, 135.
56. Shweder and Haidt, 143–67.
57. Shweder and Haidt, 154–55.
58. Shweder and Haidt, 155–56.

of sadness, or the inability to bear children in the African context which may provoke the feeling of shame. Concerning plans for management of self-esteem, people manage different emotions in varied ways. Taking the example of a person who has received good news, he may manage the joy by celebrating. A person who is ashamed may choose to withdraw from social settings while an angry person may manage anger by retaliation. A fearful person may choose to manage the fear by fleeing. The common symbolic vehicles used in the expression of emotions include: facial expression, voice change, posture change and sometimes an action.[59]

The relevance of the symbolic approach has been demonstrated in the study of *Rasādhayāya*[60] in the *Sanskrit*[61] language. The cultural study exemplified that there was no word in English which is equivalent to the word "emotion" in *Sanskrit*. Shweder and Haidt noted that the word *lajja*, which is assumed as the English equivalent of shame, is different and that *Raga* is not similar to anger. They concluded by emphasizing the value of symbolic approach, by noting that in the application of "the symbolic structure of the emotions, researchers can render the meaning of other peoples' mental states without assimilating them in misleading ways into an a priori set of familiar lexical items."[62] Having stated the relevance of the symbolic approach, the next section is on "logic" by Daniel Fessler.

2.3 Daniel M. T. Fessler's "Logic"

The third method that I use was developed by Daniel M. T. Fessler. Fessler said, "It is possible to describe an emotion in terms of what I call its 'logic,' that is, the abstracted set of conditions wherein it is experienced."[63] In this "logic," an emotion can be broken down to different levels of developmental stages, which build up to the experience of the emotion. Fessler has demonstrated

---

59. Shweder and Haidt, 155–56.
60. Rasādhayāya is an ancient piece of literature that bears a description of "human self-consciousness about the emotions."
61. Sanskrit comes from the word *saṁskrta*. It is a classical language of Hinduism and is now used mostly in religious ceremonies, in poetry and drama.
62. Shweder and Haidt, "Cultural Psychology of Emotions," 167.
63. Fessler, "Toward an Understanding," 5.

the value of this logic in his study of *malu* "shame" in Dusun Bagak.[64] In his analysis, he broke down *malu* into six levels of development. For illustrative purpose, his observation of *malu* was that it is characterized by a six-point logic[65] as follows:

> Six-point logic
> a.   Ego violates a norm
> b.   Ego is aware of his failure
> c.   An Other is also aware of Ego's failure
> d.   Ego is aware of the Other's knowledge
> e.   Other displays hostility or revulsion toward Ego
>   -OR- Ego assumes that Other experiences hostility
>   and revulsion toward Ego
> f.   Ego experiences *malu*, an aversive emotion

According to this methodology, the proposed steps reveal the set of conditions that precedes an experience of a certain emotion. The steps offer a useful guideline, which changes depending on the data that each context presents. Concerning this research, the six steps by Fessler are helpful in examining *ngoò* which is an emotion that is evoked by קָצַף.

The three methods outlined above are used in the analysis of the data for this research. The last methodology mentioned below is for data collection. Since this is a cross-cultural research, the acquisition of data from the Akamba requires a different approach from the analyzing approach. The different modes of data collection used fall under the qualitative research.

2.4 Qualitative Field Research

In my field research, I have collected my data from parts of the Ūkambani region within three counties – Machakos, Makueni and Kītui – which are largely dominated by the Akamba people and which geographically is located in the lower eastern part of Kenya. The Kīkamba language has three main dialects, but I will treat them as four because of a little known one, which

---

64. Dusun Bagak is a pseudonym for a village in Sumatra, Indonesia.

65. Since languages are different, each language will have a different set of conditions and not necessarily six as it is the case with *malu*.

is gaining prominence in the northeastern part of Kĩtui County, formerly Mwingĩ District.

In the process of data collection, I used qualitative research which, as Donna Mertens notes, "is designed to provide an in-depth description of a specific program, practice or setting."[66] The study of a practice within its setting, allows one to describe objects and events in terms of the meaning given by the local people. Qualitative research relies upon a number of methods which include: "case study; personal experience; introspection; life story; interview; artifacts; cultural texts and productions; observational, historical, interactional, and visual texts – that describe routine and problematic moments and meanings in individuals' lives."[67] Out of the above-mentioned approaches, those that are applied here are interviews, personal experience, life stories and observations. The interviews are mainly done with individuals and in focus groups. In employing these different approaches to data collection, a key point to note is that the goal of the researcher is to seek the indigenous conceptualization of the subject. The cultural setting and the social well-being of the local people play an important role in the way they shape their concepts. As Sharan Merriam notes, "the key to understanding qualitative research lies with the idea that meaning is socially construed by individuals in interaction with their world."[68] Specifically for this research, the goal is to understand the meaning of the emotion of *ngoò* based on the Akamba's world and experiences, through the process of data collection, analysis, and a description of the findings.[69]

The following section states the complementary approach that is used in this research.

2.5 Proposed Complementary Approach

In this research, I propose a complementary approach to the study of the cross-cultural study of קצף in the BHS and *ngoò* in Kĩkamba. The complexity of the data and the subject of emotion, in which a single method is insufficient,

---

66. Mertens, *Research and Evaluation*, 229.
67. Mertens, 230.
68. Merriam, "Introduction to Qualitative Research," 3.
69. Merriam, 5.

necessitate this complementary approach. The proposed complementary approach is the Fillmore-Shweder (frame semantics-symbolic) approach, the Fessler-Shweder (logic-symbolic) approach and the Shweder symbolic approach. This is the order in which the methods are applied to the analysis of the data.

In the analysis of the Kĩkamba data, in chapter 4, I will mainly use Fessler's approach and complement it with Shweder's method. Later in chapter 5, I will use Shweder's approach in the comparative analysis of both the BHS and the Kĩkamba data. This flow of the study is the basis for the proposed complementary approach: Fillmore's-Shweder's approach, Fessler's-Shweder's approach and Shweder's approach.

CHAPTER 3

The קצף Frame

This chapter examines the קצף concept in the Bible (*Biblia Hebraica Stuttgartensia*, hereafter BHS) and answers the following questions: Do קצף occurrences have any pattern? Do all the lexical items associated with קצף fit within the קצף pattern, if any? Is the קצף usage in the Aramaic texts different or similar to the קצף usage in the Hebrew texts? What are the distinctive features of קצף? This research demonstrates that the קצף occurrences fit within a specific frame, named in this project as the קצף frame. The קצף frame, I argue, is characterized by קֶצֶף being perceived as an abstract object,[1] which comes out of (comes from) the Ego, the one experiencing קצף, and follows an abstract trajectory marked by the verb היה and rests on the landmark[2] identified by the preposition על. The terms Ego, trajectory and landmark are used in cognitive grammar (the methodologies used in this research are part of cognitive grammar) to explain concepts that involve motion. For example, if someone says "New Year is approaching," New year is the trajector – the object that is moving, the visualized path of movement is the trajectory and the implied destination, that is, the New Year is soon approaching "me" is the landmark. In the case for emotions, first there is the person who is experiencing the emotion and that person is the Ego.[3] The emotion that is experienced is the קֶצֶף which is the trajector since it moves and the person or people to whom it is directed becomes the landmark. In addition, it is demonstrated

---

1. Although קֶצֶף is an emotion and, therefore, a nontangible thing, it is idiomatically talked of in the BHS as if it is something tangible. This kind of perception by the Hebrews in antiquity has informed the use of "abstract object" when referring to קֶצֶף within its frame.
2. Landmark is a term within cognitive grammar that refers to the object.
3. Fessler, "Toward an Understanding," 76–77.

later in this chapter that this frame has a vertical relationship because of, first, the syntactical function of the preposition עַל and second, because of what is termed here as "the vertical relational function" because the Ego is a superior to the landmark – a subordinate. It is important to note that while the preposition עַל has a locative function translated as "on" when used with the קֶצֶף noun forms, it has an adversative function meaning "with" or "against"[4] when used with the קָצַף verbal forms. In other words, Ego is expressing the emotion of anger against the one provoking Ego. The adversative function identifies the landmark against whom the emotion is directed. Allen Ross notes that when the preposition עַל has an adversative function, it is "especially with verbs expressing or eliciting painful emotion."[5] Other scholars have translated עַל as "with" when it is indicating the end goal of a process.[6] The קצף frame explains what this process is. Although the preposition is given two different meanings in this research, the two functions complement each other within the קצף frame.

This chapter also explains that the קצף usage in the Aramaic texts fits within the קצף frame. After examining all the Hebrew and Aramaic texts, this research analyzes the distinctive features of קצף. These features are: First, the קצף frame; second, within the frame, קצף carries the sense of "anger" when it is experienced by a superior person against a subordinate; third, when קצף is experienced by an inferior person, it carries the meaning of frustration in the qal stem, provocation of the superior to anger by the inferior in the hiphil stem and an expression of anger to a superior in the hithpael stem. Fourth, when קצף is experienced by a group, the group has a military might (superior advantage against their target) and lastly, קצף is associated mostly with punishment either actualized or intended. Because of its association with punishment,[7] קֶצֶף is argued to be a strong emotion equivalent to "wrath" in English. Wrath is variously defined as "retributory punishment for an offense

---

4. Arnold and Choi, *Guide to Biblical Hebrew*, 4.1.16f.
5. Ross, *Introducing Biblical Hebrew*, 410.
6. Van der Merwe, Naudé, and Kroeze, *Biblical Hebrew Reference Grammar*, 292.
7. In most occurences, the punishment of קצף is commensurate to the crime committed regardless of whether God or man is the subject. However, there are a few occurrences, where man is the Ego, in which the punishment is hard to justify since the context is not explicit on what the crime was. For example, Genesis 40:1 and 41:10 talk of the imprisonment of the cup bearer and the chief baker yet the nature of their crime is not specified. This example and others are explained in detail later in this chapter.

or a crime; divine chastisement"[8] or "violent or stern indignation," as or "divine vengeance or retribution";[9] as "extreme anger,"[10] and as "divine displeasure or retribution."[11] In this research, the meaning of קצף is "wrath" in the sense of "retributory punishment for an offense or a crime."[12] The first category, in the following section, focuses on the details of the קצף frame.

3.1 The קצף Frame

The analysis in this section shows that the קצף frame is comprised of the Ego (the one experiencing קֶצֶף) who is also the source of קֶצֶף, the trajector (קֶצֶף as the abstract object) which comes out of Ego, the trajectory (the path taken by the trajector) and landmark (patient[13]), the object which קֶצֶף comes (falls) on.

The קצף frame's data is analyzed in three stages: the core frame elements, the peripheral frame elements and the extrathematic frame elements. In this frame, the core frame elements of קֶצֶף can be summarized as follows: Ego (God or human) is the source of קֶצֶף, קֶצֶף is the trajector and person(s) is the landmark. The following subsection is on the core frame elements of קצף.

3.1.1 The Core Frame Elements of קצף: Investigation of קצף in the BHS

The BHS has eleven lexical items that have the sense of anger as demonstrated in the table (Table 2) below.

---

8. *Webster's New Collegiate Dictionary*, 988.
9. Patrick Hanks, *Collins Dictionary*, 1673.
10. Paul Procter, *Cambridge International Dictionary*, 1689.
11. Brown, *Shorter Oxford English Dictionary*, 3727.
12. *Webster's New Collegiate Dictionary*, 988.
13. The landmark is also treated as a patient because there is a change of state when קֶצֶף is effected. For example, Jeremiah – who was free and not wounded – was beaten (wounded) and imprisoned (denied freedom) by the Babylonians (Jer 27:15).

Table 2

Hebrew root	Lexical usage
אנף (אף)	As a noun, it means "nose, nostril, face, anger."[14] The אף meaning nose sometimes has the idea of heavy breathing through the nose because of anger (Deut 32:22).[15] At other times it refers to the reddening of the face symbolically because of anger (Gen 30:2).[16]
זעם	In its qal verbal form, it means to be indignant, to curse or to denounce.[17] In its qal passive participle form, it means to be accursed.[18] As a substantive participle, it means the cursed one. As a niphal participle, it means to be made indignant[19] or to be "inflicted by a curse."[20] In its hiphil imperfect form, it means to make indignant or cause to curse. In its noun form, it means indignation or curse.[21]
זעף	As a verb in the qal verbal form, it means to be angry or thin.[22] In its infinitive form, it means to be enraged or to be angry.[23] As a noun, it means anger[24] or rage.[25] As an adjective, it means angry or upset.[26]
חמה	In its qal verbal form, it means to see, to be hot or to be inflamed.[27] As a noun, it means venom, heat, poison or anger.[28] Depending on the context, it also has the sense of rage or wrath.[29]

---

14. Clines, "(אף) אנף," *DCH*, 1:344, 353–55.
15. Koehler and Baumgartner, "אף," *HALOT*, 1:76.
16. Koehler and Baumgartner, 76.
17. Clines, "זעם," *DCH*, 3:125–26.
18. Clines, 125–26.
19. Clines, 125–26.
20. Koehler and Baumgartner, "זעם," *HALOT*, 1:277.
21. Clines, "זעם," *DCH*, 3:125–26.
22. Clines, "זעף," *DCH*, 3:126–27.
23. Clines, 126–27.
24. Clines, 126–27.
25. Koehler and Baumgartner, "זעף," *HALOT*, 1:277.
26. Clines, "זעף," *DCH*, 3:126–27.
27. Clines, "חמה," *DCH*, 3:249–51.
28. Clines, 249–51.
29. Koehler and Baumgartner, "חמה," *HALOT*, 1:326.

Hebrew root	Lexical usage
חרה	When it is a verb in the qal stem, it means either to burn, to be kindled with anger, to be angry, to be incensed or to dwindle away.[30] In the hiphil perfect form, it means to "burn with zeal."[31] In the hithpael imperfect form, it means to show oneself angry, be annoyed.[32] It can also be used as a participle to mean "compete."[33] As a noun, it means burn, anger or wrath.[34]
כעס	As a verb in the qal perfect verbal form, it means to be angry or vexed.[35] In its piel perfect form, it means to provoke to anger.[36] In its hiphil perfect form, it means to provoke to anger, to disturb, to offend or to insult.[37] As a noun, it means anger, irritation, grief, vexation or provocation.[38]
עבר	This lexical item has a wide range of lexical usage. This entry, therefore, limits itself to the sense of anger of עבר. When it is a verb in the qal stem, it means to be angry.[39] In its hithpael form, it means to be angry, furious, enraged, impose as angry or display characteristics of being angry.[40] Other usages include incitement to anger, to infuriate, being arrogant, being headstrong and rebelling against.[41]

---

30. Clines, "חרה," DCH, 3:313–14.
31. Clines, 313–14.
32. Clines, 313–14.
33. Clines, 313–14.
34. Clines, 313–14.
35. Clines, "כעס," DCH, 4:448–50.
36. Clines, 448–50.
37. Clines, 448–50.
38. Clines, 448–50.
39. Clines, "עבר," DCH, 6:242.
40. Clines, 242.
41. Clines, 242.

Hebrew root	Lexical usage
קנא	When it is a verb in the qal verbal form, it means to be jealous, to be angry or to be zealous.⁴² In its hiphil form, it means to provoke or stir to jealousy or anger.⁴³ As an adjective, it means jealous.⁴⁴ As a noun, it means zeal, jealousy, anger, wrath, passion, redness or rust.⁴⁵ It can also mean to be excited concerning something or someone, to annoy and to hurt.⁴⁶
רוח	As a noun, it means "wind, breath, Spirit, life giving spirit, temper and anger."⁴⁷ Sometimes it can mean wind especially when translated as someone's spirit (Dan 5:20).⁴⁸
רגז	When it is a verb in the qal stem, it means to shake, tremble or quake.⁴⁹ In its hiphil form, it means to cause to "tremble, shake, disquiet, cause unrest, disturb, enrage or provoke."⁵⁰ In its hithpael form, it means rage or quarrel.⁵¹ As an adjective, it means trembling or agitated. As a noun, it means "agitation, turmoil, trouble, raging, anger, wrath, excitement or rumbling."⁵² It is also used in its construct form to mean "rumbling of."⁵³

Previous scholarship, especially by Matthew Schlimm, has identified other lexical items that occur in close relation to the BHS lexical items with sense of anger. He says,

> [T]he words with the strongest tendencies to appear with terms for anger include: [1] קנא (*jealousy*); [2] words related to the more extreme forms of violence, particularly, הרג (*kill*),

---

42. Clines, "קנא," *DCH*, 7:263–66.
43. Clines, 263–66.
44. Clines, 263–66.
45. Clines, 263–66.
46. Koehler and Baumgartner, "קנא," *HALOT*, 2:1109–10.
47. Clines, "רוח," *DCH*, 7:427–40.
48. Koehler and Baumgartner, "רוח," *HALOT*, 2:1979–80.
49. Clines, "רגז," *DCH*, 7:409–10.
50. Clines, 409–10.
51. Clines, 409–10.
52. Clines, 409–10.
53. Clines, 409–10.

שמד (*utter destruction*), חרם (*annihilate*), and כלה (*finish*); [3] word[sic] derived from the root רעע (*bad, evil, calamity*); [4] אש (*fire*) and various related terms; [5] שפך and נתך both meaning *pour out*; [6] words referring to rulers (e.g., מלך, *king*); [7] ריב (*dispute*), דין (*judge, contend*), and other words referring to angry speech; [8] שוב (*turn*); and [9] qualifiers such as מאד (*very*), ארך (*length*), and קצר (*shortness*). Finally, [10] words for anger[54] have a strong tendency to appear with one another.[55]

The data in this chapter demonstrates that the קצף frame occurs with words, which are not mentioned by Schlimm. Out of the list above, only ריב (dispute) and מאד (very) are paralleled with קצף in the poetic genre; it is explained later in this chapter that ריב (dispute) is an extrathematic frame element of the קצף frame while מאד (very) marks the degree of how the emotion is experienced. The verbs that occur with קֶצֶף, and are not mentioned by Schlimm in the above extract, probably because of the limitation of his study, are יצא (to come out), היה (to come/fall) and בוא (to enter/come). These three verbs are the main verbs in קֶצֶף clauses and show that קֶצֶף is the trajector (subject) in those clauses. Those verbs are complemented by the use of preposition עַל (on) which is usually conjugated to the object (landmark), meaning that קֶצֶף comes out of the Ego and comes on the object (landmark). In the analysis, these verbs and the preposition are the items that help the reader to focus on the predominant information in the verse or clause. The term "focus" is used in this research to mean the grammatical elements (in this research the verbs and prepositions) that draw the attention of the reader to the predominant information in the verse or clause.[56]

---

54. The ten words with the nuance of an anger that Schlimm identifies are the above-mentioned ones in table 1 with an exception of רוח and קנא. However, he adds שטם as a lexical item meaning harbored anger (Schlimm, *From Fratricide to Forgiveness*, 131).

55. Schlimm, *From Fratricide to Forgiveness*, 100.

56. Shimasaki, *Focus Structure*, 42.

3.1.1.1 The Source of קֶצֶף Is Explained By the Use of יָצָא and בוֹא Verbs, and the Preposition מִן (and Compounds of מִן) in קֶצֶף Clauses

Factoring in the above mentioned verbs and prepositions used in קֶצֶף clauses, it is evidently explained that קֶצֶף was conceptualized as an abstract object that left the Ego (experiencer) as demonstrated by the use of יצא and בוא verbs, and the preposition מִן (and compounds of מִן). In this frame, קֶצֶף is both the subject of the clause and the abstract trajector that comes out or from the Ego, and comes on the landmark. The following examples illustrate this frame. The order of the examples advanced in the research is based on the BHS order of the canon – Torah, prophets and the writings.[57] The first example is found in Numbers 17:11[16:46][58] as stated below.

1. Num 17:11[16:46]

וַיֹּאמֶר מֹשֶׁה אֶל־אַהֲרֹן קַח אֶת־הַמַּחְתָּה וְתֶן־עָלֶיהָ אֵשׁ מֵעַל הַמִּזְבֵּחַ וְשִׂים קְטֹרֶת וְהוֹלֵךְ מְהֵרָה אֶל־הָעֵדָה וְכַפֵּר עֲלֵיהֶם כִּי־יָצָא הַקֶּצֶף מִלִּפְנֵי יְהוָה הֵחֵל הַנָּגֶף:

> Then Moses said to Aaron, "take your fireholder and put fire from the altar in it and set incense on it and take it quickly to the community and make an atonement for them because (קֶצֶף) 'anger' has come out from the Lord and the plague has begun."

In this passage, Aaron makes atonement because God's קֶצֶף had come on the Israelites and the expected outcome was that God would destroy them. According to the English text, this chapter can be divided into three parts: the first part is verses 1–34 which is the destruction of the Israelites who were led by Korah to oppose Moses. The earth opened up and swallowed them (vv. 31–34). Part two is about the group of 250 men (vv. 35–38) who were consumed by fire for making an offering of incense against the law because offering of incense was to be done only by the priest. The third part (vv. 39–50) is about the grumbling of the Israelites against Moses and Aaron, accusing them of being responsible for the death of the other Israelites (v. 41). For

---

57. This order is preferred because it is the order in the BHS which is the primary text for this research. However, there are instances where this order is altered for the flow of the argument.

58. This verse, Numbers 16:46, is according to the English translations. In the BHS, it is Numbers 17:11.

the third time in this passage, God wanted to destroy the Israelites for their grumbling. It is in this latter context that Moses urged Aaron to hurry and make an atonement to appease God's קֶצֶף. Because of this atonement, the plague stopped (v. 48). Although the specifics of this plague are not stated, the context presupposes death. The role of Aaron was to avert the resultant onslaught. The intended punishment, effect of God's קֶצֶף, was destruction through death of the Israelites, the remnants of the previous two judgments.

The verse quoted above begins with וַיֹּאמֶר, which is introducing the direct speech. The conjunction וּ has a sequential syntactical function which is translated as "then"[59] because the preceding verse is about God's warning that he is about to consume the entire congregation. The order by Moses to Aaron is in the form of five imperatives קַח "take," וְתֶן־ "and put," וְשִׂים "and set," וְהוֹלֵךְ "and walk" and וְכַפֵּר "and atone."[60] Baruch Levine says, concerning this atonement, that it "expresses the spatial factor in expiatory rites, performed in close proximity to persons or objects.[61] Here Aaron was positioned between those already stricken by the plague and those still unaffected."[62] George Gray noted, "The people had sinned by means of censers and incense, so propitiation was made for them in the same way."[63] Then Moses gave the reason for all this at the end of verse 11[46], which is introduced by the particle כִּי.

The כִּי introduces a causal clause,[64] which is translated as "because," and the clause explains the cause for God's קֶצֶף, which necessitated the reason for the offering. The קֶצֶף is the subject (trajector) which is leaving (יָצָא) the Ego, hence its perception as an abstract object. The verb יָצָא when it is intransitive can be translated as "go out, come out."[65] In its transitive form, it can be translated as "go out from, leave."[66] In the passages where יָצָא is used with קֶצֶף, the verb bears the idea of exiting. The translation deemed plausible, therefore, is "come out."

---

59. Seow, *Grammar for Biblical Hebrew*, 285.

60. This is the only reference in which God's קֶצֶף is atoned. The understanding held in this research is that atonement was necessary because the sin of rebellion was in the tent of meeting.

61. Who or which needs to be atoned for.

62. Levine, *Numbers 1–20*, 420–21.

63. Gray, *Commentary on Numbers*, 213.

64. Seow, *Grammar for Biblical Hebrew*, 331.

65. Clines, "יצא," *DCH*, 4:254–65.

66. Clines, 254–65.

In the verse above, the verb יָצָא "it has come out" is a persistent perfective[67] because it is denoting the activity of destruction, which started in the past and had continued up to the present, the time of speaking. In this context, קֶצֶף resulted in the death of the Israelites. As it will be continuously stated in this chapter, קֶצֶף had a retributive effect (the retributive nature of קֶצֶף is interwoven in the exegesis and not discussed under a separate heading), either actualized or intended. The noun הַקֶּצֶף "the anger" has a definite article whose syntactical function is a definite in the imagination[68] since the context has a spate of deadly scenes because of the Israelites' rebellion. In other words, the Israelites had and were already experiencing God's anger. This last clause implies that the need for the atonement was because God's קֶצֶף had come and the plague had already begun. The verb of this clause is הֵחֵל "has begun," which is a recent act perfective[69] referring to an event that has occurred in the recent past. In this verse, קֶצֶף is the subject of the יָצָא verb. The offending situation in this verse was the offering of incense (v. 35) and the grumbling that followed (v. 41) from the Israelites accusing Moses and Aaron of killing the Israelites. This research is limited by the available data to probe this point further since the verse mentioned in the above verse is the only one in which the phrase כִּי־יָצָא הַקֶּצֶף occurs in the BHS. The phrase מִלִּפְנֵי יְהוָה "from the Lord"[70] focuses on the Ego, the source of קֶצֶף. Based on this understanding, this phrase has been translated as "קֶצֶף has come from the Lord".

There are numerous passages where יָצָא is used in the predicate to show movement of a person or thing from one point to another. This section will first give two general examples of the movement of things and second, give specific examples in which the subject of יָצָא is an emotion. First, Genesis 10 gives a record of the sons of Noah and describes how they spread to occupy the land after the flood. In verse 11, the record states, "out of the land he יָצָא 'went forth' to Assyria and built Nineveh, and the city Rehoboth, and Calah." According to this verse, Cush moved away from Babylon (v. 10) and relocated to Assyria. Second, the other example of יָצָא can be found in Exodus 21:3, which talks about the freeing of a slave once she/he has served for seven years.

---

67. Waltke and O'Connor, *Introduction to Biblical Hebrew*, 30.5.1c.
68. Waltke and O'Connor, 13.5.1e.
69. Waltke and O'Connor, 30.5.1b.
70. The מִלִּפְנֵי is a compound preposition, which means "from the presence of" (Seow, *Grammar for Biblical Hebrew*, 60).

At the end of the seventh year, the master would let his slave "יֵצֵא 'go out' (free) alone. But if he had a wife when he came, she must יָצָא 'go out' with him." In the case of the slave, there is a movement from the homestead of the slave's master to the slave's preferred destination. The two examples above are among many others that show that the concept of יָצָא is that of movement from one locality to another. However, there are many other passages where יָצָא does not imply a movement from one locality to another. Rather, יָצָא is used to signify that someone or something has gone out, or exited from a location. For example, in Genesis 19:23, we read "by the time Lot reached Zoar, the sun had risen over the land" (NIV). The phrase "the sun had risen over the land" is הַשֶּׁמֶשׁ יָצָא עַל־הָאָרֶץ which can literally be translated as "the sun came out on the land." The Hebrews' thinking is that the sun revolves (moves) around the earth and it therefore comes out in the morning. The idea of the sun coming out is replicated in the description of the stars coming out (Neh 4:15).[71] Another example is in Esther 1:17 which reads: "for the queen's conduct will become known to all the women, and so they will despise their husbands and say, 'King Xerxes commanded Queen Vashti to be brought before him, but she would not come'" (NIV). The phrase translated as "for the queen's conduct will become known" is כִּי־יֵצֵא דְבַר־הַמַּלְכָּה, which can literally be translated as "because the queen's conduct 'will come out.'" The idea of יָצָא in this verse is that of making her conduct public. Vashti is referred to as "the queen" with a definite article because she is a well-known person.[72] These examples, and many more, for instance, in Leviticus 25:30, I Samuel 2:3; 24:15, and Isaiah 51:5, among others, show that יָצָא does not necessarily indicate a literal movement of someone or something from one locality to another. This latter use of יָצָא signifying the exit of something as discussed above is replicated in passages with other words that fall within the domain of anger. The יָצָא verb is used with רוּחַ "anger" and חֵמָה "anger" with a sense of "exiting" as explained in the examples below.

---

71. In some versions like NIV, KJV and NASB, verse 15 of Nehemiah is indicated as verse 21.

72. Chisholm, *From Exegesis to Exposition*, 73.

i. Prov 29:11

כָּל־רוּחוֹ יוֹצִיא כְסִיל A fool utters all his anger;

וְחָכָם בְּאָחוֹר יְשַׁבְּחֶנָּה but a wise man keeps it back and stills it.

The relationship of this bicola is that of base-contrast.[73] The first colon can also be translated as "a fool brings out all his anger." The יוֹצִיא is translated as "brings out" and not "comes out" as in the example on קֶצֶף because in the latter example the verb is in the hiphil stem,[74] whose translation is causative.[75] The noun כָּל־ "all his anger" is a non-cognate effected accusative[76] meaning the accusative is the effect/result of the verb. The noun רוּחוֹ has a third person masculine affix, which can be regarded as a genitive suffix.[77] It is, therefore, translated as a genitive of authorship[78] meaning that a fool expresses his anger as opposed to a wise man who holds it back. Richard Clifford describes the fool as one who lets loose his anger in the sense of breathing fast in agitation.[79] The character of the fool in this verse is similar to the character mentioned in verse 9 which depicts him as someone who lets out everything.[80]

The conjunction וְ in colon b has an adversative syntactical function[81] meaning "but" since it is contrasting the deeds of the fool and the wise. The חָכָם is a substantive adjective, which can be translated as either the wise one or the wise man.[82] What the wise man does is he is בְּאָחוֹר "keeping it in" which literally can be translated as "in back part." The verb of this clause יְשַׁבְּחֶנָּה "he keeps still," which carries a meaning of "keeping it within,"[83] is taken in this research to have a habitual non-perfective,[84] denoting that whenever a wise man is angered he repeatedly keeps his anger still.

---

73. Wendland, *Analyzing the Psalms*, 74.
74. Although a good parallel to Numbers 17:11 would have been a verb in the qal stem, this verse is preferred because יָצָא is used in the context of a Hebrew word carrying anger meaning.
75. Seow, *Grammar for Biblical Hebrew*, 181.
76. Joüon and Muraoka, *Grammar of Biblical Hebrew*, 125a.
77. Van der Merwe, Naudé, and Kroeze, *Biblical Hebrew Reference Grammar*, 200.
78. Chisholm, *From Exegesis to Exposition*, 62.
79. Clifford, *Proverbs: A Commentary*, 252.
80. Koptak, *Proverbs: From Biblical Text*, 640.
81. Seow, *Grammar for Biblical Hebrew*, 284.
82. Arnold and Choi, *Guide to Biblical Hebrew*, 2.5.3.
83. Murphy, *Proverbs*, 220.
84. Van der Merwe, Naudé, and Kroeze, *Biblical Hebrew Reference Grammar*, 148.

In the example given above, יָצָא does not signify the movement of רוּחַ "anger" from one locality to another, but explains anger leaving Ego in the sense of verbalized anger. The following section gives two examples in which יָצָא is used with חֵמָה "anger" signifying movement from Ego, but the idea of transitioning from one locality to another is missing.

ii. Jer 4:4

הִמֹּלוּ לַיהוָה circumcise yourselves to the Lord

וְהָסִרוּ עָרְלוֹת לְבַבְכֶם and take away the foreskin(s) of your heart,

אִישׁ יְהוּדָה וְיֹשְׁבֵי יְרוּשָׁלָם you men of Judah and inhabitants of Jerusalem,

פֶּן־תֵּצֵא כָאֵשׁ חֲמָתִי וּבָעֲרָה lest my anger will come out like fire and burn

וְאֵין מְכַבֶּה מִפְּנֵי רֹעַ מַעַלְלֵיכֶם so that none can quench it, because of the evil of your doings.

This passage is about God's call to the Israelites to repent. The sentence begins with an idiom "Circumcise yourselves to God, and take away the foreskins of your heart," which is understood as an idiomatic way of calling for repentance. William McKane says this "is a demand for a dedication to Yahweh which is inward and profound and is not exhausted by an external rite."[85] John Bright shares similar thoughts and adds, "let repentance be from the heart."[86] The verb הִמֹּלוּ "circumcise yourselves" is a niphal stem which has a reflexive meaning, that is, the subject is also the object receiving the action of the verb.[87] This request is perhaps motivated by the practice of the ritual of circumcision, which was not "preceded by a right disposition within."[88] The phrase "circumcise the foreskin(s) of your hearts" is also mentioned in Deuteronomy 10:16. In both passages, the message is that of a call to repentance. This call to repentance is addressed to the men of Judah and the inhabitants of Jerusalem. However, it is important to establish the meaning of

---

85. McKane, *Commentary on Jeremiah*, 88.
86. Bright, *Jeremiah*, 25.
87. Seow, *Grammar for Biblical Hebrew*, 288.
88. Calvin and Owen, *Commentaries*, 206.

"Judah and Jerusalem" (and not "Judah and inhabitants of Jerusalem") since it is repeated in many other verses that are discussed later on.

The names "Judah and Jerusalem" are both figures of speech as used in this passage and in other passages quoted in this research. The understanding given here is therefore retained in the other places where it occurs without replication of the explanation. Judah has two possibilities of interpretation. First, it can mean a metonymy of the cause for the effect.[89] That is, Judah is the ancestor and the reference is to his posterity who is the effect. Second, Judah can also refer to the region, meaning it is a metonymy of the subject for the adjunct.[90] That is, Judah is the substitute for the inhabitants. Since the author talks of Judah and Jerusalem, and Jerusalem is a place, the understanding advanced here is that both Judah and Jerusalem are a metonymy of the subject for the adjunct, meaning they are used as a substitute for the inhabitants of Judah and Jerusalem (Judah and Jerusalem being a region and its main city, respectively). In the address in the verse above, they were warned to heed the call פֶּן־תֵּצֵא כָאֵשׁ חֲמָתִי "lest my (God's) anger like fire will come out" and consume them.

In this example, יָצָא is used to show an emotion exiting from Ego but not necessarily emanating from one locality for another. The last example in which יָצָא is used with a lexical item with a sense of anger is in Jeremiah 21:12.

iii. Jer 21:12

בֵּית דָּוִד כֹּה אָמַר יְהוָה O house of David, thus says the Lord,

דִּינוּ לַבֹּקֶר מִשְׁפָּט judge with justice in the morning,

וְהַצִּילוּ גָזוּל מִיַּד עוֹשֵׁק and deliver the robbed one out of the hand of the oppressing one,

פֶּן־תֵּצֵא כָאֵשׁ חֲמָתִי וּבָעֲרָה lest my anger come out like fire and burn

וְאֵין מְכַבֶּה מִפְּנֵי רֹעַ מַעַלְלֵיהֶם so that none can quench it, because of their evil deeds.

In this verse, Zedekiah, the king of Judah, inquired of God concerning the impending siege by the Babylonians. God assured him that he would hand them over to the Babylonians who would kill them (v. 6) and destroy their

---

89. Bullinger, *Figures of Speech*, 544.
90. Bullinger, 587.

city by fire (v. 10). However, in this prophecy of destruction God urged them, the Israelites, to exercise justice (vv. 12–14).

This verse begins with the noun בֵּית "house" which is a metonymy of the subject for the adjunct,[91] meaning household in the sense of a family. The proper name "David" is a metonymy of the cause for the effect,[92] meaning David is the ancestor and his posterity is the effect. The phrase "house of David" with this same meaning has been used in 1 Samuel 19:11; 20:16; 2 Samuel 3:1; 3:6; 1 Kings 12:20; 2 Kings 17:21; and Isaiah 7:13; 22:22. The speaker in this context is God whose speech is affirmed by the phrase כֹּה אָמַר יְהוָה "thus says the Lord." God's address is to the "house of David." This address means the posterity of David is supposed to דִּינוּ לַבֹּקֶר מִשְׁפָּט וְהַצִּילוּ גָזוּל מִיַּד עוֹשֵׁק "judge with justice in the morning, and deliver the robbed one out of the hand of the oppressing one." The verbs דִּינוּ "judge" and וְהַצִּילוּ "and deliver" are both imperatives of command,[93] signifying the sense of the importance of the task and its urgency. The object of the first command is מִשְׁפָּט "justice," which is an accusative of manner,[94] describing how the judgment should be done. This justice is to be done לַבֹּקֶר "in the morning" which has a preposition לְ whose syntactical function is a temporal function and so its translation as "in" denoting a specified period. The specified time is "in the morning" referring to the earliest time of the day, probably signifying that there should be no delay in dispensing justice.

Thus far, the verse is about God's instruction on what should be done. These instructions are to be followed פֶּן־תֵּצֵא כָאֵשׁ חֲמָתִי "lest (God's) anger will come out like (the) fire." The verb תֵּצֵא is a qal imperfect of a specific future,[95] implying that unless God's instruction to administer justice is followed, then inevitably his חֵמָה "anger will come out on them. The phrase "anger of God" will come out כָאֵשׁ "like the fire" is a simile of resemblance.[96] This simile is complemented by the following clause which states that, once this anger comes out, it will: וּבָעֲרָה וְאֵין מְכַבֶּה מִפְּנֵי רֹעַ מַעַלְלֵיהֶם "burn so that none can quench it, because of the evil of your deeds." Its burning is an idiom

---

91. Bullinger, 573.
92. Bullinger, 625.
93. Chisholm, *From Exegesis to Exposition*, 105.
94. Gibson, *Davidson's Introductory Hebrew Grammar*, 117 Rem. 1c.
95. Gibson, 64a.
96. Bullinger, *Figures of Speech*, 726.

stating how severe God's punishment will be, since, like fire "his judgment will blaze until everything is destroyed."⁹⁷ The reason this punishment will be visited on them is caused by their evil deeds. The phrase מִפְּנֵי רֹעַ מַעַלְלֵיהֶם occurs also in Jeremiah 4:4.

The examples above are focused on passages where the יָצָא verb is used, both in general passages where the subject is not an emotion and in specific passages where the verb occurs with other words with the sense of anger other than קֶצֶף. When יָצָא is used with קֶצֶף as the subject, the idea is that of a thing moving from one locality to another. Similarly, in the general transitive passages, it has been explained that יָצָא has the idea of movement of a person or a thing from one locality to another. However, in the passages with other words (other than קֶצֶף) that refer to anger, the only idea retained is that of exiting from the source because they do not share the same frame as קֶצֶף.⁹⁸

The second example that identifies קֶצֶף as an abstract object leaving its Ego is found in 2 Chronicles 32:26. The action of leaving is marked by the verb בוֹא. The verse reads as follows:

2. 2 Chr 32:26

וַיִּכָּנַע יְחִזְקִיָּהוּ בְּגֹבַהּ לִבּוֹ הוּא וְיֹשְׁבֵי יְרוּשָׁלָ͏ִם וְלֹא־בָא עֲלֵיהֶם קֶצֶף יְהוָה בִּימֵי יְחִזְקִיָּהוּ׃

But Hezekiah humbled himself for the pride of his heart, both he and the inhabitants of Jerusalem, therefore the (קֶצֶף) "anger" of the Lord did not come out on them in the days of Hezekiah.

The context of this verse is about God delivering Hezekiah the king of Judah from the hand of Sennacherib king of Assyria. The Assyrian king wrote an intimidating message to Hezekiah (vv. 10–15) and he insulted and mocked the God of Israel (vv. 16–19). In return, Hezekiah and Isaiah, the son of Amoz, prayed and God delivered them from the hand of Sennacherib through a fighting angel. The king of Assyria fell under the sword of his own sons (vv. 20–21). Because of this success, Hezekiah became proud but God punished him with illness, which almost took his life (vv. 24–25; cf. 2 Kgs 20:1--11).

---

97. McKane, *Commentary on Jeremiah*, 1:510.

98. The idea of קֶצֶף exiting from one person and falling on another person shows how different the קֶצֶף frame was from the other Hebrew words with the sense of anger. However, other than the frame, in some instances the antecedent conditions and the effects of all the other words with the sense of anger are similar.

In response, he humbled himself from his pride as stated in verse 26 quoted above. What provoked God's קֶצֶף in this context was Hezekiah's pride and the penalty was intended death (2 Kgs 20:1).

The verse begins with a conjunction וְ, which has an adversative syntactical function[99] meaning "but" because it is contrasting the pride of Hezekiah (vv. 24–25) and his humility and repentance (v. 26). The verb וַיִּכָּנַע is an ingressive perfective[100] which explains what Hezekiah began doing, humbling himself. The ingressive perfective is supported by the change of attitude, from pride (v. 25) to humility (v. 26). Hezekiah's repentance was not only for himself but also for the inhabitants of Jerusalem. For that reason, then וְלֹא־בָא עֲלֵיהֶם קֶצֶף יְהוָה "the קֶצֶף of the Lord did not come out on them."

The verb of this clause is בוֹא, which depending on the context can be translated as either to "go away (come out) . . . or enter."[101] This verb identifies the source from which the abstract object – trajector, leaves. The result of Hezekiah's repentance is that God's קֶצֶף did not come out on them. In this verse, the verb בָא is taken to have a simple present[102] function, meaning in this situation the action did not occur at the time of speaking. Looking back, they can confirm that the קֶצֶף did not come, leave the source (Ego), on them during the reign of Hezekiah. The preposition עַל has a locative function[103] with a vertical relationship in which it comes over or on the object. (It is discussed later in this research that the קצף frame is a vertical frame relationship between the Ego and the landmark). The time when the effect of this repentance lasted is stated as בִּימֵי יְחִזְקִיָּהוּ "in the days of Hezekiah." The preposition בְּ has a temporal function[104] since it conveys a point in time when an action took place. That is why it is translated as "in." It is clear in this verse that קֶצֶף originated from the Lord and it was conceptualized to move from the Ego to the landmark. This is the only verse in the BHS where the verb בוֹא occurs with קֶצֶף.

There are many other passages where בוֹא is used, but it is only in one of those many references that carries the meaning of anger. The following section

---

99. Seow, *Grammar for Biblical Hebrew*, 284.
100. Gibson, *Davidson's Introductory Hebrew Grammar*, 57 Rem. 2.
101. Clines, "בוֹא," *DCH*, 2:102.
102. Chisholm, *From Exegesis to Exposition*, 87, 97–98.
103. Arnold and Choi, *Guide to Biblical Hebrew*, 4.1.16a.
104. Arnold and Choi, 4.1.5b.

will give two examples from some of those passages in which the subject of בוֹא is not a person or a thing, and then cite the only reference where the subject of בוֹא is an emotion.

　　i. Gen 29:9

עוֹדֶנּוּ מְדַבֵּר עִמָּם וְרָחֵל ׀ בָּאָה עִם־הַצֹּאן אֲשֶׁר לְאָבִיהָ כִּי רֹעָה הִוא׃

While he was still talking with them, Rachel came in with her father's sheep, for she was the one who tended them.

The context of this passage is about Jacob arriving in Paddan Aram. Verses 4 to 8 record the conversation that Jacob had with the people of Harran before Rachel arrived as recorded in verse 9 above. According to the context, Rachel (בָּאָה) came in the middle of the conversation between Jacob and the people of Haran. That is why the adverb עוֹדֶנּוּ is translated as "while." It is clear in this verse that the verb בָּאָה is used in a context signifying movement from one locality to another.

This is the first of two examples given here to show that the verb בוֹא has an idea of movement from one place to another.

　　ii. 2 Kgs 4:25

וַתֵּלֶךְ וַתָּבוֹא אֶל־אִישׁ הָאֱלֹהִים אֶל־הַר הַכַּרְמֶל וַיְהִי כִּרְאוֹת אִישׁ־הָאֱלֹהִים אֹתָהּ מִנֶּגֶד וַיֹּאמֶר אֶל־גֵּיחֲזִי נַעֲרוֹ הִנֵּה הַשּׁוּנַמִּית הַלָּז׃

So she travelled and came to the man of God at Mount Carmel. When he saw her in the distance, the man of God said to his servant Gehazi, "Look! There is the Shunammite!"

The context of this verse is about a woman from Shunem whose son had died and she decided to go and look for Elisha. In verse 25, it is recorded that "she בוֹא 'came' to Mount Carmel. That's where the man of God was." She had moved from Shunem to Mount Carmel. Elisha came to her house in the company of Gehazi and resurrected the boy (v. 27–37).

The passage begins with the description of how the Shunammite woman went to look for Elisha. The first clause says וַתֵּלֶךְ וַתָּבוֹא אֶל־אִישׁ הָאֱלֹהִים אֶל־הַר הַכַּרְמֶל "So she travelled and came to the man of God at Mount Carmel." The verb וַתֵּלֶךְ "she travelled" is a definite past-time reference[105] because it is

---

105. Waltke and O'Connor, *Introduction to Biblical Hebrew*, 30.5.1b.

a onetime occurrence of the action denoted by the verb. The complementing verb, וַתָּבוֹא "and came" has a telic perfective function[106] because it is stating the end of the action of travelling. She travelled אֶל־אִישׁ הָאֱלֹהִים אֶל־הַר הַכַּרְמֶל "to the man of God at Mount Carmel." This phrase has double use of the preposition אֶל but each has a different function. The first preposition אֶל has a terminative function[107] because it explains movement toward a goal; in this case, the goal of the Shunammite's movement was to reach Elisha. The second preposition אֶל has a spatial function[108] because it indicates where Elisha was.

The examples above are only two of many other passages where בוא is used to indicate a movement from one locality to another. When בוא is used with קֶצֶף, it indicates the same idea of movement of departure from the Ego to the offender. The only reference where בוא is used with a lexical item in the BHS whose semantic range includes anger, other than קֶצֶף, is in Job 3:26. The context of this verse is about the reflection Job had after he lost his wealth, his children and his health. Verse 26 is therefore a reflection of his suffering in general and not only on his health as stated in chapter 3.

iii. Job 3:26

לֹא שָׁלַוְתִּי	I have no peace,
וְלֹא שָׁקַטְתִּי	I have no ease,
וְלֹא־נָחְתִּי	I have no rest,
וַיָּבֹא רֹגֶז	for trouble has come

With this arrangement, it is noticeable that each line of the tricola, a to c, begins with a negation marker "לֹא" and all the verbs in that tricola are in the qal stem, perfect first person. It is therefore taken here that lines abc parallel line d. The conjunctions וְ at the beginning of line b and c mark sequence[109] and are better left untranslated. All the verbs are perfects with the syntactical function of present perfective[110] because they are denoting the current state of the subject because of a past act. The poetic relationship of line a with b and

---

106. Waltke and O'Connor, 30.2.1d.
107. Arnold and Choi, *Guide to Biblical Hebrew*, 4.1.2a.
108. Arnold and Choi, 4.1.2f.
109. Seow, *Grammar for Biblical Hebrew*, 285.
110. Gibson, *Davidson's Introductory Hebrew Grammar*, 57d.

c is that of synonymous parallelism base-restatement.[111] In other words, line b and c are restating what line a has already said. However, the relationship of line a to c and line d is that of non-temporal correlation, result-reason[112] because the content of line d is the cause of the event described in line a to c. The conjunction וְ prefixed to וַיָּבֹא is translated as "for" because it is introducing a causal clause.[113] The reason Job has no peace, ease and rest is caused by the trouble that he has encountered. The verb וַיָּבֹא "has come" has a persistent perfective meaning,[114] denoting an activity which started in the past but continued to the present. He had lost his wealth and his children, and now he was losing his health. The subject of this verb is רֹגֶז "trouble," which is an emotion but presented as the subject – just like קֶצֶף – and is a reference to the pain of his losses.

Thus far, section 3.1.1.1 above has looked at the broad use of the verbs יָצָא and בּוֹא in specific passages where קֶצֶף is the subject. The examined passages have explained that the two verbs are central in understanding the source of קֶצֶף in the קצף frame, which is advanced in this research. The source of קצף, as demonstrated in the above mentioned section, is enhanced by the use of מִן "from" (and מִן compound) prepositions in the קֶצֶף clauses. The following references demonstrate how מִן "from" (and מִן compound) prepositions point to the source of this frame. In the two references given below, מִן is interpreted to denote a movement in direction from one point. When מִן is used to signify a movement in direction or a position in reference or relation to the subject, it can have one of five senses. First, it can mean "from" in the sense of "away from" an object. In this sense, it is used to show movement from an object. Second, it can mean "from" with a sense of "positioned away from." In this sense, it means something is positioned away from another but an actual movement may not be involved. Third, it can mean "from" in the sense "out of." The idea in this case is that something or someone was inside of something and has come out. Fourth, it can have the meaning of "originating from" (identifying the source). In this case, "from" is used to show the place of origin. For example, once in a while we hear news reporters say

---

111. Wendland, *Analyzing the Psalms*, 63.
112. Wendland, 81.
113. Seow, *Grammar for Biblical Hebrew*, 331.
114. Waltke and O'Connor, *Introduction to Biblical Hebrew*, 30.5.1c.

"this is a message from the head of state" signifying the source of the message. In this usage, "from" shows the source of the message. Lastly, it can mean "from" with a focus on the starting point. For example, one can say she is from Nairobi, meaning she began her journey at Nairobi.[115] The preposition מִן when used with קֶצֶף means "from" in the sense of stating the origin. This observation is in tandem with Waltke and O'Connor's assertion that מִן has a spatial sense, meaning "a place where a thing or person originated."[116] The first example examined with the preposition מִן is found in 2 Chronicles 19:2 and reads as follows:

3. 2 Chr 19:2

וַיֵּצֵא אֶל־פָּנָיו יֵהוּא בֶן־חֲנָנִי הַחֹזֶה וַיֹּאמֶר אֶל־הַמֶּלֶךְ יְהוֹשָׁפָט הֲלָרָשָׁע
לַעְזֹר וּלְשֹׂנְאֵי יְהוָה תֶּאֱהָב וּבָזֹאת עָלֶיךָ קֶצֶף מִלִּפְנֵי יְהוָה

When Jehu the seer, son of Hanani, went out to his presence and he asked King Jehoshaphat, "Should you help the wicked and love those who hate the Lord? For this reason, the קֶצֶף from God (from the face/presence of God) is on you."

The context of this verse is that of King Jehoshaphat of Judah who had just returned to his palace after helping Ahab in the war against the Syrians (ch. 18). In the war, Ahab died in the battle, after disregarding the message given to him by Micaiah. Through God's intervention, Jehoshaphat survived (vv. 31–32) and returned to his palace. As soon as he arrived, Jehu, the seer, went to meet him with the message which is recorded in chapter 19:2.

Jehu, is described as יֵהוּא בֶן־חֲנָנִי "Jehu son of Hanani." The construction בֶן־חֲנָנִי is a genitive of relation,[117] giving a hint to his lineage. The significance of this detail is probably because Jehu's father had given Asa, the father of Jehoshaphat, a similar warning (2 Chr 16:7–9). Jehu is also mentioned as הַחֹזֶה "the seer" with a definite article whose function is that of indicating a well-known person.[118] The identification of his office explains the divine authority he possessed to face the king. The narrator identifies Jehu with his office, the seer, and identifies Jehoshaphat with his office, the king. Just like the priest,

---

115. Clines, "מִן," *DCH*, 337.
116. Waltke and O'Connor, *Introduction to Biblical Hebrew*, 213.
117. Van der Merwe, Naudé, and Kroeze, *Biblical Hebrew Reference Grammar*, 198.
118. Waltke and O'Connor, *Introduction to Biblical Hebrew*, 13.5.1c.

the king has a definite article with a function of a well-known person.[119] The message Jehu brought to the king was introduced with a rhetorical question, "Should you help the wicked and love those who hate the Lord?" In this question, the adjective הָרָשָׁע "the wicked is a substantive adjective,[120] which can also be translated as "the wicked ones." The king was not only helping the wicked but also loved those who hate the Lord. The king's love תֶּאֱהָב has a function of a non-perfective of deliberation[121] because it is a deliberative question concerning his action. The word וּלְשֹׂנְאֵי is interpreted as an independent relative participle[122] meaning "and those who hate." The details discussed so far form the immediate context in which God's קֶצֶף "anger" was to come upon Jehoshaphat. In this context, what provoked God's קֶצֶף was Jehoshaphat's association with ungodly kings and the result was military defeat (2 Chr 20:35–37). The קֶצֶף came from God as indicated by the phrase מִלִּפְנֵי יְהוָה "from God (from the face of God)" which is a synecdoche of the part for the whole[123] where a body part is mentioned to mean the whole person. In this example discussed above, the compound preposition מִלִּפְנֵי "from" is used to signify the origin of קֶצֶף. Another example where the compound form of the מִן "from" preposition is used and identifies the origin of קֶצֶף, is in Zechariah 7:12, which reads as follows:

4. Zech 7:12

וְלִבָּם שָׂמוּ שָׁמִיר מִשְּׁמוֹעַ אֶת־הַתּוֹרָה וְאֶת־הַדְּבָרִים אֲשֶׁר שָׁלַח
יְהוָה צְבָאוֹת בְּרוּחוֹ בְּיַד הַנְּבִיאִים הָרִאשֹׁנִים וַיְהִי קֶצֶף גָּדוֹל מֵאֵת
יְהוָה צְבָאוֹת:

And they made their hearts as hard as stone so as not to obey the instruction and the words that the Lord of hosts had sent by his spirit through the earlier prophets. So קֶצֶף גָּדוֹל great anger, came/fell from the Lord of hosts.

The context of this verse is the hardening of the hearts of the Israelites so that they did not pay attention to the message God had given through

---

119. Waltke and O'Connor, 13.5.1c.
120. Arnold and Choi, *Guide to Biblical Hebrew*, 2.5.3.
121. Waltke and O'Connor, *Introduction to Biblical Hebrew*, 30.5.1c.
122. Waltke and O'Connor, 37.5a.
123. Bullinger, *Figures of Speech*, 641.

the earlier prophets. As a result, God's great קֶצֶף came/fell on them. The verse above begins with וְלִבָּם שָׂמוּ שָׁמִיר "and they made their hearts as hard as stone" with the conjunction וְ having a copulative function,[124] hence its translation as "and." The preceding verse is already talking of body parts: shoulder, ears and now heart in verse 12. The author associates each part of the body he has mentioned with a specific role. They had shrugged their shoulders and stopped their ears from hearing. Therefore, the heart should be understood in this context to mean the central part of the body which the Jews thought was the center for response in obedience.[125] The phrase וְלִבָּם "and their hearts" is a metonymy of the subject for the adjunct.[126] It means "the hearts" is mentioned in the place of "the will" which is responsible for their inability to obey the law and the message which came to them from the prophets. The verb שָׂמוּ "they made" is a definite past perfective[127] since the author is reporting what happened in the past. The hardening of their hearts is likened to a stone. In this case, the noun שָׁמִיר "hard" is a simile of resemblance[128] comparing the hardness of the heart to that of the stone. They have hardened their hearts and the result is they cannot hear (obey). The verb מִשְּׁמוֹעַ "to obey" is an infinitive construct which is used as a purpose clause[129] meaning the effect of the hardening of their hearts was that they did not obey. What they refused to obey is אֶת־הַתּוֹרָה וְאֶת־הַדְּבָרִים "the law and God's words" which are both marked by the direct object marker and both have definite articles of a well-known thing,[130] since the law and God's word had been with them for a long time. These words are qualified further by a relative clause אֲשֶׁר "which" which states that they are the words God שָׁלַח "had sent." The verb שָׁלַח "had sent" is past perfect (pluperfect)[131] because it is a reference to a past state, which is a precursor to another past state – hardening of the hearts. The source of this message, Zechariah reminds the Hebrews, was יְהוָה צְבָאוֹת the "God of hosts," a title that occurs forty-eight

---

124. Seow, *Grammar for Biblical Hebrew*, 284.
125. Meyers and Meyers, *Haggai, Zechariah 1–8*, 402.
126. Bullinger, *Figures of Speech*, 567.
127. Waltke and O'Connor, *Introduction to Biblical Hebrew*, 30.5.1b.
128. Bullinger, *Figures of Speech*, 726.
129. Waltke and O'Connor, *Introduction to Biblical Hebrew*, 36.2.3d.
130. Arnold and Choi, *Guide to Biblical Hebrew*, 2.6.1.
131. Gibson, *Davidson's Introductory Hebrew Grammar*, 58 (a).

times in the book of Zechariah. The term "host" in the BHS can be used in two possible ways. First, it is used with a military theme in which God is the leader of the troops (1 Sam 17:45). Second, it is used to refer to heavenly beings (Judg 5:20; 1 Kgs 22:19; Neh 9:6; Job 1:6; 2:1; and others). The most likely meaning of יְהוָה צְבָאוֹת in the book of Zechariah is that "the Lord of hosts" refers to God presiding over a heavenly council, since the context of the book is marked by a series of heavenly events Zechariah experienced in the form of eight visions, recorded from chapter 1:7 to chapter 6:8.

The means through which this message got to the people was בְּרוּחוֹ בְּיַד הַנְּבִיאִים הָרִאשֹׁנִים "through his spirit by the hand of the earlier prophets." The noun "hand" is used figuratively here to mean "power."[132] It is used the same way in Exodus 9:35 where Pharaoh is said to have hardened his heart as God had said through (the power) of Moses. The understanding of "the hand" to mean "power" has influenced the translation of the phrase בְּיַד הַנְּבִיאִים הָרִאשֹׁנִים as "through the earlier prophets" since the power is understood to be inherent in the messenger. The prophet Zechariah also uses this same figure of speech in Zechariah 7:7 and the phrase הַנְּבִיאִים הָרִאשֹׁנִים in Zechariah 1:4. The earlier prophets, most likely, refer to the periods of Joshua, Judges, Samuel and Kings[133] because this is the designation according to the Palestinian canon which grouped the Old Testament books into law, prophets and writings. This canon targeted the Palestinian Jews and the order of books was guided by the dates of acceptance of the books and their perceived degree of authority. This order is different in the Alexandrian canon which groups the Old Testament books into law, history, poetry and prophecy.[134]

The details in this verse so far form the background for the message in the last clause of this verse. This clause begins with וַיְהִי קֶצֶף גָּדוֹל whose translation is "therefore קֶצֶף גָּדוֹל (great anger) came/fell." The adjective גָּדוֹל "great" is an attributive[135] serving as an intensifier of קֶצֶף. The entire construction קֶצֶף גָּדוֹל occurs five more times in the BHS: Deuteronomy 29:27; 2 Kings 3:27; Jeremiah 21:5; 32:37, and Zechariah 1:15. In five out of the six occurrences, the object of קֶצֶף גָּדוֹל is the Israelites. Only once is "the nations" the object.

---

132. Koehler and Baumgartner, "יָד," *HALOT*, 1:388.
133. Ap-Thomas, *Primer of Old Testament*, 3.
134. Ap-Thomas, 3.
135. Gesenius, *Gesenius' Hebrew Grammar*, 126u.

There is no clear-cut difference to explain the use of קֶצֶף גָּדוֹל and the קֶצֶף in different passages although the former is most commonly used in contexts where the antecedent condition was idolatry (Deut 29:27; Jer 21:5; 32:37; Zech 7:12). Other contexts where קֶצֶף occurs have to do with "lesser evils." However, there are exceptions to this. For example, in 2 Chronicles 24:18 God had קֶצֶף against the Israelites and the antecedent condition is idolatry. The references in which קֶצֶף גָּדוֹל "great anger" occurs and the antecedent condition does not seem to be idolatry are 2 Kings 3:27 and Zechariah 1:15). All the passages in which the construction קֶצֶף גָּדוֹל "great anger" occurs are discussed later in detail.

Although it has been stated at the beginning of this verse that קֶצֶף גָּדוֹל "great anger" was caused by hardening of hearts by the Israelites, a close examination of the context explains that the root cause was idolatry. As recorded in verse 11, the prophet said "but they refused to pay attention; stubbornly they turned their backs and covered their ears" (NIV). This verse is the background of verse 12 which talks about hardening of hearts in which we get the construction קֶצֶף גָּדוֹל. The phrase in verse 11 translated as "stubbornly they turned their backs" is וַיִּתְּנוּ כָתֵף סֹרָרֶת and it occurs only once in the BHS, with a minor variation, in Nehemiah 9:29 where it is worded as וַיִּתְּנוּ כָתֵף סוֹרֶרֶת. The message in these two passages is very similar. For example, Nehemiah talks of the Israelites being ignorant of God's law (Neh 8:26) and so does Zechariah in chapter 7:12. Nehemiah talks of how they rebelled and killed the prophets (Neh 8:26) and similarly Zechariah talks of them paying no attention to the message that came from the earlier prophets (Zech 7:12). With this kind of similarity in the content of the two chapters, it is possible that there is a similarity of the two phrases: וַיִּתְּנוּ כָתֵף סֹרָרֶת and וַיִּתְּנוּ כָתֵף סוֹרֶרֶת which are used in Zechariah and Nehemiah, respectively. The context of Nehemiah 9 is about the Israelites abandoning their God and casting an image for themselves in the form of a calf (Neh 9:18). So when the phrase וַיִּתְּנוּ כָתֵף סוֹרֶרֶת "they stubbornly turned their backs" is used later in verse 29, it is understood in the context of idolatry. The passage in Nehemiah sheds light in understanding the phrase וַיִּתְּנוּ כָתֵף סֹרָרֶת "they stubbornly turned their backs" in Zechariah 7:11 as one that meant the Israelites had turned away from their God and turned to idols. Subsequently, the hardening of hearts in verse 12 is a characteristic of people who had a focus on idols and as a result God experienced קֶצֶף גָּדוֹל. Therefore, the root problem in Zechariah 7:12 is idolatry (v. 11) as an antecedent condition of קֶצֶף גָּדוֹל. The result of קֶצֶף גָּדוֹל "great anger" coming/falling on them was captivity (vv. 13–14).

The source of קֶצֶף גָּדוֹל is יְהוָה צְבָאוֹת "God of hosts" who is identified by the compound preposition מֵאֵת "from" which puts focus on God who is experiencing קֶצֶף, and from him the קֶצֶף came to the Israelites. The phrase יְהוָה צְבָאוֹת "God of hosts" is repeated twice in this verse and has an emphatic force since in both cases it signifies origin. In the first usage, it explains the origin of the instructions and the second explains the origin of קֶצֶף.

The four verses given above demonstrate that קֶצֶף is an abstract object, which leaves the (Ego). The following section gives examples that show the trajectory taken by קֶצֶף, the abstract object, and its final destination – the landmark. Both the trajectory and the landmark are identified by the use of the verb הָיָה (to come/fall) together with the preposition עַל in the קֶצֶף clauses.

3.1.1.2 The הָיָה Verb and the Preposition עַל

The accompanying use of verb הָיָה (to come/fall) with the preposition עַל in the phrases where קֶצֶף is the subject, connects the perceived motion of the trajector from the Ego to the end location – landmark. Both the verb הָיָה and the preposition עַל occur nine times with the noun form of קֶצֶף as explained in the following references.

In addition to the discussion on the preposition עַל discussed in section 3.0, this preposition has a wide range of usage but the specific interest for this research is how the authors of the BHS used it with verbs of motion. Scholars point out that the preposition עַל, when used with verbs of motion, has locational spatial sense. However, verbs of motion can indicate vertical motion or horizontal motion.[136] When the preposition עַל has a sense of "on" or "over,"[137] it has a locational spatial sense but implies a vertical motion. For example, in Genesis 1:2 the author said, "now the earth was formless and empty, darkness was over (עַל) the surface of the deep, and the Spirit of God was hovering over the waters" (NIV). Another example is in Genesis 19:23, which says, "by the time Lot reached Zoar, the sun had risen over (עַל) the land" (NIV). This vertical view is also held by Allen Ross who notes that "the

---

136. Arnold and Choi, *Guide to Biblical Hebrew*, 4.1.16a.
137. Waltke and O'Connor, *Introduction to Biblical Hebrew*, 216.

preposition עַל has the fundamental idea 'on' or 'upon' to express location ('on, above, over'), [and] termination ('upon, to')."[138]

When the preposition עַל is used with a sense of a horizontal motion, it can be translated as "against, at or around."[139] For example, 1 Kings 6:5 reads, "against (עַל) the walls of the main hall and inner sanctuary he built a structure around the building, in which there were side rooms" (NIV). A second example is from Numbers 20:23, which says, "at (עַל) mount Hor, near the border of Edom, the Lord said to Moses and Aaron" (NIV). The last example is from 1 Samuel 25:16 in which the author said, "night and day they were a wall around (עַל) us the whole time we were herding our sheep near them" (NIV). The context is the only determinant as to whether עַל should be translated as "on," "at," "around" or "against."

This research demonstrates that the contextually fitting translation of the preposition עַל in passages where קֶצֶף is the subject, the trajector, is "on." This means that the קֶצֶף frame has a vertical relationship between the Ego and the landmark. Because of the vertical relationship frame, it is argued that the verb הָיָה "to come/fall" can also be translated as "to fall" since the implied movement is that of vertical, from top to bottom. This section specifically examines passages in which both the verb הָיָה and the preposition עַל are used together with קֶצֶף being the subject. The examples are in the following section beginning with those in the Torah.

3.1.1.2.1 The Torah

5. Num 1:53

וְהַלְוִיִּם יַחֲנוּ סָבִיב לְמִשְׁכַּן הָעֵדֻת וְלֹא־יִהְיֶה קֶצֶף עַל־עֲדַת בְּנֵי יִשְׂרָאֵל וְשָׁמְרוּ הַלְוִיִּם אֶת־מִשְׁמֶרֶת מִשְׁכַּן הָעֵדוּת׃

But the Levites shall camp around the tabernacle of the covenant to ensure that קֶצֶף may not come/fall on the congregation, the children of Israel. The Levites shall keep charge of the tent of the meeting.

The larger context of this passage is when the Israelites are about to set out from Mount Sinai toward Kadesh. The immediate context of this verse is a

---

138. Ross, *Introducing Biblical Hebrew*, 53.3.
139. Arnold and Choi, *Guide to Biblical Hebrew*, 4.1.16a.

census of all the Israelites by Moses (v. 2) and a specific census of the men for war (v. 45). The preceding verse (v. 52) is about the Israelites pitching their tents according to their camps. The instruction in verse 52 is different from the instructions in verse 53 in which the Levites were not supposed to pitch their tents according to their camp like the rest of the Israelites, instead, they were to pitch them surrounding the tent of meeting. With this understanding, the conjunction וְ at the beginning of verse 53 is adversative[140] meaning "but" because it contrasts how the people were to pitch their tents and how the Levites were to pitch theirs. The instructions in verse 53 are a direct address to הַלְוִיִּם "the Levites." The instruction from Moses is that the Levites יַחֲנוּ סָבִיב לְמִשְׁכַּן הָעֵדֻת "shall encamp around the tent of meeting." The instruction to the Levites on pitching their tents is to encamp around לְמִשְׁכַּן הָעֵדֻת "the tent of meeting" which is a genitive of purpose;[141] the purpose of the tent is to hold meetings for religious practices. However, encamping around the tent was not only because they had primary role in caring for the tent (v. 50), but also to ensure that God's קֶצֶף did not come/fall on the people. Preventing God's קֶצֶף is clearly stipulated in the words of Moses as he said וְלֹא־יִהְיֶה קֶצֶף עַל־עֲדַת בְּנֵי יִשְׂרָאֵל "so that קֶצֶף might not come/fall on the congregation of the children of Israel." The conjunction וְ introduces a purpose clause,[142] thus it is translated as "so that." The verb יִהְיֶה is a non-perfective of possibility,[143] suggesting the possibility of קֶצֶף coming/falling on the Israelites if the instructions given are breached. The verb יִהְיֶה, also identifies the trajectory taken by קֶצֶף which rests on the landmark marked by the preposition עַל. The landmark is the עַל־עֲדַת בְּנֵי יִשְׂרָאֵל "the congregation of the children of Israel." The phrase "children of Israel" constitutes a pleonasm[144] – that is to say, it is contextually redundant, since if refers to the congregation in question. Although this verse does not say who the source of קֶצֶף is, it is clear from the context that it is God, who is a superior to the Israelites. The fact that God is the Ego of קֶצֶף, supports the argument in this research that the קצף frame had a vertical relationship – from a superior to an inferior.

---

140. Seow, *Grammar for Biblical Hebrew*, 284.
141. Chisholm, *From Exegesis to Exposition*, 63.
142. Van der Merwe, Naudé, and Kroeze, *Biblical Hebrew Reference Grammar*, 299.
143. Waltke and O'Connor, *Introduction to Biblical Hebrew*, 31.4e.
144. Bullinger, *Figures of Speech*, 405.

The last sentence of this verse is giving more details on what encamping around the tent of meeting entailed. The purpose of encamping was to אֶת־מִשְׁמֶרֶת מִשְׁכַּן הָעֵדוּת "charge of the tent of the meeting." Since the noun מִשְׁמֶרֶת has the sense of ensuring the proper conduct in regard to the ceremonial priestly function[145] in the tent of meeting, the encamping ensured that there is no infringement of the code of conduct (contamination) within the tent. This clause is the object of the verb since a definite object marker introduces it. In this verse, קֶצֶף is the subject doing the action of "coming/falling on" the Israelites.

It is also important to note that camping around the tent of meeting guarded it because the penalty of trespassing was death. George Gray takes note of this and says, "the whole people are to encamp in an orderly manner around the tabernacle, but kept from immediate proximity to it by the Levites. This inner position of the Levites is to prevent even accidental contact of the non-Levites with the tabernacle, and, consequently, any such sudden and destructive outburst of Yahweh's anger."[146] The penalty of death was for all, both Israelites and aliens. The author of Numbers 1:51 states this penalty; the reference says, "whenever the tabernacle is to move, the Levites are to take it down, and whenever the tabernacle is to be set up, the Levites shall do it. Anyone else who approaches it is to be put to death" (NIV). The word translated as "anyone else" is הַזָּר which when used as a participle can mean a stranger, a strange one, a foreigner in relation to an Israelite or a stranger in the sense of someone who is forbidden or unauthorized. The context in Numbers 1:53 implies that the noun הַזָּר "alien" is used, meaning someone who is forbidden or not authorized,[147] and that includes both Israelites and aliens. Since הַזָּר "alien" is an adjective, it has a substantive adjective function[148] operating as a noun. Other passages that pronounce the death penalty for הַזָּר "unauthorized people" coming to the tent of gathering are Numbers 3:10, 38 and 18:7. The intended penalty of God's קֶצֶף is death.

---

145. Koehler and Baumgartner, "שמר," *HALOT*, 2:1583.
146. Gray, *Commentary on Numbers*, 16.
147. Clines, "זור," *DCH*, 3:98.
148. Van der Merwe, Naudé, And Kroeze, *Biblical Hebrew Reference Grammar*, 235.

The next reference in which the verb הָיָה (to come/fall) is used with the preposition עַל to show the trajectory and the landmark of קֶצֶף is in Numbers 18:5.

6. Num 18:5

וּשְׁמַרְתֶּם אֵת מִשְׁמֶרֶת הַקֹּדֶשׁ וְאֵת מִשְׁמֶרֶת הַמִּזְבֵּחַ וְלֹא־יִהְיֶה עוֹד קֶצֶף עַל־בְּנֵי יִשְׂרָאֵל:

You are to keep charge of the tabernacle and the altar, so that קֶצֶף may not come/fall again on the Israelites.

The context of this passage is Aaron instructing the Levites on how to care for the tabernacle. These instructions were given just before the Israelites, who had been on a journey from Mount Sinai, entered Kadesh. Verse 5 is a continuation of the instructions which Aaron has been giving from verse 1. The instruction begins with וּשְׁמַרְתֶּם "you take care" which is a non-perfective of command.[149] The larger context of the book of Numbers has informed this understanding since it demonstrates that the work of Levites in caring for the tabernacle was ongoing before Aaron gave the instructions. The cognate internal accusatives of the verb are אֵת מִשְׁמֶרֶת הַקֹּדֶשׁ וְאֵת מִשְׁמֶרֶת הַמִּזְבֵּחַ "the tabernacle and the altar." The two phrases: מִשְׁמֶרֶת הַקֹּדֶשׁ "charge of the tabernacle" and מִשְׁמֶרֶת הַמִּזְבֵּחַ "charge of the altar" are both genitives of advantage[150] since both the tabernacle and the altar are worth guarding.[151] The noun מִשְׁמֶרֶת is used in the two constructions with a sense of the guarding function of a ceremonial office/function.[152] Both the הַקֹּדֶשׁ "the tabernacle" and הַמִּזְבֵּחַ "the altar" have definite articles of a unique referent.[153]

The last clause of this verse is a purpose clause[154] introduced by a conjunction וְ. Thus it is translated as "so that." The Levites were to ensure proper conduct in the place of worship וְלֹא־יִהְיֶה עוֹד קֶצֶף עַל־בְּנֵי יִשְׂרָאֵל "so that קֶצֶף may not come/fall again on the Israelites." The verb יִהְיֶה is a non-perfective of

---

149. Chisholm, *From Exegesis to Exposition*, 94, 101.
150. Joüon and Muraoka, *Grammar of Biblical Hebrew*, 129e.
151. The constructs are not translated for idiomatic reading of the verse.
152. Koehler and Baumgartner, "שמר," *HALOT*, 2:1583.
153. Chisholm, *From Exegesis to Exposition*, 73.
154. Van der Merwe, Naudé, and Kroeze, *Biblical Hebrew Reference Grammar*, 299.

possibility,[155] meaning if the Levites do not fulfill the conditions of taking care of the tabernacle, there is a possibility that קֶצֶף may come/fall on the Israelites.

In this last clause, God warns the priests and the Levites to care for the tabernacle and the altar so that God's קֶצֶף does not come/fall on the Israelites again, עוֹד. The use of the particle עוֹד "again" evokes the memories of the destructions in chapter 16 (in the English Bible) or 17 (in the BHS) – in which the קֶצֶף is also used. Therefore, the precaution is that if the Levites do not take good care of the tabernacle and the altar – by ensuring the proper offering of sacrifices – then God in his קֶצֶף would punish[156] the Israelites. This is another example of intent of punishment associated with קֶצֶף. The need for the proper care of the altar is underscored by Cole who said, "The holiness and purity of the sanctuary may be at risk should a people become rebellious and attempt to usurp the power of the divinely ordained priesthood or endeavor to present impure or unclean sacrifices in the realm of the holy."[157] The charge in the verse above was given to both the priests and the Levites, hinted by the use of the affirmative plural you, וּשְׁמַרְתֶּם "you keep." The responsibility is therefore on the shoulders of the priests and Levites as noted by Gray, who said, "The priests and Levites – alike must keep their charge if the Israelites are to be prohibited from outbreaks of the divine wrath."[158] Failure to heed this advice would lead to destruction similar to that mentioned in chapter 16 (or 17 in the BHS) in which fire consumed 250 Israelites who offered sacrifices but had neglected the set rules for offering sacrifices.

In summary, Numbers 18:5 is a record of God's instruction to Aaron and the Levites to care for the tabernacle so that his קֶצֶף will no longer come/fall on the Israelites. In addition to the vertical function of the preposition עַל, the fact that God is a superior and the Israelites are subordinates supports the argument that the קצף frame has a vertical relationship. The noun קֶצֶף is the subject coming on the Israelites. These examples are the only ones in the Torah where the verb הָיָה and the preposition עַל are used together in the קֶצֶף clauses. The following section has more examples from the prophets.

---

155. Waltke and O'Connor, *Introduction to Biblical Hebrew*, 31.4e.

156. The kind of punishment meted out on the Israelites is varied, but in this case, the implied punishment is death based on the events of chapter 16 (in the English Bible) or 17 (in the BHS).

157. Cole, *Numbers*, 281.

158. Gray, *Commentary on Numbers*, 220.

3.1.1.2.2 The Prophets

7. Josh 9:20

זֹאת נַעֲשֶׂה לָהֶם וְהַחֲיֵה אוֹתָם וְלֹא־יִהְיֶה עָלֵינוּ קֶצֶף עַל־הַשְּׁבוּעָה אֲשֶׁר־נִשְׁבַּעְנוּ לָהֶם׃

This is what we will do to them: we allow them to live, so that God's קֶצֶף anger will not come/fall on us because of the oath, which we swore to them.

The context of this passage is about the deception of the Israelites by the Gibeonites. The Gibeonites pretended that they were aliens from a far country who had come to Israel because of the fame of the God of the Israelites (vv. 9–15). It was after only three days (v. 16) that they learned that these aliens were their neighbors. After this discovery, the Israelites set out to attack the Gibeonites but the Israelites' leaders could not allow them to do so since they had sworn an oath to the Gibeonites by the God of Israel (v. 18). Therefore, the Israelites decided to let them live in their midst so that God's קֶצֶף would not come/fall on them. Breaking of an oath sworn to God would provoke God's קֶצֶף and attract punishment because all oaths were binding (Exod 20:7; Lev 19:12; 1 Sam 14:24). This oath was later disregarded by Saul and the result was the killing of his five sons by the Gibeonites (2 Sam 21:1–9). Before this brutal killing, there was famine in the land and David attributed it to the breaking of the oath between the Israelites and the Gibeonites by Saul (2 Sam 21:1–2). David Howard observes that the famine was a result of the breaking of this oath as he notes, "many years later Saul killed the Gibeonites in violation of this oath, the Lord brought famine upon the land and this would have been the type of wrath the leaders feared."[159] Therefore, Saul, the one who disregarded the oath taken in God's name, which Joshua did not want to break, lost his family as a form of punishment from God's קֶצֶף.

This verse, Joshua 9:20, begins with a near demonstrative זֹאת "this" which is cataphoric pointing to the content of the speech which follows. The leaders beseeched the Israelites saying this is what נַעֲשֶׂה לָהֶם וְהַחֲיֵה אוֹתָם "we will do to them: we let them live." The verb נַעֲשֶׂה "we will do" has a specific future function[160] meaning they will certainly honor their commitment. Their

---

159. Howard, *Joshua*, 229.
160. Gibson, *Davidson's Introductory Hebrew Grammar*, 64a.

commitment is וְהַחֲיֵה "allow (them) to live," which is an infinitive absolute[161] continuing the action of the preceding verb.

The reason for this plea by the leaders to allow the Gibeonites to live is וְלֹא־יִהְיֶה עָלֵינוּ קֶצֶף "so that God's קֶצֶף 'anger' will not come/fall on us." The conjunction וְ is indicating a sequence of events hence its translation as "so that."[162] The יִהְיֶה "will (not) come/fall" verb is a non-perfective of possibility,[163] meaning there is a possibility that God's קֶצֶף will come/fall on them if the oath is broken. The subject of this clause is קֶצֶף, which would come on the landmark עָלֵינוּ "on us" identified by the preposition עַל. This verse explains both the vertical syntactical function relationship because of the preposition עַל and the vertical relational function since the Ego is superior to the landmark.

The leaders' duty was to ensure the Israelites understood that the קֶצֶף of God would come/fall on them if they failed to keep an oath they had made. The content of the last clause is: עַל־הַשְּׁבוּעָה אֲשֶׁר־נִשְׁבַּעְנוּ לָהֶם "because of the oath which we swore to them." This last clause is introduced by the preposition עַל which has a causal function[164] hence its translation as "because." The object of the preposition is הַשְּׁבוּעָה "the oath." The manner in which the oath was dealt with is explained in a relative clause אֲשֶׁר־נִשְׁבַּעְנוּ לָהֶם "which we swore to them." The context implies that this swearing was binding. Joshua 22:20 is the next reference in which הָיָה (to come/fall) verb is used with the preposition עַל to show the trajectory and the landmark of קֶצֶף.

8. Josh 22:20

הֲלוֹא עָכָן בֶּן־זֶרַח מָעַל מַעַל בַּחֵרֶם וְעַל־כָּל־עֲדַת יִשְׂרָאֵל הָיָה קָצֶף
וְהוּא אִישׁ אֶחָד לֹא גָוַע בַּעֲוֹנוֹ׃

Achan, son of Zerah, acted treacherously by violating (on) the ban. Was it not, therefore, on the entire community of Israel that קֶצֶף "anger" came/fell? He did not die alone for his guilt.

The context of this verse is about a warning to Gilead – comprised of Reuben, Gad and the half tribe of Manasseh – against disobeying God and building an altar other than that of God. If the tribes of Gilead did go on to

---

161. Waltke and O'Connor, *Introduction to Biblical Hebrew*, 35.5.2b-d.
162. Seow, *Grammar for Biblical Hebrew*, 285.
163. Waltke and O'Connor, *Introduction to Biblical Hebrew*, 31.4e.
164. Arnold and Choi, *Guide to Biblical Hebrew*, 4.1.16d.

build an altar to another god, then their rebellion would attract God's קֶצֶף and result in punishment to the entire nation, just as God's קֶצֶף fell on the Israelites when Achan acted unfaithfully regarding the sacred items. The author of Joshua 7:1–26 records the sin of Achan, who was stoned to death, and how Israel suffered defeat at the hands of their enemies.[165] The reminder of Achan's judgment is a warning to the people of Israel to take heed, lest they sin again and suffer another defeat. Howard noted, "Israel had never truly rid itself of this sin that it always flirted with – if not participated in – idolatry and the allure of pagan religious systems. Achan's case was proof of this, and the Cisjordan tribes feared that this altar represented another such case."[166] Therefore, disregarding this warning meant God's קֶצֶף would bring military defeat (punishment) in this context.

The verse begins with a rhetorical question: Did not wrath come/fall upon the whole community? What brought the misfortune was the act of Achan עָכָן בֶּן־זֶרַח מָעַל מַעַל בַּחֵרֶם "Achan son of Zerah acted treacherously by violating the ban." The verb מָעַל "acted" is a definite past[167] and the noun מַעַל is a cognate internal accusative[168] since it shares the root as the verb and it is expressing Achan's conduct which should be avoided by the current audience. The sin of Achan was primarily that of breaking the covenant by stealing things that were devoted for destruction (6:18; 7:10–15). Similarly, the perceived sin in Joshua 22:20 is possible erecting an altar to the idols (7:11, 19) other than an altar to God. God's instructions were that they should completely destroy all the altars to idols as written in Exodus 34:12–13 which says, "Watch yourself that you make no covenant with the inhabitants of the land into which you are going, or it will become a snare in your midst. But rather, you are to tear down their altars and smash their sacred pillars and cut down their Asherim." In this case the altars are devoted for destruction. Because of his action, the Israelites were punished וְעַל־כָּל־עֲדַת יִשְׂרָאֵל הָיָה קָצֶף. This clause begins with a conjunction וְ, which is introducing the consequences[169] and explaining the consequences of violation of the ban by Achan. The phrase וְעַל־כָּל־עֲדַת יִשְׂרָאֵל

---

165. In this passage, the author uses אַף in Numbers 7:1, 26, and not קֶצֶף. The relationship of these two lexical items is explained later in this chapter.
166. Howard, *Joshua*, 408.
167. Joüon and Muraoka, *Grammar of Biblical Hebrew*, 112c.
168. Gibson, *Davidson's Introductory Hebrew Grammar*, 93.
169. BDB, 254c.

"all the congregation of Israel" has the preposition עַל, which has a locative function identifying the location on which קֶצֶף falls.[170] The noun קֶצֶף is the subject of the verb הָיָה "came/fell," which is a definite (simple) past perfective.[171] This marks the end of the rhetorical question, after which, in the last clause, the author emphatically states that Achan did not die alone. In this example, a superior experienced קֶצֶף over an inferior, which is in line with the קצף frame's proposition that it had a vertical relationship. In addition, the reminder of the destruction of the Israelites due to the sin of Achan is an evidence that קֶצֶף had a retributive effect.

The last phrase of this verse is a further explanation of the entire congregation being punished. It says וְהוּא אִישׁ אֶחָד לֹא גָוַע בַּעֲוֺנוֹ "he did not die alone for his guilt." The phrase הוּא אִישׁ which can literally be translated as "he, man" has the pronoun הוּא whose function is to show "the focus of an utterance confirming the personal or exclusive role of the referent of the pronoun in an event."[172] In the context of this verse, Achan is specifically responsible for what is happening and the author draws the readers' attention to that fact. Although entirely responsible, Achan did not die alone in his iniquity. The author of this reference explains Achan's death further in that it was בַּעֲוֺנוֹ "in his iniquity." The preposition בְּ has a semantic function of cause[173] which means "in (because of) his iniquity." The affix in בַּעֲוֺנוֹ is a genitive suffix, his iniquity, whose syntactical function is a genitive of quality – the affix did what amounts to iniquity.[174] The next example in which the הָיָה verb and the preposition עַל are used with קֶצֶף as the subject is in 2 Kings 3:27.

9. 2 Kgs 3:27

וַיִּקַּח אֶת־בְּנוֹ הַבְּכוֹר אֲשֶׁר־יִמְלֹךְ תַּחְתָּיו וַיַּעֲלֵהוּ עֹלָה עַל־הַחֹמָה וַיְהִי
קֶצֶף־גָּדוֹל עַל־יִשְׂרָאֵל וַיִּסְעוּ מֵעָלָיו וַיָּשֻׁבוּ לָאָרֶץ:

Then he took his son, the firstborn, who was to become king after him, and offered him as a burnt offering upon the wall/

---

170. Arnold and Choi, *Guide to Biblical Hebrew*, 4.1.16a.
171. Chisholm, *From Exegesis to Exposition*, 86.
172. Van der Merwe, Naudé, and Kroeze, *Biblical Hebrew Reference Grammar*, 253.
173. Van der Merwe, Naudé, and Kroeze, 282.
174. Van der Merwe, Naudé, and Kroeze, 198.

altar. Therefore, great קֶצֶף "anger" came/fell on Israel that they retreated from him and returned to their own land.

The context of this passage is about a war between the Israelites and the Moabites, whose army marched and staged war at the Israelites' camp. However, the Moabites were defeated and they retreated as the Israelites pursued. When they arrived at Kir-hareseth, the king of the Moabites took his eldest son and offered him as a burnt offering on the wall. Then great קֶצֶף came/fell on the Israelites and they retreated.

This verse begins with וַיִּקַּח "then he took" with the conjunction ו which is indicating a logical sequence[175] of events hence its translation as "then." What he took was his son who was not only a firstborn child, but also אֲשֶׁר־יִמְלֹךְ תַּחְתָּיו "was to become king after him" which is a relative clause introduced by אֲשֶׁר "who." The verb יִמְלֹךְ is a historical future non-perfective[176] since the author is looking at what he would have begun being at some point after the era of his father. After the king took his son, he וַיַּעֲלֵהוּ עֹלָה עַל־הַחֹמָה "offered him as a burntoffering on the wall." The verb וַיַּעֲלֵהוּ "and he offered him" is a simple past perfective.[177] The phrase וַיַּעֲלֵהוּ עֹלָה "and he offered him as a burntoffering" is a double accusative of the person acted on (the object) and the complement of how he was acted upon,[178] while the first object is the person acted upon, affix ו "him," translated with the verb as "offered him," and a complement of how the offering was done עֹלָה, "burnt offering." The offering was עַל־הַחֹמָה "on the wall." The preposition עַל indicates locality in the sense of on top of an object[179] – which is הַחֹמָה "the wall." The use of the preposition עַל implies that the offering was on top of the wall. Although there are passages in Scripture that show that the Moabites' altars were built on public high places (1 Kgs 11:7; 2 Kgs 23:13) and that meant the sacrifice was done in public for everybody to see,[180] this offering on the wall meant the wall was not a conventional altar but it served the purpose of the offering being displayed in public.

---

175. Seow, *Grammar for Biblical Hebrew*, 285.
176. Waltke and O'Connor, *Introduction to Biblical Hebrew*, 31.6.2c.
177. Chisholm, *From Exegesis to Exposition*, 86.
178. Waltke and O'Connor, *Introduction to Biblical Hebrew*, 10.2.3e.
179. Arnold and Choi, *Guide to Biblical Hebrew*, 4.1.16a.
180. Daviau and Steiner, "Moabite Sanctuary," 8.

וַיְהִי קֶצֶף־גָּדוֹל עַל־יִשְׂרָאֵל וַיִּסְעוּ מֵעָלָיו וַיָּשֻׁבוּ לָאָרֶץ The king's action meant that "great קֶצֶף came/fell on Israel and they retreated from him and returned to their own land." The verb וַיְהִי has a conjunction וְ, which is indicating a sequence of events,[181] meaning "then." The subject of the verb is קֶצֶף "anger" with גָּדוֹל being an attributive adjective[182] modifying the noun. The construction עַל־יִשְׂרָאֵל "on Israel" has the preposition עַל showing the landmark of קֶצֶף. The verbs, וַיִּסְעוּ and וַיָּשֻׁבוּ "retreated and returned" form a hendiadys[183] since they are two words expressing one idea.. The Israelites returned to the land לָאָרֶץ – that is their own land (v. 27).

This passage is silent on who the source of קֶצֶף־גָּדוֹל is, and that silence has created room for speculation. This section offers a summary of the main different views and also states the position held in this research on the matter. The varying views on the source of קֶצֶף־גָּדוֹל are the Israelites,[184] the king of the Moabites,[185] the Israelites' God[186] and the Moabite god – Chemosh.[187] The following section reviews all these possible Egos of קֶצֶף־גָּדוֹל. First, it is not possible that the Israelites experienced קֶצֶף־גָּדוֹל caused by the detestable act, and decided to retreat. The reason this is not possible is because of the preposition עַל which identifies them as the object of the preposition. Second, it is unlikely that it is the Moabites who got angry since they had already retreated. Furthermore, when the Israelites returned it was not a flight in fear of being pursued by the Moabites (2 Kgs 3:20–27). Third, there are textual clues that suggest that the source was the Israelites' God although this research argues against that view. The possibility of the source being the Israelites' God is that, first of all, considering all the six places where קֶצֶף־גָּדוֹל occurs (Deut 29:27; 2 Kgs 3:27; Jer 32:37; 21:5; Zech 1:15; 7:12), in five out of those passages, excluding this one, God is the Ego. Therefore, in the strength of the Ego of the other occurrences of קֶצֶף־גָּדוֹל being God and not a human being or another deity, the evidence of occurrence supports that God is the source from whom קֶצֶף־גָּדוֹל came/fell. Second, other than God being the

---

181. Seow, *Grammar for Biblical Hebrew*, 285.
182. Gibson, *Davidson's Introductory Hebrew Grammar*, 41.
183. Bullinger, *Figures of Speech*, 657.
184. Cogan and Tadmor, *11 Kings*, 47.
185. Wiseman, *1 and 2 Kings*, 202.
186. Conti, Pilara, and Oden, *1–2 Kings*, 154.
187. Montgomery, *Book of Kings*, 364.

Ego, all those passages where קֶצֶף־גָּדוֹל is used show that idolatry was involved as the central event that was the antecedent of קֶצֶף־גָּדוֹל. Although idolatry is practiced in this passage in the sense of offering of human sacrifice, the Israelites were not directly responsible or involved. Moreover, there is no reason given in the text which would explain why the Israelites' God was the source of קֶצֶף־גָּדוֹל. The position held in this research is that the source of קֶצֶף־גָּדוֹל was Chemosh, the god of the Moabites. Contextually, there is a direct link between the offering of the son on the wall/altar in verse 26 and the קֶצֶף־גָּדוֹל falling on the Israelites in verse 27.

There are other passages which show that the Israelites believed in the superstition[188] that was associated with human sacrifice (Judg 11:24; 2 Kgs 16:3; Mic 6:7).[189] However, this position does not go unchallenged. One of the scholars who oppose this position is Robert Cohn who says, "biblical scholars would not ascribe wrath to a god whose power they would not acknowledge."[190] But the biblical references given above imply that the biblical writers recorded that the Jewish people had fallen into this superstition. James Montgomery puts it well when he asserts that Israelites believed in קֶצֶף־גָּדוֹל coming from Chemosh because "the superstitious fears of the soldiery must have been more alive in a land that was not theirs."[191] The study on "The Wrath of Moab" by Patricia J Berlyn holds this view that the קֶצֶף־גָּדוֹל was from Chemosh.[192] Another scholar, Klaas Smelik, has the same thoughts as Berlyn when he noted that for the Moabites, it is Chemosh who delivered them and not king Mesha since the king's army had already lost the battle.[193] In light of this belief, the author of this dissertation argues that קֶצֶף־גָּדוֹל is associated with God or a deity. In this context, the antecedent condition of קֶצֶף־גָּדוֹל is the attack of the Moabites by the Israelites and the result was Israelites' army retreated.

This passage supports the argument in this research that where either קֶצֶף־גָּדוֹל or קֶצֶף is the subject with the verb הָיָה and the preposition עַל, the relationship of the Ego and the landmark is that of a superior to a subordinate – vertical relationship. Out of all of the possible proposed Egos of

---

188. The belief that idols were alive and could be worshiped.
189. Montgomery, *Book of Kings*, 363.
190. Cohn, *2 Kings*, 24.
191. Montgomery, *Book of Kings*, 364.
192. Berlyn, "Wrath of Moab," 217.
193. Smelik, "King Mesha's Inscription," 22.

קֶצֶף־גָּדוֹל in this passage, only God or a deity qualifies to be a superior to the Israelites. The next examples that demonstrate these characteristics of the קצף frame are in the section of "writings" according to the BHS.

3.1.1.2.3 The Writings
The first example to be considered in this category is from 1 Chronicles 27:24.

10. 1 Chr 27:24

יוֹאָב בֶּן־צְרוּיָה הֵחֵל לִמְנוֹת וְלֹא כִלָּה וַיְהִי בָזֹאת קֶצֶף עַל־יִשְׂרָאֵל וְלֹא עָלָה הַמִּסְפָּר בְּמִסְפַּר דִּבְרֵי־הַיָּמִים לַמֶּלֶךְ דָּוִיד

Joab, son of Zeruiah, began to count, but he did not complete it, for because of it קֶצֶף came/fell on Israel. Therefore, the number was not recorded in the book of chronicles of King David.

This chapter is about the order by David concerning the counting of the Israelite's fighting men. He ordered Joab to take the census but Joab did not number all the people (v. 21–24; cf. 1 Chr 21:1–6). Because of this census, which was amounting to relying on the fighting men instead of God, God's קֶצֶף came/fell on the Israelites. The punishment from this was a plague – the killing of seventy-thousand men (2 Sam 24:13–17). Since these passages form a corpus, the reason for God's קֶצֶף was David's act of counting the people without God's approval (1 Chr 21:6–7).

In the example from 1 Chronicles 27:24, we begin with the introduction of the subject of the verb יוֹאָב בֶּן־צְרוּיָה "Joab, son of Zeruiah" who הֵחֵל לִמְנוֹת "began to count" but the verse does not specify what he was counting. However, it is clear according to verse 23 that he was taking a census of the Israelites which David had not taken for many years. The exclusion of the object of the verb is not abnormal since with infinitive constructs, the subject or the object of the verb may be omitted in the specific verse if it is clear in the immediate context.[194] The verb preceding the infinitive is הֵחֵל whose syntactical function is definite past,[195] since the author is referring to an activity that took place in the past. What he began to do was לִמְנוֹת "to count", which is an infinitive construct with a preposition לְ, and used as an accusative of verbal

---

194. Gibson, *Davidson's Introductory Hebrew Grammar*, 106 Rem. 1.
195. Waltke and O'Connor, *Introduction to Biblical Hebrew*, 30.5.1b.

complement[196] of what he began to do. Although Joab began counting, the narrator quickly notes that וְלֹא כִלָּה "but he did not finish." The conjunction וְ has an adversative function,[197] meaning "but" because it is contrasting the counting process and the failure to complete that process.

Because of this counting, God's קֶצֶף came/fell on them. The clause describing God's קֶצֶף is וַיְהִי בָזֹאת קֶצֶף עַל־יִשְׂרָאֵל "because of it God's קֶצֶף came/fell on Israel." The conjunction וְ has a syntactical function of introducing the consequences,[198] that is, the consequences of the failure to count everyone among the Israelites is the coming/falling of God's קֶצֶף on them. The verb יְהִי "it came/fell" identifies the trajectory taken by קֶצֶף. The object, landmark, of קֶצֶף is עַל־יִשְׂרָאֵל "on Israel." The preposition עַל has a locative meaning[199] because it points to the location of the movement of קֶצֶף. Its contextually fitting translation is "on" which means the landmark has a vertical relationship with the Ego. In this verse as in other examples given above, קֶצֶף is a subject of the verb הָיָה and the Ego of קֶצֶף is a superior to the landmark.

Because of this form of judgment, וְלֹא עָלָה הַמִּסְפָּר בְּמִסְפַּר דִּבְרֵי־הַיָּמִים לַמֶּלֶךְ דָּוִיד, "the number was not recorded in the book of chronicles of King David." The specific reference to which this number was not recorded is דִּבְרֵי־הַיָּמִים "the words of the days (chronicles)" of King David. The genitive "of the days" in the construction דִּבְרֵי־הַיָּמִים is a genitive of content,[200] meaning the words spoken in the days (period) of King David. The construction דִּבְרֵי־הַיָּמִים occurs in the BHS thirty-eight times. It can be translated as "the chronicles" referring to the written records.

This passage shows that the Ego of קֶצֶף was a superior to the landmark. It exemplifies the argument that קֶצֶף functions within a vertical relationship frame. The next passage that demonstrates this frame is 2 Chronicles 19:10.

11. 2 Chr 19:10

וְכָל־רִיב אֲשֶׁר־יָבוֹא עֲלֵיכֶם מֵאֲחֵיכֶם הַיֹּשְׁבִים בְּעָרֵיהֶם בֵּין־דָּם לְדָם
בֵּין־תּוֹרָה לְמִצְוָה לְחֻקִּים וּלְמִשְׁפָּטִים וְהִזְהַרְתֶּם אֹתָם וְלֹא יֶאְשְׁמוּ לַיהוָה
וְהָיָה קֶצֶף עֲלֵיכֶם וְעַל־אֲחֵיכֶם כֹּה תַעֲשׂוּן וְלֹא תֶאְשָׁמוּ

---

196. Waltke and O'Connor, 36.2.3b.
197. Seow, *Grammar for Biblical Hebrew*, 284.
198. BDB, 254c.
199. Arnold and Choi, *Guide to Biblical Hebrew*, 14.1.16a.
200. Van der Merwe, Naudé, and Kroeze, *Biblical Hebrew Reference Grammar*, 200.

And every dispute that comes to you from your brothers, who are living in their cities, whether it concerns bloodguilt or questions of law, command, statutes, or ordinances, warn them not to offend the Lord. Otherwise, קֶצֶף will come/fall on you and on your brothers. Now, you will do (this) and you will not offend.

In summary, this chapter concerns the appointment of Levites, priests and heads of families by King Jehoshaphat. The appointees are to settle disputes among the Hebrews. Instructions from the leaders are recorded in the preceding verse (2 Chr 19:9) which state "you must serve faithfully and wholeheartedly in the fear of the Lord" (v. 9). The content in verse 10 concerns additional instruction and it begins with the clause וְכָל־רִיב אֲשֶׁר־יָבוֹא עֲלֵיכֶם מֵאֲחֵיכֶם "and in every dispute that comes on you from your brothers." The conjunction וְ is a copulative[201] meaning "and" since it is a continuation of the instructions given in the previous verses. What forms the subject matter for the instructions in this verse is כָל־רִיב "every dispute" and the author of the text gives details on how the leaders should handle them.

The verb of the first clause יָבוֹא "may come" is a non-perfective of possibility[202] because it denotes the possibility of the subjects, the brothers, having disputes. These disputes are likely to come מֵאֲחֵיכֶם "from your brothers," who are a synecdoche of the part for the whole[203] meaning the entire community regardless of the gender and age. The author of the text explains further that these people are הַיֹּשְׁבִים בְּעָרֵיהֶם "who are living in their cities." The verb הַיֹּשְׁבִים is a participle with a predicate use[204] meaning "who are living." The place they are living is בְּעָרֵיהֶם "in their cities" with the preposition בְּ which has a spatial function[205] indicating localities where people live.

After describing the brothers and where they live, the narrator now changes focus to the nature of their disputes בֵּין־דָּם לְדָם בֵּין־תּוֹרָה לְמִצְוָה לְחֻקִּים וּלְמִשְׁפָּטִים "between blood and blood, law and commandments, and between statutes and judgments." It is noticeable that בֵּין is repeated twice but is translated only once. Bill Arnold and John Choi note, "בֵּין is paired with itself in order

---

201. Seow, *Grammar for Biblical Hebrew*, 284.
202. Waltke and O'Connor, *Introduction to Biblical Hebrew*, 31.4e.
203. Bullinger, *Figures of Speech*, 648.
204. Gibson, *Davidson's Introductory Hebrew Grammar*, 113a.
205. Arnold and Choi, *Guide to Biblical Hebrew*, 4.1.5a.

to denote the interval between two points or two parties, in which case the second בֵּין is not repeated in translation."²⁰⁶ The only other place where this formula is used is in Deuteronomy 17:8 which says:

> כִּי יִפָּלֵא מִמְּךָ דָבָר לַמִּשְׁפָּט בֵּין־דָּם לְדָם בֵּין־דִּין לְדִין וּבֵין נֶגַע לָנֶגַע דִּבְרֵי רִיבֹת בִּשְׁעָרֶיךָ וְקַמְתָּ וְעָלִיתָ אֶל־הַמָּקוֹם אֲשֶׁר יִבְחַר יְהוָה אֱלֹהֶיךָ בּוֹ׃

> If there is a case for judgment which proves too baffling for you to decide, in a matter of bloodshed or of law or of injury, matters of dispute within your gates, you shall then go up to the place which the Lord, your God, will choose (NAB).

Jehoshaphat's instruction to the priests, Levites and headmen was clear and concise. He instructed them to וְהִזְהַרְתֶּם אֹתָם וְלֹא יֶאְשְׁמוּ לַיהוָה "warn them not to offend the Lord." The verb וְהִזְהַרְתֶּם is a non-perfective of command²⁰⁷ because it implies that the warning was to be observed at the present time and in the future. This warning is further elaborated by the phrase וְלֹא יֶאְשְׁמוּ לַיהוָה, "not to offend the Lord." The negative particle לֹא "not" is key since it means not offending the Lord equals to קֶצֶף not וְהָיָה "coming/falling" on the Israelites. The verb יֶאְשְׁמוּ "offend" is a non-perfective of injunction²⁰⁸ since it shows what the speaker, in a position of authority, would not want to see his subordinates do. This verb יֶאְשְׁמוּ "offend" occurs in the BHS seven times (2 Chr 19:10; Ps 34:22–23; Jer 2:3; Hos 5:15; 10:2; Zech 11:5) and has a nuance of being guilty. It is repeated twice in this verse although in different form. The charge to the Levites and the priests was that they should ensure no one is guilty of bloodshed, God's law, command, statutes or ordinances.²⁰⁹ Being guilty of such was to result in God's קֶצֶף coming/falling on them.

The reason for all these instructions is that וְהָיָה־קֶצֶף עֲלֵיכֶם וְעַל־אֲחֵיכֶם כֹּה תַעֲשׂוּן וְלֹא תֶאְשָׁמוּ "otherwise קֶצֶף will come/fall on you and on your brothers. Now, you will do (this) and you will not offend." This clause begins with a conjunction וְ which has an alternative function²¹⁰ meaning "or, otherwise"

---

206. Arnold and Choi, 4.1.16.
207. Chisholm, *From Exegesis to Exposition*, 94, 101.
208. Arnold and Choi, *Guide to Biblical Hebrew*, 3.2.2(d.4).
209. All these mentioned wrongs are examples of what is introduced as disputes at the beginning of the verse.
210. Van der Merwe, Naudé, and Kroeze, *Biblical Hebrew Reference Grammar*, 298.

because the last clause is an alternative of what will happen if the instructions are not heeded. The first verb in this clause is וְהָיָה "will come/fall," which is a specific future,[211] denoting that if God is offended then קֶצֶף (from God) וְהָיָה "will come/fall" עֲלֵיכֶם "on them," hence the charge not to disobey. The prepositional phrase עֲלֵיכֶם וְעַל־אֲחֵיכֶם "on you and on your brothers," has the preposition עַל showing locality, the goal movement of the subject.[212]

Having clearly delineated the laws by which they should live, King Jehoshaphat ended by urging the leaders that כֹּה תַעֲשׂוּן וְלֹא תֶאְשָׁמוּ "you will do (this) and you will not offend." This final clause begins with particle כֹּה which is an adverb of manner "introducing the content of the speech."[213] The verb תַעֲשׂוּן is a non-perfective of command[214] denoting that the speaker wanted to be followed without wavering. If this command is followed, they would not be guilty before God and his קֶצֶף would not come/fall on them.

In summary, 2 Chronicles 19:10 concerns King Jehoshaphat's instruction to the leaders of the community who were to warn the Israelites not to trespass against the Lord so that his קֶצֶף does not come/fall on them. Trespassing against God's laws is an antecedent of his קֶצֶף, which would come/fall on them. The verse has demonstrated that קֶצֶף is the subject of its clause whose trajectory is identified by the verb הָיָה and its landmark by the preposition עַל. In addition, the meaning of the preposition עַל further demonstrates that קצף frame had a vertical syntactical relationship. Since the Ego of קֶצֶף is superior to the landmark, it explains a vertical relationship and the two complement each other. It is also true of this passage that there is an intended punishment.

Another example that exemplifies these characteristics of the קצף frame is 2 Chronicles 24:18.

12. 2 Chr 24:18

וַיַּעַזְבוּ אֶת־בֵּית יְהוָה אֱלֹהֵי אֲבוֹתֵיהֶם וַיַּעַבְדוּ אֶת־הָאֲשֵׁרִים וְאֶת־הָעֲצַבִּים וַיְהִי־קֶצֶף עַל־יְהוּדָה וִירוּשָׁלַ͏ִם בְּאַשְׁמָתָם זֹאת׃

They abandoned the house of Yahweh, the God of their forefathers, and began to serve the Asherahs and the idols; therefore,

---

211. Waltke and O'Connor, *Introduction to Biblical Hebrew*, 31.6.2a–b.
212. Arnold and Choi, *Guide to Biblical Hebrew*, 14.1.16a.
213. Arnold and Choi, 4.2.9.
214. Waltke and O'Connor, *Introduction to Biblical Hebrew*, 31.3d.

because of this crime of theirs, קֶצֶף came/fell upon Judah and Jerusalem.

The larger context of this verse is about King Joash and Jehoiada, the priest, who mobilized the Israelites to rebuild the house of God and subsequently restored proper worship in the house of God (vv. 1–16). After the death of Jehoiada, the officials of the king came to pay homage to King Joash and apparently misled him, causing him to abandon the temple of God (vv. 17–18). Because of this act of retreat into idolatry, God's קֶצֶף came/fell on Judah and Jerusalem. The people abandoned their true God and began to worship idols. The end result was military defeat at the hands the army of Aram (v. 23), a punishment characteristically associated with קצף frame.

The specific verse, which is the focus in this research, is verse 18 which began with a sad statement of a sinful act by the Hebrews. It says וַיַּעַזְבוּ אֶת־בֵּית יְהוָה אֱלֹהֵי אֲבוֹתֵיהֶם "they abandoned the house of the Lord, the God of their fathers." The verb וַיַּעַזְבוּ "they abandoned" is an ingressive perfective,[215] which refers to the beginning of an action. The plural afformative is contextually referring to the king and the officials of Judah (v. 17). The object of the verb is אֶת־בֵּית "the house." This house is explained further by a genitive יְהוָה "house of Yahweh" which is a possessive genitive,[216] but a possession which is metaphorical, meaning the house called by God's name and associated with worship. After describing the house, the author, redirects the readers' focus to who this God is. He is אֱלֹהֵי אֲבוֹתֵיהֶם יְהוָה "Yahweh, God of their forefathers." The two אֱלֹהֵי יְהוָה nouns are in apposition, a common noun in apposition to a proper noun.[217]

There is a direct link between the first verb וַיַּעַזְבוּ, "they left" and the second, וַיַּעַבְדוּ, "they served." The action of the former set the stage for the action of the latter. Just like the former, the latter is also an ingressive perfective[218] denoting what they began to do – serve other gods. The objects of the verb וַיַּעַבְדוּ, "they served" are אֶת־הָאֲשֵׁרִים וְאֶת־הָעֲצַבִּים "the Asherahs and the idols."

The first part of this verse, as discussed above, sets the background for the last clause, which says וַיְהִי־קֶצֶף עַל־יְהוּדָה וִירוּשָׁלַם בְּאַשְׁמָתָם זֹאת "therefore,

---

215. Gibson, *Davidson's Introductory Hebrew Grammar*, 57 Rem. 2.
216. Van der Merwe, Naudé, and Kroeze, *Biblical Hebrew Reference Grammar*, 198.
217. Waltke and O'Connor, *Introduction to Biblical Hebrew*, 12.3e.
218. Waltke and O'Connor, 30.2.1b.

because of this crime of theirs, קֶצֶף came/fell upon Judah and Jerusalem." The conjunction וְ at the beginning of this clause is introducing a consequence[219] meaning "therefore." With this understanding, it is possible to note that the conjunction וְ at the beginning of this clause has a direct connection with בְּאַשְׁמָתָם זֹאת "because of this guiltiness." The preposition בְּ has a causal syntactic function[220] meaning it should be translated as "because." The near demonstrative זֹאת "this" is anaphoric pointing to "their crime" which was the reason God's קֶצֶף anger, יְהִי "came/fell" on Judah and Jerusalem. The verb יְהִי "came/fell" is a definite past[221] and in this research, it identifies the trajectory of the קצף frame. The prepositional phrase עַל־יְהוּדָה וִירוּשָׁלַם "on Judah and Jerusalem" is marked by the preposition עַל which explains locality,[222] the goal of the movement of קֶצֶף. The result was that punishment by God's קֶצֶף was manifested by the invasion of Hazael (v. 23).[223] As mentioned earlier in the section under reference 4, the antecedent condition of קֶצֶף is the "lesser of two evils," when compared to references where קֶצֶף־גָּדוֹל is used with idolatry as the antecedent condition. However, this context is the only exception to the claim that idolatry provoked קֶצֶף־גָּדוֹל since the antecedent condition of קֶצֶף in this passage is idolatry.

In 2 Chronicles 29:8, קֶצֶף is the subject of its clause. Its trajectory is identified by the הָיָה verb and its landmark is identified by the preposition עַל.

13. 2 Chr 29:8

וַיְהִי קֶצֶף יְהוָה עַל־יְהוּדָה וִירוּשָׁלָם וַיִּתְּנֵם לְזַעֲוָה לְשַׁמָּה וְלִשְׁרֵקָה כַּאֲשֶׁר אַתֶּם רֹאִים בְּעֵינֵיכֶם:

> Therefore, the קֶצֶף of (from) the Lord came/fell on Judah and Jerusalem; he has made them an object of terror, horror, and hissing, as you are seeing with your own eyes.

The context of this passage is about a reminder of how God's קֶצֶף came/fell on Judah and Jerusalem after their ancestors sinned against God. The setting is during the reign of King Hezekiah. Since Hezekiah feared God

---

219. BDB, 254c.
220. Arnold and Choi, *Guide to Biblical Hebrew*, 4.1.5f.
221. Joüon and Muraoka, *Grammar of Biblical Hebrew*, 30.5.1b.
222. Arnold and Choi, *Guide to Biblical Hebrew*, 4.1.16a.
223. Curtis and Madsen, *Books of Chronicles*, 437.

and wanted to please him (v. 2), he reopened the temple and repaired its doors (v. 3). He also brought priests and Levites and asked them to sanctify themselves and the temple (vv. 4–5). The reasons for the sanctification were the sins of their ancestors. Their sins, according to 2 Chronicles 29:6–7, were as follows: They forsook God and turned their faces against God; they closed the doors of the temple; they put off the fire – believed to be "the lamps of the golden 'candle stick' which burned until morning (Exod 25:31; 30:7; 40:24; Lev 24:3)."[224] Therefore, their sins and the defilement of the temple provoked God's קֶצֶף. The result was probably referring to the devastating attack and destruction by the king of Aram, the events in 2 Chronicles 28:5–8. William Johnstone argues for the Aramean invasion by saying that "the defeat in battle and captivity of women and children, which Judah has just experienced (2 Chr 28:5–8), are to be understood as evidence of the anger of the Lord."[225] However, the language that the chronicler uses here of God making the forefathers "an object of dread and horror and scorn," resonates with Jeremiah's message before the Israelites were taken into captivity by the Babylonians (Jer 19:8; 25:9, 18; 29:18; 51:37).

This verse begins with וַיְהִי קֶצֶף יְהוָה עַל־יְהוּדָה וִירוּשָׁלָ͏ם "therefore, the קֶצֶף of the Lord came/fell on Judah and Jerusalem." The verb וַיְהִי has a conjunction וְ which is introducing a consequence[226] because in this narrative the reasons mentioned in verses 7–8 are the basis on which קֶצֶף came/fell on the Israelites. The וַיְהִי verb is a persistent present perfective[227] meaning this happened at some point in the past and had continued in Hezekiah's time. The subject of the verb is קֶצֶף which occurs in the construction קֶצֶף יְהוָה "anger of the Lord." This construction is a genitive of source[228] meaning that קֶצֶף came/fell from the Lord. This understanding is in line with the קצף frame advanced in this research since the argument is that קֶצֶף is an abstract object which comes/falls from Ego – the experiencer of קֶצֶף . The effect of קֶצֶף coming on them is explained in the clause that follows, that is וַיִּתְּנֵם לְזַעֲוָה לְשַׁמָּה וְלִשְׁרֵ־ קָה כַּאֲשֶׁר אַתֶּם רֹאִים בְּעֵינֵיכֶם "he has made them an object of terror, horror,

---

224. Curtis and Madsen, 376.
225. Johnstone, *1 and 2 Chronicles*, 191.
226. BDB, 254c.
227. Waltke and O'Connor, *Introduction to Biblical Hebrew*, 30.5.1c.
228. Joüon and Muraoka, *Grammar of Biblical Hebrew*, 191.

and hissing, as you see with your own eyes." The verb וַיִּתְּנֵם "he has made them" is a persistent present perfective[229] meaning this activity of punishing them began in the past and continues into the present. What they became is לְזַעֲוָה לְשַׁמָּה וְלִשְׁרֵקָה "object of terror, horror and hissing," which will be evident as stated in the last relative clause which says כַּאֲשֶׁר אַתֶּם רֹאִים בְּעֵינֵיכֶם "as you are seeing with your own eyes." The verb רֹאִים is a participle whose syntactical function is predicate use, present time with a durative sense.[230] The construction בְּעֵינֵיכֶם "with your own eyes" has an emphatic function[231] meaning it was self-evident. The offence of their forefathers was that they abandoned God and the service/worship in the temple (2 Chr 29:6–7).

This passage (2 Chr 29:8) has demonstrated that קֶצֶף is the subject of its clause whose trajectory is identified by the verb הָיָה and its landmark is marked by the preposition עַל. The Ego is superior to the subordinate and there is pronouncement of punishment. The last example in which the trajectory is identified by the verb הָיָה and its landmark by the preposition עַל is 2 Chronicles 32:25.

14. 2 Chr 32:25

וְלֹא־כִגְמֻל עָלָיו הֵשִׁיב יְחִזְקִיָּהוּ כִּי גָבַהּ לִבּוֹ וַיְהִי עָלָיו קֶצֶף וְעַל־יְהוּדָה וִירוּשָׁלָ͏ִם

But Hezekiah did not respond with kindness (given) him, for he had become proud. Therefore, קֶצֶף came/fell on him and on Judah and Jerusalem.

This verse concerns Hezekiah and Sennacherib, the king of Assyria. The Assyrians invaded Judah (v. 1) and Hezekiah's first response to the attack was to block all the water springs (vv. 3–4). Later, Sennacherib sent his officials to Hezekiah with a message describing how mighty he was, and mocking the God of the Israelites (vv. 9–19). In response to Sennacherib's message, Hezekiah and Isaiah prayed to God (v. 20). God heard the prayers offered and he subjected the Assyrians to disgraceful defeat (v. 21). In celebration of what the Lord did, many people brought gifts to the Lord and to Hezekiah (v. 23). Later, during these days of peace and success, Hezekiah became ill almost to

---

229. Waltke and O'Connor, *Introduction to Biblical Hebrew*, 30.5.1c.
230. Joüon and Muraoka, *Grammar of Biblical Hebrew*, 121c, d.
231. Seow, *Grammar for Biblical Hebrew*, 93.

the point of death but he prayed and God healed him (v. 24). Instead of being grateful, he became proud and God was angry with him (v. 25).

This sentence begins with conjunction וְ which has an adversative function[232] being translated as "but" because it contrasts the healing of Hezekiah by God and his response which was pride. This verb is followed by a negation clause וְלֹא־כִגְמֻל עָלָיו הֵשִׁיב "but Hezekiah did not respond with kindness (given) him." The noun כִגְמֻל "kindness" has a preposition כְּ which has a comparative syntactical function,[233] comparing his arrogance to the kindness granted him. The noun גְּמוּל has the idea of benefit in the sense of acting in a manner to the benefit of someone.[234] It is used with the same sense in Psalm 103:2. The construction כִגְמֻל עָלָיו "kindness (given to) him" is two prepositional phrases delineating the recipient of the kindness. The verb הֵשִׁיב "return" is a telic perfective[235] looking at the end of his action, namely, that Hezekiah did not do what was expected of him.

The reason he did not act in kindness was כִּי גָבַהּ לִבּוֹ "because he became proud." The כִּי is introducing a causal clause.[236] The construction גָבַהּ לִבּוֹ "his heart was high" is an idiom meaning he became proud. This construction is also used in 2 Chronicles 26:16, again in reference to Hezekiah. Edward Curtis and Albert Madsen note that "he should have taken pride not in his wealth but in Yahweh his God and deliverer."[237] The consequence of his pride was that קֶצֶף came/fell on him, and Judah and Jerusalem. The conjunction וְ introduces a consequence[238] being translated as "therefore." The object is עָלָיו . . . וְעַל־יְהוּדָה וִירוּשָׁלָם "on him and on Judah and Jerusalem." Even though the wrong is attributed to Hezekiah, God's קֶצֶף came/fell on all the people as Johnstone states, "Since the king is also the representative of his people, that anger falls on 'Judah and Jerusalem.'"[239] They, however, experienced a reprieve after they prayed and repented. Therefore, God's קֶצֶף did not come/

---

232. Seow, 284.
233. Arnold and Choi, *Guide to Biblical Hebrew*, 4.2.10a.
234. Koehler and Baumgartner, "גְּמוּל", *HALOT*, 1:197.
235. Waltke and O'Connor, *Introduction to Biblical Hebrew*, 10.2.3b.
236. Seow, *Grammar for Biblical Hebrew*, 331.
237. Curtis and Madsen, *Books of Chronicles*, 491.
238. Bergman, *Cambridge Biblical Hebrew Workbook*, 20.
239. Johnstone, *1 and 2 Chronicles*, 2:220.

fall on them immediately (2 Chr 32:26).²⁴⁰ The relationship of verses 25 and 26 is that in verse 25 Hezekiah is proud and for that reason God's קֶצֶף comes/falls on him and the Israelites. However, after repenting, they found reprieve as mentioned in verse 26.

In this verse as in the preceding ones, קֶצֶף is the subject of the clause. The trajectory is identified by verb הָיָה and the landmark by the preposition עַל whose syntactical function is that of a vertical relationship between the Ego and the landmark. Other than the syntactical function, the vertical relationship is supported by the Ego and the landmark relationship, which is that of a superior and the subordinate, respectively.

According to the examples examined so far, the קצף frame can be illustrated in the diagram below.

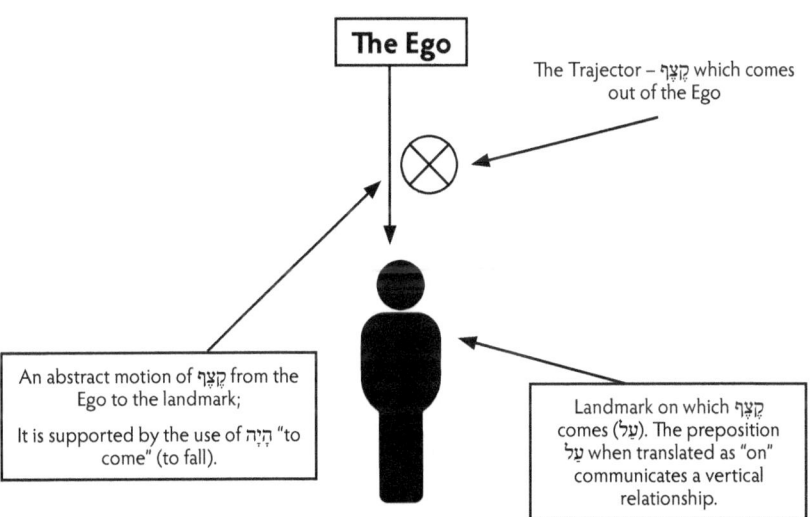

Chart 1

Understanding this frame is profitable for biblical exegesis in areas where קֶצֶף occurs. Some authors of Old Testament commentaries have already mentioned some aspects of the frame, for example, William Johnstone, who is quoted earlier in this chapter, notes the retributive nature associated with קֶצֶף.

---

240. This passage is discussed in section 3.1.1.1 number 2.

However, the entire frame is needed as background information for proper exegesis. Charles Fillmore underscores the benefit of frames in that they "play an important role in how people perceive, remember, and reason about their experiences, how they form assumptions about the background and possible concomitants of those experiences, and even how one's life experiences can or should be enacted."[241]

The section 3.1.1.2 above has identified the frame elements of the Ego who is experiencing קֶצֶף. However, all the passages considered demonstrate that no one experienced קֶצֶף without a cause. The causes of קֶצֶף are the antecedent conditions and they are part of the core frame elements. These conditions amount to what Richard Shweder calls the decomposable slots – the subparts of an emotion that make it complete.[242]

3.1.1.3 The Antecedent Conditions of קֶצֶף

The Scripture references in which קֶצֶף occur explain that there were conditions that preceded the experience of קֶצֶף before it was experienced. Some of these conditions have been discussed in the references given above and others are discussed in the following section. These conditions are: opposition to a leader (Num 16:22, 46; Josh 9:20), lack of proper care for the altar (Num 18:5), breaking of vows (Eccl 5:6), rebellion (Deut 1:34; 9:7–8, 22; Josh 22:18, 20), idolatry (Deut 29:26; 2 Chr 24:18), breaking of an oath (Josh 9:20), disobedience (1 Chr 27:24), forsaking cultic worship (2 Chr 29:8), and pride (2 Chr 32:25–26).[243] So far, the core frame elements of קֶצֶף can be summarized in table 3.

The frame elements are comprised of at least two people – the one provoking and the one being provoked – and the antecedent conditions. It is hard to imagine any event where קֶצֶף is experienced where these three elements are not present: the person causing a provocation, the person being provoked, and the situation in which the conflict unfolds. These frame elements fit within a scenario in which we have a provoking, provoked and a provocative situation and that is the reason they form the core frame elements of the קצף frame.

---

241. Fillmore and Baker, "Frames Approach," 314.

242. Shweder and Haidt, "Cultural Psychology of Emotions," 155–56.

243. Some of the passages mentioned here are discussed later under different subheadings. When they are discussed later, a mention is made to affirm the stated antecedent conditions.

In addition to these frame elements, emotions are usually accompanied by non-verbal gestures which Shweder calls iconic symbols.

Table 3

Frame	Core frame elements
קצף	Sin
	Disobedience
	Opposing a leader
	Breaking a vow
	Rebellion
	Idolatry
	Breaking of an oath
	Pride
	Ego – the *experiencer*
	Trajector
	Landmark

3.1.1.4 Iconic Symbols

Iconic symbols are expressions or gestures that reveal the kind of emotion that person is displaying. The iconic symbols for קצף frame are two as discussed below.

3.1.1.4.1 Hiding of Face

Vorwahl Heinrich notes that facial expressions associated with anger in the Old Testament include winking of the eyes (Job 15:12), frowning of face (Dan 3:19), gazing of the eye (Amos 9:4), hiding of the face (Job 13:24), and breathing heavily (Ps 18:9).[244] These facial expressions carry a variety of meanings which can be deduced from the context. For example, the hiding of the face can also indicate shame (Esth 6:12). Out of the facial expressions mentioned above, only the hiding of face is associated with קֶצֶף. In Isaiah 54:8, God said, "'In an outburst of קֶצֶף 'anger' I hid my face from you for a moment, But with everlasting loving kindness I will have compassion on

---

244. Vorwahl, *Die Gebärdensprache*, 18.

you,' says the Lord your Redeemer."²⁴⁵ However, while Vorwahl's description of "the hiding of the face" assumes a physical approach, I have taken it figuratively as a synecdoche of the part for the whole,²⁴⁶ and as an expression which implies forsaking – in קֶצֶף management – of the party who experienced קֶצֶף by symbolically withdrawing from the person or scene of provocation.²⁴⁷ The "hiding of face" is therefore one of the iconic symbols of קֶצֶף. the second iconic symbol is "laying of hands/sending a hand."

3.1.1.4.2 Laying of Hand(s)

In addition to the facial expressions, Vorwahl has also examined bodily gestures associated with anger in the Old Testament and notes the following: stretching hands (Isa 10:4), raising up hands (Job 31:21) and clapping of hands (Job 27:23).²⁴⁸ Another scholar, Nili Fox, has findings which are in agreement with Vorwahl's study of clapping of hands. Fox notes that תקע, נבה, חאם and ספק are the main verbs associated with anger, and which are given the English translation of either to strike or to clap. In addition, Fox wrote that clapping of hands was also accompanied by stamping of feet. An example is Ezekiel 6:11, which says, "Thus says the Lord GOD, 'clap your hand, stamp your foot and say, "Alas, because of all the evil abominations of the house of Israel, which will fall by sword, famine and plague!"'" (NASB).²⁴⁹ However, these gestures are not specific to anger expressions only; their correct interpretation is dependent on the context. For example, in 2 Kings 11:12, we read, "Then he brought the king's son out and put the crown on him and gave him the testimony; and they made him king and anointed him, and they clapped their hands and said, 'Long live the king!'" In this verse, the clapping of hands is a sign of approval.

Max Rogland singles out תקע as used by Fox and notes that in some contexts it is better translated as "striking a hand" – meaning two people striking their hands as opposed to one person clapping his hands. In his monograph – "Striking a Hand" (*tq' kp*) in biblical Hebrew – he says,

---

245. This verse is discussed in detail later in this chapter.
246. Bullinger, *Figures of Speech*, 640.
247. This verse is discussed later in detail under a different heading. The purpose of this section was to highlight the symbolic icon element without detailed study of the verse.
248. Vorwahl, *Die Gebärdensprache*, 18.
249. Fox, "Clapping Hands," 51–52.

In the book of Proverbs *TQ' KP* occurs in parallelism with forms of *'RB* ("to act as surety"), where it appears to be a gesture which accompanies the giving of a pledge: vi 1 "My son, if you have become surety for your neighbour, if you have struck your hands for a stranger (*tq't lzr kpyk*)"; xvii 18 "A man lacking judgment strikes a hand (*twq' kp*), becomes surety before his neighbour"; xxii 26 "Be not among those who strike a hand (*btq'y kp*), who become surety for debts." It is most likely that "striking a hand" in these instances refers to giving a handshake, which in the context is understood as an official seal to some sort of agreement. It should be noted that this "striking a hand" involves the hand of someone else and is clearly different than "clapping one's hands," which refers to striking one's own hands together.[250]

This observation by Rogland explains the need for taking Fox's identified verbs: תקע, נכה, חאם and ספק within their specific contexts. This research has ascertained that the aforementioned verbs do not occur with קֶצֶף, which is the specific Hebrew lexical item this research focuses on. On the contrary, קצף occurs with לִשְׁלֹחַ יָד which can be literally translated as "send hand" or "lay hand" in Esther 2:21. This phrase – לִשְׁלֹחַ יָד, occurs five times in the book of Esther (2:21; 3:6; 6:2; 8:7;[251] 9:2) although it is a gesture associated with קֶצֶף only in Esther 2:21. As opposed to the analysis by Fox and Rogland, which showed that the clapping and striking of hands was a hand-to-hand contact, the "lay hand" is not limited to only-hands contact. The examples below demonstrate how לִשְׁלֹחַ יָד "send hand" is a hand-to-body contact and/or a figurative use meaning to harm someone.

The first example is Esther 2:21 which reads: "During the time Mordecai was sitting at the king's gate, Bigthana and Teresh, two of the king's officers who guarded the doorway, became angry (קצף) and conspired to assassinate King Xerxes" (NIV). The word translated as "conspired" is לִשְׁלֹחַ יָד "to send of hand." This same story is recapped in Esther 6:2 as the narrator revisits the events preceding the honoring of Mordecai. The intention of these two officials was to assassinate (send their hands on) the king. In this case, "sending

---

250. Rogland, "'Striking a Hand,'" 107.

251. In this reference, it is not an infinitive construct but it carries the same meaning of "sending a hand."

of hand" is a hand-to-body contact or a figurative expression which also demonstrates the intention of retribution.

The second example is from Esther 3:6 which reads: "Yet having learned who Mordecai's people were, he scorned the idea of killing only Mordecai. Instead, Haman looked for a way to destroy all Mordecai's people, the Jews, throughout the whole kingdom of Xerxes" (NIV). The phrase translated as "killing" is לִשְׁלֹחַ יָד "to send of hand." Haman's idea was to kill Mordecai and the Jews. The idiom "to send hand" is hereby used figuratively to mean "to kill."

The third example is in Esther 8:7 which says: "King Xerxes replied to Queen Esther and to Mordecai the Jew, 'Because Haman attacked the Jews, I have given his estate to Esther, and they have impaled him on the pole he set up'" (NIV). The word translated as "Haman שָׁלַח יָדוֹ attacked the Jews" literally means "Haman sent his hand on the Jews." In this context שָׁלַח יָדוֹ "to send a hand" is used to mean physically harming someone.

The fourth and the last example is from Esther 9:2 which reads: "The Jews assembled in their cities in all the provinces of King Xerxes to attack those seeking their destruction. No one could stand against them, because the people of all the other nationalities were afraid of them" (NIV). The word translated as "to attack" is לִשְׁלֹחַ יָד "to send of hand." While לִשְׁלֹחַ יָד has been used previously against Hebrew(s), it is now used in this verse in reference to the Jews against (attacking) their oppressors. Out of the five references given above, only one reference explicitly states that לִשְׁלֹחַ יָד "to send of hand" is associated with קֶצֶף (Esth 2:21) and therefore a non-verbal communication from which קֶצֶף is implied. In addition, the general use of the idiom לִשְׁלֹחַ יָד "to send of hand" in the book of Esther enhances the understanding that it symbolizes an act of punishment or revenge (actualized or intended, explicit or implicit), an idea that is associated with קֶצֶף.

The section 3.1.1 above has discussed the core frame elements of the קצף frame. The following section examines the peripheral frame elements.

3.1.2 Peripheral Frame Elements

Charles Fillmore notes that time, place and manner usually form part of the peripheral frame elements. Let us reconsider the example given in chapter 2 section 2.1.3.2 which says "Moses bought a shirt on Monday along Tom Mboya Street after bargaining for twenty minutes." According to Fillmore's view, the mention of Monday (time), Tom Mboya Street (place) and the twenty minutes of bargaining (manner) are evoked peripheral frame elements. This means that the manner in which the shirt was bought, the place and the time are not necessary conditions evoked in every commercial transaction. However, depending on the kind of frame, the aforementioned trio can be part of the core frame elements.

Concerning the קצף frame, there are no biblical references that mention the specific time and manner in which God or an individual experienced קצף. However, the following verses take note of where, the place, the Israelites were when God's קצף came/fell on them. The places are mentioned in Deuteronomy 9:7–8, 22 and in Psalm 106:32. Since these verses are discussed in detail later under another subheading, they are only quoted here (and numbered differently) for illustrative purposes without discussion.

Deut 9:7

זְכֹר אַל־תִּשְׁכַּח אֵת אֲשֶׁר־הִקְצַפְתָּ אֶת־יְהוָה אֱלֹהֶיךָ בַּמִּדְבָּר לְמִן־הַיּוֹם אֲשֶׁר־יָצָאתָ מֵאֶרֶץ מִצְרַיִם עַד־בֹּאֲכֶם עַד־הַמָּקוֹם הַזֶּה מַמְרִים הֱיִיתֶם עִם־יְהוָה׃

Remember and do not forget how you provoked to anger the Lord, your God, in the wilderness. Because, from the day when you left the land of Egypt until you came to this place you have been rebellious toward the Lord.

This verse singles out a general place, wilderness, as a name of a place where they angered God.

Deut 9:8

וּבְחֹרֵב הִקְצַפְתֶּם אֶת־יְהוָה וַיִּתְאַנַּף יְהוָה בָּכֶם לְהַשְׁמִיד אֶתְכֶם׃

Also at Horeb you so provoked to anger the Lord and he became angry with you to destroy you.

The place mentioned in this verse is Horeb.

Deut 9:22

וּבְתַבְעֵרָה וּבְמַסָּה וּבְקִבְרֹת הַתַּאֲוָה מַקְצִפִים הֱיִיתֶם אֶת־יְהוָה׃

Likewise, at Taberah, at Massah, and at Kibroth-hattaavah you were the ones provoking to anger the Lord.

The first three nouns are names of where Israel was encamped when God was angered.

Ps 106:32

וַיַּקְצִיפוּ עַל־מֵי מְרִיבָה וַיֵּרַע לְמֹשֶׁה בַּעֲבוּרָם׃

They provoked to anger (the Lord) at the waters of Meribah and Moses felt bad for their sake.

This verse highlights Meribah as a place of waters where God was angered.

The significance of these places is that they mark historical moments during the wanderings of the Israelites when they angered their God. The fact that only few references are given, is a testament to how peripheral they are in the קצף frame.

The analysis of the קצף frame so far has stated that both the core and the peripheral frame elements are central to the understanding of any particular frame. Other components, which are important but not central to the main frame, are the extrathematic frame elements. The usage of קצף in poetry brings to light some of these extrathematic frame elements.

3.1.3 Extrathematic Frame Elements: Parallelism in Poetry

While the discussion thus far has focused on the core frame elements of the קצף frame, the parallelisms in poetry illustrate the extrathematic frame elements. Fillmore elaborates the extrathematic frame elements as those elements that "introduce information that is not a necessary part of the description of the central frame. In many cases such phrases introduce a new frame."[252] As it is shown in the verse analyzed below, קֶצֶף occurs in the primary colon – the one bearing the primary meaning – in its entire noun forms. This primary colon is the first line of the parallelism under comparison. The קֶצֶף is paralleled with חֵמָה "anger," זַעַם "anger" and חֶסֶד "kindness." Similar to the noun forms, the קצף verbal forms also occur in the primary colon except in two instances. It is shown in those two cases that the primary colon bears the action that evokes Ego to be קצף "angry." The two verbs which appear in the first colon are מָאַס "to reject" and רִיב "to strive." The analysis done later in this section shows that these two verbs, מָאַס "to reject" and רִיב "to strive," are

---

252. Fillmore and Baker, "Frames Approach," 326.

antecedent conditions of קָצַף "angry". In other passages, קֶצֶף is paralleled with חָלַל "to wound," עָוֺן "to have iniquity," רָצוֺן "to show favor," גָּעַר "to rebuke" and חָטָא "to sin." The first category examined below is on the parallelism of קֶצֶף.

3.1.3.1 Parallelism of קֶצֶף in Poetry

This section examines the lexical items that are paralleled with קֶצֶף with the understanding that "parallelism promotes the perception of a relationship between the elements of which parallelism is composed and this relationship is one of correspondence. The nature of the correspondence varies, but in general it involves repetition or the substitution of things which are equivalent on one or more linguistic levels."[253] These frame elements will be given in bold style for the purpose of clarity. Since the passages considered in this pericope are in poetry, the verses are quoted and arranged according to their parallelisms. The first example under consideration is Psalm 38:2[1][254].

15. Ps 38:2[1]

This is a psalm of David in which he expresses a need for relief from illness (v. 3). Not only was he suffering from illness, his enemies were also working for his downfall (vv. 12, 16, 19–20). In the context of this psalm, David implied, because of the causative form of the verbs and the preposition בְּ, that the illness and the attack from his enemies was a result of God's קֶצֶף. What provoked God's קֶצֶף was caused by sin. Although in this psalm sin is not mentioned, it is implied since in Psalm 39:12[11], being rebuked and disciplined is associated with sin. Psalm 38:2[1] says,

יְהוָה אַל־בְּקֶצְפְּךָ תוֹכִיחֵנִי O Lord, do not rebuke me in your קֶצֶף

וּבַחֲמָתְךָ תְיַסְּרֵנִי Or discipline me in your חֵמָה

Psalm 38:2[1] begins with יְהוָה "O Lord" which is a vocative of address[255] since the prayer by the psalmist is directed to him. The description of this bicola is as follows. Both קֶצֶף in line a and חֵמָה in line b have a preposition בְּ. The preposition בְּ in both lines has a state function[256] denoting the state in

---

253. Berlin, *Dynamics of Biblical Parallelism*, 2.
254. The number in the square brackets is for the corresponding verse number in the English versions.
255. Van der Merwe, Naudé, and Kroeze, *Biblical Hebrew Reference Grammar*, 249.
256. Köhler and Baumgartner, "בְּ," *HALOT*, 1:103–5.

which God might be in order to rebuke or discipline. This state function is supported by the use of a hiphil verb תוֹכִיחֵנִי "rebuke me" which has a causative function[257] and can be literally translated as "caused to rebuke me." This verb תוֹכִיחֵנִי "rebuke me" is paralleled with תְיַסְּרֵנִי "discipline me" in line b.

Both verbs are jussives of request[258] since the two verbs connote a passionate plea from an inferior to a superior. The ו conjunction at the beginning of line b has an alternative function[259] meaning "or" since line b is basically an alternative of the message in line a. The bicola is, therefore, a synonymous parallelism in the category of base-restatement[260] because the second line does not add any significant meaning to the content of line a.

In addition to the parallelism of ideas, this bicola has also parallelism of sounds. Berlin notes, "Sound pairing enhances the perception of correspondence between the lines ... The sound pair plays a crucial role in forging the union between the lines."[261] The first set of words end with ךָ and the second set of words end with נִי. As the verse quoted above implies, David is attributing his suffering to God's קֶצֶף. The use of חֵמָה in the second colon is that of semantic equivalence – notice it is not in the primary colon, the first one. However, as already explained at the beginning of this chapter, the meaning of חֵמָה is not a replica of קֶצֶף, so חֵמָה evokes a different frame[262] beyond the frame advanced in this research, and hence its treatment as an extrathematic frame element. Both קֶצֶף and חֵמָה are viewed to be semantically similar, and they are used together in contexts of judgment. Their similarity can be compared to the same way חֵטְא "sin" is paralleled with עָוֹן "transgression" in Psalm 38:18. According to verse 18, David attributes his current suffering to sin, which he says he will confess. Therefore, the reason God is rebuking David in his קֶצֶף is because he has sinned. A similar parallelism of קֶצֶף and חֵמָה is stated in Isaiah 34:2 as explained in the following reference.

---

257. Seow, *Grammar for Biblical Hebrew*, 181.
258. Van der Merwe, Naudé, and Kroeze, *Biblical Hebrew Reference Grammar*, 152.
259. Seow, *Grammar for Biblical Hebrew*, 284.
260. Wendland, *Analyzing the Psalms*, 67.
261. Berlin, *Dynamics of Biblical Parallelism*, 111.
262. The diagram at the end of this section will elaborate this.

16. Isa 34:2

כִּי קֶצֶף לַיהוָה עַל־כָּל־הַגּוֹיִם Because קֶצֶף "anger" of (from) the Lord is on all the nations

וְחֵמָה עַל־כָּל־צְבָאָם (his) חֵמָה "anger" is on all their armies

הֶחֱרִימָם he has placed them under the ban

נְתָנָם לַטָּבַח he has given them to the slaughter

The context of this chapter is on judgment against the nations, eschatologically referring to the whole world. Verse 2 quoted above is specifically on God's anger which precedes his judgment. Line a and b are a verbless bicola. The word קֶצֶף – in line a is paralleled with חֵמָה – in line b. The last clause of each line is syntactically paralleled with a preposition followed by two nouns in each colon and all are connected with a *maqqep*. The syntactically paralleled prepositional phrases are עַל־כָּל־הַגּוֹיִם and עַל־כָּל־צְבָאָם. The pronoun "his" in line d is supplied since it is not part of the text.

The particle כִּי is introducing a causal clause[263] meaning it should be translated as "because" since the content of the speech in verse 2 is the motivation for the appeal in verse 1 in which the prophet is calling upon all the nations to obey God's message. The verb "to be" is supplied and the subject of this verb is קֶצֶף לַיהוָה "anger of the Lord" whose contextual usage means that קֶצֶף came/fell from the Lord. The target of God's קֶצֶף is עַל־כָּל־הַגּוֹיִם "on all the nations." The preposition עַל, in both line c and d has a locative function[264] showing the location of קֶצֶף and חֵמָה respectively.

The parallelism of line a and b is synonymous, general-specific.[265] The message in line a is קֶצֶף coming from God on הַגּוֹיִם "the nations" which has a definite article of particular reference[266] since it has been introduced in verse 1. In line b, the message is חֵמָה "anger" which is coming on all their armies, which is a specific example of what the nations are, with the particle כִּי governing both lines and with line d having an ellipsis of לַיהוָה "of the Lord." Since "their armies" is a part and a specific example of the nations, so is חֵמָה a part of קֶצֶף in the קצף frame – again, קֶצֶף is in the primary colon which carries

---

263. Arnold and Choi, *Guide to Biblical Hebrew*, 4.3.4a.
264. Arnold and Choi, 4.1.16a.
265. Wendland, *Analyzing the Psalms*, 72.
266. Gibson, *Davidson's Introductory Hebrew Grammar*, 30a.

the main idea. However, both words are usually used in the same context in passages that have to do with judgment.

The effect of God's anger on the nations is הֶחֱרִימָם נְתָנָם לַטָּבַח "He has placed them under the ban, has given them to slaughter." Just as in line a and b, the bicola of line c and d is synonymous parallelism, general-specific[267] because line d is specific on what kind of "ban" it will be – slaughter. The verbs חָרַם and נָתַן have a prophetic perfective function[268] because the verbs represent the speaker's confidence in the fulfillment of the prophecy.

The message of Isaiah is that of judgment against the nations. The reason for this judgment, desolation, is a vengeance for the Israelites (v. 8). Similarly, the same way קֶצֶף and חֵמָה are paralleled in Psalm 38 when David sinned, the two lexical items are also paired in Isaiah 34 when the nations sinned against God by attacking the Israelites. As mentioned above in this chapter, sin is an antecedent condition of קֶצֶף. However, חֵמָה – appearing in the second colon – is an extrathematic frame element because, although a close semantic equivalent to קֶצֶף, it evokes a different frame on its own.

While the above two references have looked at the parallelism of קֶצֶף and חֵמָה, the following two examples show how זַעַם and קֶצֶף are used together in poetry. The first reference is in Psalm 102:10–11[9–10].

17. Ps 102:10–11[9–10]

כִּי־אֵפֶר כַּלֶּחֶם אָכָלְתִּי for I eat ashes like bread

וְשִׁקֻּוַי בִּבְכִי מָסָכְתִּי and mingle my drink with tears

מִפְּנֵי־זַעַמְךָ וְקִצְפֶּךָ because of your זַעַם and קֶצֶף " great anger"

כִּי נְשָׂאתַנִי וַתַּשְׁלִיכֵנִי so that you have lifted me up to cast me down

The context of this psalm is of an afflicted person who is praying to God for help. In verse 9[10], the psalmist describes his current state in which he has been made a laughing stock by his enemies (v. 8[9]). The reason for his suffering, which in turn has led to scorn from his enemies, is because of God's קֶצֶף and זַעַם as mentioned in verse 11[10]. What caused God's זַעַם and קֶצֶף is not specified in this psalm. However, since it is suggested that the setting of this psalm is Babylon, the cause would be sin.

---

267. Wendland, *Analyzing the Psalms*, 72.
268. Joüon and Muraoka, *Grammar of Biblical Hebrew*, 112h.

The relationship of lines ab and lines cd is that of base-reason because he is stating his predicament first and then gives the reason for it. Narrowing down to line a and b, their relationship is that of temporal correlation, base-simultaneous,[269] meaning both events happen approximately at the same time. Line a begins with כִּי which is introducing a causal clause[270] hence its translation as "because." The psalmist is explaining the cause for the scorning he is receiving from his enemies in the previous verse. This bicola is figuratively worded to exemplify the suffering of the psalmist. First, the phrase כִּי־אֵפֶר כַּלֶּחֶם אָכָלְתִּי "for I eat ashes like bread" is a simile. In addition, the message in the bicola of eating of ash like bread and taking of his drink mingled with tears is figurative language, metonymy of effect for the thing causing it,[271] meaning suffering. The reason for this suffering is explained in line c and d.

The relationship of line c and d is that of synthetic parallelism, non-temporal correlation reason-result[272] because line c states the event which causes the result of the event in line d. Line c begins with a מִפְּנֵי "because of," a compound preposition which has a causal function,[273] translated as "because of." The use of both זַעַם and קֶצֶף in line c is a repetition of semantically equivalent nouns for emphatic purpose so that the pair can be translated as "great anger." They are used together for emphasis.

The particle כִּי, is introducing a result clause[274] and so is translated as "so that," and the result being introduced is נְשָׂאתַנִי וַתַּשְׁלִיכֵנִי "you have lifted me up to cast me down." The two verbs are, therefore, present perfectives[275] representing a resultant state in the present time from the standpoint of the speaker. This phrase fits well as a metaphor for a strong wind which could lift the Israelites and cast them down as used in Isaiah 64:6 and Job 27:21; 30:22. This metaphor symbolizes punishment. The conjunction וְ joining the two verbs is introducing a clause that is expanding the preceding clause, which is, the reason he was lifted up was so that he can be cast down. This understanding has guided the translation of the conjunction as "to."

---

269. Wendland, *Analyzing the Psalms*, 92.
270. Seow, *Grammar for Biblical Hebrew*, 331.
271. Bullinger, *Figures of Speech*, 563.
272. Wendland, *Analyzing the Psalms*, 81.
273. Arnold and Choi, *Guide to Biblical Hebrew*, .4.1.14c.
274. Seow, *Grammar for Biblical Hebrew*, 331.
275. Waltke and O'Connor, *Introduction to Biblical Hebrew*, 30.5.1b.

The next passage in which זַעַם and קֶצֶף are used together in poetry is in Jeremiah 10:10.[276]

18. Jer 10:10

וַיהוָה אֱלֹהִים אֱמֶת But the Lord is the true God

הוּא־אֱלֹהִים חַיִּים וּמֶלֶךְ עוֹלָם he is the living God and the eternal King

מִקִּצְפּוֹ תִּרְעַשׁ הָאָרֶץ because of his קֶצֶף the earth trembles

וְלֹא־יָכִלוּ גוֹיִם זַעְמוֹ And his זַעַם the nations cannot endure

The context of this verse is about the contrast of the true God and carved idols that people worshiped. Unlike the gods, the God of the Israelites is true, living and eternal (v. 10a). Line b of this verse describes the character of this God, "because of his קֶצֶף 'anger' the earth trembles and his זַעַם 'anger' the nations cannot endure." Since this verse is describing the nature of the true God, then God experiencing קֶצֶף is one of his attributes.

The relationship of line a and b is that of synonymous parallelism, base amplification.[277] The meaning of the two lines is very similar but the second line adds some significant details. Line a has the construction וַיהוָה אֱלֹהִים "the Lord God" which is an apposition of common name to a proper noun[278] and can be understood to mean God is true. God as true in the sense of being genuine and not false[279] is explained further in line b as the living God who is also the eternal king. The conjunction וְ at the beginning of the verse has an adversative function meaning "but"[280] since the author is contrasting the idols carved from wood (v. 9), who neither do any harm nor any good, and God of the Israelites who is the living God. This declaration of who God is forms the background of the message in bicola c and d.

The parallelism of line c and d is that of synonymous parallelism, general-specific[281] because "the nations" in line d is a specific example of "the earth" as mentioned in line c. Line c begins with מִקִּצְפּוֹ "because of his anger" which has the preposition מִן prefixed to the noun. This preposition has a causative

---

276. The order of books is altered at this stage for the sake of the flow of the argument.
277. Wendland, *Analyzing the Psalms*, 71.
278. Arnold and Choi, *Guide to Biblical Hebrew*, 2.4.5.
279. BDB, 54b.
280. Seow, *Grammar for Biblical Hebrew*, 284.
281. Wendland, *Analyzing the Psalms*, 72.

function,²⁸² meaning "because of." Both pronouns זַעְמוֹ and מִקִּצְפּוֹ are genitives of source²⁸³ denoting where this anger came from. According to line c, because of his קצף, תִּרְעַשׁ הָאָרֶץ "the earth trembles." The earth in this case is referring to the inhabitants of the earth who shake out of fear. The verb תִּרְעַשׁ "trembles" is a hyperbole which is emphasizing how powerful God's קֶצֶף is, that is, it can make all the inhabitants of the earth shake in fear.²⁸⁴ The idea of being powerful is implied in the verb כּוּל "(cannot) endure" which has a habitual non-perfective function,²⁸⁵ meaning every time God is angry he punishes his people in anger. In essence, no one can withstand his punishment.

In this bicola, קֶצֶף in line c is paralleled with זַעַם in line d. Comparing this parallelism with the way הֵטְא "sin" is paralleled with עָוֹן "transgression" in Psalm 38:18 and in Psalm 103:10, it is plausible to assert that in poetry, זַעַם, קֶצֶף and חֵמָה have overlapping meanings but each is distinct, as explained earlier in this chapter.²⁸⁶ The diagram below illustrates this.²⁸⁷

Chart 2

---

282. Arnold and Choi, *Guide to Biblical Hebrew*, 4.1.13d.
283. Van der Merwe, Naudé, and Kroeze, *Biblical Hebrew Reference Grammar*, 199.
284. Bullinger, *Figures of Speech*, 423.
285. Van der Merwe, Naudé, and Kroeze, *Biblical Hebrew Reference Grammar*, 148.
286. One of the distinctive differences between these lexical items is that קֶצֶף functions within a specific frame as advanced in this research. This frame is not shared by the other lexical items with the sense of anger. Therefore, the conceptualization of קֶצֶף in itself sets it apart from the rest.
287. The meaning of זַעַם is already discussed in section 1.6.1 while that of חֵמָה is discussed in 3.2.2.1. Those discussions show how the two lexical items are different from קצף and any further detailed research is beyond the limits of this research.

In the following reference קֶצֶף is paralleled with עוֹלָם.

19. Isa 54:8

בְּשֶׁצֶף קֶצֶף הִסְתַּרְתִּי פָנַי רֶגַע מִמֵּךְ In a flood of קֶצֶף I hid my face from you for a moment

וּבְחֶסֶד עוֹלָם רִחַמְתִּיךְ But in everlasting kindness I will show compassion on you

אָמַר גֹּאֲלֵךְ יְהוָה Says the Lord, your redeemer

The context of this passage is the future restoration of the Israelites. In this chapter, God gives illustrations that demonstrate that he will restore the Israelites. From verse 1 to verse 6, the Lord gives an example of a barren woman and a widow. Israel like a barren woman is urged to rejoice because she will have more children than the woman who has a husband (and already has children) (vv. 1–3). Like a widow her shame and disgrace will be taken away (vv. 4–6). From verse 7 to verse 9, the author gives another example of the flood and he reminds the Israelites how he will restore them. Verses 8 and 9, which are the verses of focus in this section are understood and discussed with the example of Noah's flood, which is compared to God forsaking his people in anger as explained in the context. Because of the comparison of this passage with the events of Noah's time, the implied cause for God's קֶצֶף was sin and the implied penalty was captivity.

The relationship of the bicola, line a and b is that of contrastive parallelism[288] because God is contrasting what he did in line a and what he will do in line b. The message in line a begins with a preposition בְּ which has an instrument function.[289] The noun בְּשֶׁצֶף "in (with) a flood" means the flood is the instrument. Since this is an illustration of the flood during Noah's time, קֶצֶף is being compared to the judgment in the form of the flood. According to Noah's story, the cause of the flood was God's judgment. The flood was the instrument of God's judgment. With this understanding, the construction בְּשֶׁצֶף קֶצֶף "in a flood of anger" is a hypocatastasis since it is comparing a real flood with the greatness of קֶצֶף and hence the translation "in great anger." Therefore, the significance of the metaphorical usage שֶׁצֶף "flood" is that it

---

288. Wendland, *Analyzing the Psalms*, 74.
289. Arnold and Choi, *Guide to Biblical Hebrew*, 4.1.5c.

brings out the comparative aspect of judgment and anger, and is in tandem with the argument in this research that קֶצֶף is associated with punishment. It is also worth noting that this is the only place the noun שֶׁצֶף occurs as an attributive genitive of anger.

According to the context, when God experienced קֶצֶף, he hid his face. The object of the verb is "face" in the phrase פָּנַי רֶגַע מִמֵּךְ "I hid my face from you for a moment." This phrase "I hid my face from you" is linked with "I forsook you" in verse 7. These two phrases are used together in contexts where God's anger is in view, that is, Deuteronomy 31:17 and Psalm 27:9. The relationship of "hiding one's face and forsaking" is that the two words are communicating the same idea, that is, to hide one's face is the figurative way of saying "I forsake you." For example, Psalm 27:9 says, "Do not hide your face from me, do not turn your servant away in anger; you have been my helper. Do not reject me or forsake me, God my Savior" (NIV).[290] The lexical item with a sense of anger used in the two references given above is אַף. The use of אַף and קֶצֶף in similar contexts implies that both of them have a close relation. The lexical meaning of אַף has already been discussed at the beginning of this chapter in section 3.1.1. Later in this chapter, אַף is discussed in other contexts in which it occurs with קֶצֶף. Because of its wide semantic range, it is fitting to consider it as a peripheral frame element of קֶצֶף.

This message in colon a, however, is contrasted in the next colon, line b which begins with וּבְחֶסֶד עוֹלָם "but in everlasting kindness" – this is the only place this phrase occurs. The ו conjunction has an adversative function,[291] meaning "but." The preposition בְּ has an instrumental function,[292] meaning the kindness was the instrument of his compassion. The word עוֹלָם is an attributive genitive because the construct, kindness, is characterized by the noun in the genitive "everlasting," hence the translation "everlasting kindness." What God will do is רִחַמְתִּיךְ "I will show you compassion" which is a prophetic perfective[293] because it affirms confidence in what God will do without fail. This colon explains that חֶסֶד, which means "joint obligation between

---

290. Bullinger, *Figures of Speech*, 657.
291. Seow, *Grammar for Biblical Hebrew*, 284.
292. Arnold and Choi, *Guide to Biblical Hebrew*, 4.1.5c.
293. Gesenius, *Gesenius' Hebrew Grammar*, 106n.

relatives, friends, host and guest, master and servant; closeness, solidarity,"[294] is an antonym of קֶצֶף, implying the presence of קֶצֶף could mean the absence of חֶסֶד. Therefore, its usage is larger than its pairing with קֶצֶף and therefore, an extrathematic frame element of קֶצֶף.

As mentioned earlier, the context of this passage is on the future restoration of the Israelites. In the specific verse quoted above, God is contrasting what he did and what he plans to do. That is, in the past he hid his face from them in קֶצֶף but in future, in חֶסֶד he will show compassion. In this same context, in Isaiah 60:10, God promises that although he struck them when he was קָצַף "angry," in רָצוֹן "favor" he will show them mercy.

20. Isa 60:10

וּבָנוּ בְנֵי־נֵכָר חֹמֹתַיִךְ foreigners will build your walls

וּמַלְכֵיהֶם יְשָׁרְתוּנֶךְ and their kings shall minister to you

כִּי בְקִצְפִּי הִכִּיתִיךְ although in קֶצֶף I struck you

וּבִרְצוֹנִי רִחַמְתִּיךְ in רָצוֹן "favor" I will show you mercy

The context of this passage is about the restoration of Israel. It begins with a call to arise because God's glory is upon them (v. 1). Their restoration is not only spiritual but also of material wealth (vv. 4–9). In verse 10, which is the verse in focus, the author notes that foreigners will serve them. According to the setting of Isaiah's prophecy, the implied cause for God's קֶצֶף is sin and the penalty was life in captivity.

The relationship of the first bicola, line a and b, is a completive correlation, base-addition[295] because the line a elaborates further line b in that the foreign kings will be their servants. The first colon, line a, begins with a conjunction וּ, which is left untranslated because it marks sequence of the narrative. The verb of line b is וּבָנוּ "they will rebuild," which is a specific future non-perfective[296] because this is an event that will happen in the future. The subject of this clause is "sons" who are further described as בְנֵי־נֵכָר "sons of foreigners" which is a genitive of relation,[297] understood to be a social rela-

---

294. Köhler and Baumgartner, "חסד," *HALOT*, 1:336.
295. Wendland, *Analyzing the Psalms*, 94.
296. Gibson, *Davidson's Introductory Hebrew Grammar*, 64a.
297. Van der Merwe, Naudé, and Kroeze, *Biblical Hebrew Reference Grammar*, 198.

tion not limited to kinship, hence the translation as "foreigners." The object of the verb is "walls" in the construction חֹמֹתֶיךָ "your walls." The affix in this construction is a genitival suffix of possession.[298]

The subject of the second colon, line b, is kings. The pronoun in the construction "and their kings" is a genitive of relation,[299] in this case a political relation. The verb of this colon יְשָׁרְתוּנֶךְ "shall minister[300] to you" is a specific future non-perfective[301] since this will certainly happen.

The bicola, line a and b, forms the context for understanding the next bicola. This bicola, line c and d are a base-contrast parallelism[302] in which קֶצֶף is contrasted with רָעוֹן. Both line c and d are prepositional phrases and are syntactically paralleled ending with תִיךָ sound in both lines. Line c begins with the particle כִּי, which has a concessive force function,[303] meaning "although." The כִּי particle guides the reader to see the contrast in which God, because of בְקִצְפִּי "anger," struck them in the past. The noun בְקִצְפִּי has a preposition בְּ which has state function,[304] meaning "in." The verb הִכִּיתִיךָ "I struck you" is in the hiphil stem with a causative function,[305] meaning God was caused to strike them.

Although God struck them in the past, he now assures them that וּבִרְצוֹנִי רִחַמְתִּיךָ "because of favor I will show you mercy." The conjunction וּ is left untranslated because it is marking sequence in the narration. In this line the noun בִרְצוֹנִי "in favor" has a preposition בְּ which has a state function,[306] meaning "in." The verb in this clause is רִחַמְתִּיךָ "he will show you mercy" which is a perfect of confidence[307] since God will do it.

The context of this passage explains that קֶצֶף led to punishment, a subject which is discussed earlier in this chapter in detail. In addition, קֶצֶף is paralleled with רָעוֹן which can carry a variety of meanings – that is, "good will,

---

298. Joüon and Muraoka, *Grammar of Biblical Hebrew*, 129d.
299. Waltke and O'Connor, *Introduction to Biblical Hebrew*, 9.5.1i.
300. Minister is used with a sense of "serve."
301. Arnold and Choi, *Guide to Biblical Hebrew*, 3.2.2a.
302. Wendland, *Analyzing the Psalms*, 74.
303. Seow, *Grammar for Biblical Hebrew*, 332.
304. Köhler and Baumgartner, "בְּ," *HALOT*, 1:103–5.
305. Seow, *Grammar for Biblical Hebrew*, 181.
306. Köhler and Baumgartner, "בְּ," *HALOT*, 1:104–5.
307. Joüon and Muraoka, *Grammar of Biblical Hebrew*, 112h.

favour, acceptance, will [desire]."³⁰⁸ Therefore, רָעוֹן has a wider usage than the sense that is implied in its pairing with קֶצֶף, hence it is an extrathematic element in the קצף frame.

While section 3.1.3.1 above has examined the parallels of קֶצֶף in poetry, the following section examines the parallels of קָצַף in poetry.

3.1.3.2 Parallelism of קָצַף in Poetry

The following examples concern the lexical items that are paralleled with קָצַף "angry." Like the noun forms, they will exemplify that קָצַף "angry" is a strong emotion.

> 21. Isa 47:6
>
> קָצַפְתִּי עַל־עַמִּי I was קָצַף "angry" with my people
>
> חִלַּלְתִּי נַחֲלָתִי I "wounded" my heritage
>
> וָאֶתְּנֵם בְּיָדֵךְ and gave them into your power
>
> לֹא־שַׂמְתְּ לָהֶם רַחֲמִים but you showed them no mercy
>
> עַל־זָקֵן הִכְבַּדְתְּ עֻלֵּךְ מְאֹד on the aged you laid a very heavy yoke

The context of this passage is a reminder to the Babylonians of how God was קָצַף "angry" at the Israelites and thus punished them by sending them to captivity. Given the setting of this prophecy, the implied reason for God being קָצַף "angry" was sin and the result was suffering and death involved in life in captivity. The first bicola, line a and b are a synonymous parallelism, base-amplification³⁰⁹ because line b adds some significant details to line a. In this parallelism, "wounding" is synonymously paralleled with קָצַף implying that קָצַף would have led to חָלָל. The one wounded is עַל־עַמִּי "with (over) my people," which, although this construction is mainly used to mean that leaders have an oversight role "over the people" (1 Sam 9:16; 2 Sam 7:8, 11; 1 Kgs 8:16; 14:7; 16:2; 1 Chr 11:2; 17:7, 10; 2 Chr 6:5–6; Ezra 38:16), in this verse it means inflicting punishment on the Israelites – the people. Therefore, line b explains further what God did when he was קָצַף "angry," he wounded them. The two verbs קָצַפְתִּי "I was angry" and חִלַּלְתִּי "I wounded" are both

---

308. BDB, 953c.

309. Wendland, *Analyzing the Psalms*, 71.

definite past[310] perfectives referring to the time the Babylonians attacked the Israelites. God's anger is directed to עַמִּי "my people" in line a which is paralleled with נַחֲלָתִי "my inheritance" in line b. The noun "my inheritance" is a metonymy of the adjunct for the subject[311] referring to the Israelites who are God's inheritance. The phrase חִלַּלְתִּי נַחֲלָתִי occurs only here in the BHS but the construction נַחֲלָתִי "my inheritance" refers to the Israelites and is used with the same meaning in Ruth 4:6; 2 Kings 21:14; Psalm 119:111; and Jeremiah 12:7–9; 16:18; 50:11.

Within the קצף frame, the discussion advanced above fits with the frame in that קֶצֶף and קָצַף led to punishment and when averted, it showed the intention of punishment. In addition, this verse is in agreement with the proposition that the focus of קָצַף is the Ego, the one experiencing קֶצֶף.[312] However, חָלַל "to wound" is not limited to the קצף frame, it means "to pierce or wound."[313] In other passages, it can also mean "to profane, to dishonor, to defile, to pollute."[314] It has a wide semantic range since even in passages where חָלַל means "to wound," the wounding can be a literal wounding (Isa 53:5) or it can be figurative, referring to suffering and pain but not a physical wound (Ps 109:22). Therefore, on its own it evokes a different frame, hence its categorization as an extrathematic frame of the קצף frame. The result of God קָצַף being angry and wounding his people is explained further in line c, which says, בְּיָדְךָ וָאֶתְּנֵם "I gave them over to your power." The verb אֶתְּנֵם "I gave them" has a telic perfective function[315] since it is a judgment action taken as the result of the erring Israelites. The word בְּיָדְךָ "into your power" which literally means "into your hand," is a metonymy of the cause[316] with the "hand" being the instrument that will keep the Hebrews under the control of the Babylonians, hence the translation of the phrase as "into your power."

---

310. Chisholm, *From Exegesis to Exposition*, 86, 95.

311. Bullinger, *Figures of Speech*, 587.

312 The focus of Ego with קָצַף is discussed in detail later in this research. However, this point is mentioned here to avoid its reduplication when discussing other passages where קָצַף occurs.

313. BDB, 319c.

314. BDB, 320a.

315. Waltke and O'Connor, *Introduction to Biblical Hebrew*, 30.2.1d, 5.1b.

316. Bullinger, *Figures of Speech*, 547.

When the Babylonians captured the Hebrews, God was concerned that they treated them unjustly. He said, לֹא־שַׂמְתְּ לָהֶם רַחֲמִים עַל־זָקֵן הִכְבַּדְתְּ עֻלֵּךְ מְאֹד "(d) but you showed them no mercy, (e) on the aged you laid a very heavy yoke." Line a is parallel to line b, c to d and cd to e. Their actions described in line d shows that the outcome in line e is not what God expected from them, and that is what he is punishing them for. The relationship of line d and e is that of synthetic parallelism, completive correlation, base-attribution.[317] The content of line e is explaining in detail what "no mercy" means as stated in line d. In Isaiah 47:6, God summarizes why he had given over his people to the Babylonians – because he was קָצַף "angry," therefore he חָלַל "wounded" them. In the following example, קָצַף "to be angry" is paralleled with גָּעַר "to rebuke."

22. Isa 54:9

Specifically, this passage is about God making a promise that he would not be קָצַף "angry" with the Israelites. In light of verse 8, קָצַף is used in verse 9, emphasizing the commitment that God is making. The commitment that God will not destroy them is compared to the commitment that God made during Noah's time – that he would not destroy the earth with water again. The experience of exile and the destruction of the earth during Noah's time are evidences of "God's wrath as revealed in word and deed."[318] Given the reference to Noah's time in relation to the swearing in this passage, the implied reason for God getting קָצַף "angry" was sin. Isaiah 54:9 says:

כִּי־מֵי נֹחַ זֹאת לִי for to me the waters of Noah are this

אֲשֶׁר נִשְׁבַּעְתִּי מֵעֲבֹר מֵי־נֹחַ עוֹד עַל־הָאָרֶץ As I swore then that the waters of Noah should never again flood the earth

כֵּן נִשְׁבַּעְתִּי **מִקְּצֹף עָלַיִךְ** So I have sworn that I will neither be קָצַף "angry" with you

וּמִגְּעָר־בָּךְ(כֵּן נִשְׁבַּעְתִּי) nor will I גָּעַר "rebuke" you

The relationship between line b and c is that of synonymous parallelism, base-comparison,[319] with line a serving as an introduction and line d as a conclusion of the content contained in line b and c. The speech in the first

---

317. Wendland, *Analyzing the Psalms*, 91.
318. Koole, *Isaiah 111*, 371.
319. Wendland, *Analyzing the Psalms*, 93.

colon, line a has a כִּי particle which is introducing a causal clause[320] hence its translation as "for." The construction מֵי נֹחַ "waters of Noah" is a genitive of association[321] since the genitive, Noah, is related to the water/flood of his time. The construction evokes in the reader's mind the flood which is mentioned earlier in verse 8. The near demonstrative זֹאת is cataphoric pointing forward to the content of what happened during the waters of Noah. This is a verbless clause and the verb "to be" is supplied. This phrase on the מֵי נֹחַ "waters of Noah" links well with בְּשֶׁצֶף קֶצֶף "in a flood of anger" as used in verse 8.

The above discussed colon, line a, is paralleled with the following colon, line b. This parallelism is that of completive correlation, base-attribution,[322] meaning line b has the details that are modifying further the previous line as signaled by the זֹאת "this" near demonstrative. The second colon b has the verb נִשְׁבַּעְתִּי "I swore" which is used twice in this verse and is associated with oaths.[323] God reminds the people of the oath he took during the judgment period (waters of Noah) and that he is taking a similar oath. The content of the oath during Noah's time was that God would not destroy the earth again with water. Now he is taking an oath that he will not be angry with them to the point of completely destroying them in anger as when it rains but the rains do not completely destroy the earth.

The third colon, c, begins with כֵּן "so" which has a comparative function[324] since it is comparing what God did during Noah's flood and what he is doing now. The content of this colon is that of God saying נִשְׁבַּעְתִּי מִקְּצֹף עָלַיִךְ "I swear I will neither be angry with you." The verb מִקְּצֹף has a preposition מִ attached which has a comparative function[325] comparing the content of line b with that of line c, hence its translation as "neither."

Line d says nor will he (כֵּן נִשְׁבַּעְתִּי)וּמִגְּעָר־בָּךְ, nor will he גְּעָר "rebuke" you with an ellipsis of כֵּן נִשְׁבַּעְתִּי as mentioned in line c. The וּ conjunction has an alternative function[326] being translated as "or." The relationship of line c and

---

320. Seow, *Grammar for Biblical Hebrew*, 331.
321. Van der Merwe, Naudé, and Kroeze, *Biblical Hebrew Reference Grammar*, 199.
322. Wendland, *Analyzing the Psalms*, 91.
323. Seow, *Grammar for Biblical Hebrew*, 301.
324. Arnold and Choi, *Guide to Biblical Hebrew*, 4.2.10a.
325. Seow, *Grammar for Biblical Hebrew*, 73.
326. Seow, 284.

d is that of synonymous parallelism, base-amplification[327] since although the two lines are very similar, the mention of גָּעַר "rebuke" in the second line adds an additional detail, that קֶצֶף results in גָּעַר "rebuke." The understanding of the use of גָּעַר "rebuke" is that it is a metonymy of the cause, an action for the thing produced by it. In this case, "to rebuke" is put for the punishment produced by it. Other passages in which גָּעַר is used to show punishment[328] are in Psalm 106:9 which says, "He rebuked the Red Sea, and it dried up; he led them through the depths as through a desert" (NIV) and Nahum 1:4 which says, "He rebukes the sea and dries it up; he makes all the rivers run dry. Bashan and Carmel wither and the blossoms of Lebanon fade" (NIV). This research has shown that קֶצֶף "angry" is associated with punishment. It occasions no surprise, therefore, that it is paralleled with גָּעַר in this bicola. In this bicola, syntactically, מִגְּעָר has a preposition מִן attached to the verb and the same preposition is attached to the verb מִקְצֹף. The preposition מִן on both verbs has a restraint function[329] since the speaker is stating what he will restrain himself from doing – not to be angry and not to rebuke his people, respectively. The two verbs mentioned above "to be angry" and "to rebuke" are objects of the preposition – stating the negative consequences that will not befall the Israelites. The object of the verb in line d is בָּךְ "you."

The verb גָּעַר "rebuke" has a sense of "fighting either for or against, but it can also have a sense of rejecting"[330] much as God rejected the offerings which were not worthy (Mal 2:3). Since it evokes these different senses, it is regarded in this research as an extrathematic frame element of קֶצֶף "to be angry." However, in this passage it clearly confirms that קֶצֶף "to be angry" is associated with punishment and therefore a strong emotion.

Since this passage concerns the restoration of the Israelites, the same theme is continued in Isaiah 57:16 in which קֶצֶף is paralleled with רִיב "strive."

23. Isa 57:16

כִּי לֹא לְעוֹלָם אָרִיב For I will not רִיב "strive" forever

וְלֹא לָנֶצַח אֶקְצוֹף Nor will I be קָצַף "be angry" always

---

327. Wendland, *Analyzing the Psalms*, 71.
328. BDB, 172a.
329. BDB, 583a.
330. BDB, 172a.

כִּי־רוּחַ מִלְּפָנַי יַעֲטוֹף because without me they would fail

וּנְשָׁמוֹת אֲנִי עָשִׂיתִי the people I have created

The context of this verse concerns God who is offering comfort to the heartbroken and weak. In verse 16, God assures the contrite that he will not be קָצַף "angry" forever. In verse 17, God reiterates that although the contrite were sinful, and as a result he became קָצַף "angry," he will heal, guide, restore and comfort them (v. 18).

In this first bicola, רִיב "to strive" is paralleled with קָצַף "be angry." The two lines are syntactically parallel, both bearing a negation marker and with a prepositional phrase introduced by the preposition לְ. This bicola is a synonymous parallelism, base-amplification[331] since colon b expands the thought of colon a in that, strive preceded God being קָצַף. The first colon, line a, has a כִּי particle which is introducing a causal clause[332] meaning "because." The verbs in the bicola אָרִיב and אֶקְצוֹף are both specific future non-perfective[333] since they are pointing to future time when this resolve by God will take place; the context implies that it won't fail. In this bicola, the objects are periods of time as indicated by the nouns לְעוֹלָם "forever" and לָנֶצַח "always." Both of these nouns have a preposition לְ which has an "amounting to"[334] function whose most accurate translation would be "during forever" and "during always." For an idiomatic translation, "during" is omitted. In the context of this passage, to קָצַף "be angry" is paralleled with רִיב "strive." רִיב has a wide semantic range including "attack, dispute, strife, quarrel and disputing matters of law."[335] It is used in this verse to signify the contention within a legal dispute.[336] This legal dispute scenario means the offender is proven guilty of the offense and that judgment/punishment is carried out by Ego while he is קָצַף "angry." The verb אָרִיב in this construction occurs also in Isaiah 49:25, Jeremiah 2:9 and 12:1 with the sense of justification of one's guilt. The understanding of רִיב in this passage is that justification of one's guilt preceded God being קָצַף "be angry."

---

331. Wendland, *Analyzing the Psalms*, 63.
332. Seow, *Grammar for Biblical Hebrew*, 331.
333. Gibson, *Davidson's Introductory Hebrew Grammar*, 64a.
334. Clines, "לְ," *DCH*, 4:478–84.
335. BDB, 936d, 937a.
336. Clines, "רִיב," *DCH*, 7:479–82.

Going by the above semantic range of רִיב, it evokes another frame beyond the קצף frame. It is therefore an extrathematic frame element in the קצף frame.

The next bicola, c and d, explain the reason for the first bicola, that is, the second bicola is explaining the reason why God would not קָצַף "be angry" with them forever. The second set of bicola, like the first one, begins with a כִּי particle whose syntactical function is to introduce a causal clause,[337] that is, without God the people would fail. The use of the noun רוּחַ "spirit" is a reference to God's life-giving breath,[338] that is, without the God-given breath they would fail. The noun רוּחַ "spirit" is used with this same sense in Job 17:1 and 34:14 among other verses. The verb of line c יַעֲטוֹף "would fail" has the sense of universal truth, meaning the Israelites (by extension everybody), without God, would definitely fail in the sense of being faint on the account of distress.[339]

The relationship of line c and d is that of synonymous parallelism, base-amplification[340] since line d is adding some details to the content of line c. The noun וּנְשָׁמוֹת "the breath" fits well with the discussion in the above paragraph about the רוּחַ "spirit" in that it is God's spirit that gives breath/life. The verb עָשִׂיתִי "I have created" is a definite past perfective[341] because the focus is the past action of creation.

The next reference, Isaiah 57:17, which shares the same context with this verse, demonstrates that the קָצַף verbal form is associated with punishment just as its noun form as discussed earlier in this chapter. In Isaiah 57:17, the reason God was קָצַף "angry" was because of the Israelites' wicked greed.

24. Isa 57:17

בַּעֲוֹן בִּצְעוֹ **קָצַפְתִּי** because of their wicked greed **קָצַפְתִּי** "I became angry"

וְאַכֵּהוּ הַסְתֵּר וְאֶקְצֹף I punished them and hid while אֶקְצֹף angry

וַיֵּלֶךְ שׁוֹבָב בְּדֶרֶךְ לִבּוֹ but they turned back following the way of their own heart

---

337. Seow, *Grammar for Biblical Hebrew*, 331.
338. BDB, 925c.
339. Clines, "עטף," *DCH*, 6:350–51.
340. Wendland, *Analyzing the Psalms*, 71.
341. Waltke and O'Connor, *Introduction to Biblical Hebrew*, 30.5.1b.

This is a tricola with line a being parallel to lines bc. The relationship of line a to line b is that of non-temporal correlation, reason-result.[342] Line a states the reason and line b states the result. The relationship of the first two lines with the third, line c, is that of a temporal, base-sequential.[343] God was angry and punished them. As a result they turned away from their sins.

The first colon, line a, begins with a preposition בְּ which is introducing a causal clause[344] hence its translation as "because." The noun בֶּצַע refers to an "unjust gain"[345] which in this case is the sin God is accusing them of. This noun בֶּצַע is used with the same sense in Isaiah 33:15; 56:11 and Jeremiah 22:17 among many other passages. The reason God was angry with them was because of בַּעֲוֹן בִּצְעוֹ "their wicked greed" – that is, they were wicked because of this greed. The verb קָצַפְתִּי "I became angry" is an ingressive perfective[346] referring to the beginning of the action. Because of his anger he וָאַכֵּהוּ "punished him (them)." The affix is translated as plural since "singular suffixes can have a collective reference"[347] and therefore can be translated in plural.

The verbs וָאַכֵּהוּ "I punished" them and הַסְתֵּר "I hid" both have a causative function,[348] meaning the wickedness of the Israelites caused God to be angry. The idea of God hiding (his face) has been discussed under section 3.1.1.4 on iconic symbols of anger. In section 3.1.1.4, it has been argued that hiding of face is a figurative way of withdrawing from the provoking sin or person(s) in the form of anger management. This idea is discussed further in section 3.1.3.1 number 21 and was shown that hiding of one's face is paralleled with "forsaking," which complements the "withdrawal" aspect. The latter has a subordination function[349] since the former is a *waw*-consecutive imperfect. The last verb in this clause וָאֶקְצֹף, is translated as "while angry" because it has a conjunction וְ which has a circumstantial function.[350] The verb וָאֶקְצֹף

---

342. Wendland, *Analyzing the Psalms*, 81.
343. Wendland, 78.
344. Arnold and Choi, *Guide to Biblical Hebrew*, 4.1.5f.
345. BDB, 180c.
346. Gibson, *Davidson's Introductory Hebrew Grammar*, 57 Rem. 2.
347. Waltke and O'Connor, *Introduction to Biblical Hebrew*, 16.3.3b.
348. Seow, *Grammar for Biblical Hebrew*, 181.
349. Van der Merwe, Naudé, and Kroeze, *Biblical Hebrew Reference Grammar*, 161.
350. Seow, *Grammar for Biblical Hebrew*, 284.

has a stative non-perfective[351] function since it connotes a situation that has not changed. It is noticeable that the author employs change of verbal forms in the phrase קָצַפְתִּי וְאַכֵּהוּ הַסְתֵּר וְאֶקְצֹף beginning with perfect, imperfect, infinitive, imperfect and *waw*-consecutive imperfect. The significance of this verbal form change is that it represents different actions happening at different times. For example, the first verb קָצַפְתִּי "I became angry" is in perfect because it is in reference to an already committed sin. But the verb that follows, הַסְתֵּר, "I will smite" is in future because at the time of the utterance the punishment had not been effected. The infinite הַסְתֵּר "hiding" has a nominative function[352] since God is affirming what he will do. The smiting and hiding will happen in the future and the Lord will still be angry. This understanding has led to the translation of וְאֶקְצֹף as "while angry."

The Israelites responded in rebellion, they וַיֵּלֶךְ שׁוֹבָב בְּדֶרֶךְ לִבּוֹ "turned back (in apostasy turning their back to the Lord) following the way of their own heart." The conjunction וְ has an adversative function[353] meaning "but." In disobedience וַיֵּלֶךְ "they walked around" which figuratively means "to live,"[354] implying that they had chosen to live a life that is against the values of their God. This is exemplified by the שׁוֹבָב "turned back,"[355] which has an accusative adjective[356] function like an accusative of specification,[357] meaning "they abandoned the way of the Lord." For the purposes of a smooth translation, the translation given above is "they turned back." The phrase בְּדֶרֶךְ לִבּוֹ [they walked] "in the way of their heart," has a preposition בְּ whose figurative syntactical function is of route[358] because the preceding verbs have a motion sense. The Israelites' action described by the phrase בְּדֶרֶךְ לִבּוֹ [they walked] "in the way of their heart" refers to their character[359] which was displeasing to God. This phrase is used with the same sense in Ecclesiastes 11:9.

---

351. Waltke and O'Connor, *Introduction to Biblical Hebrew*, 31.3d.
352. Waltke and O'Connor, 35.3.3a.
353. Seow, *Grammar for Biblical Hebrew*, 284.
354. BDB, 234c.
355. BDB, 1000a.
356. Arnold and Choi, *Guide to Biblical Hebrew*, 2.5.3.
357. Van der Merwe, Naudé, and Kroeze, *Biblical Hebrew Reference Grammar*, 245.
358. Arnold and Choi, *Guide to Biblical Hebrew*, 4.1.5a.
359. BDB, 203c.

This verse does not show synonyms or antonyms of קָצַף, however, it demonstrates evil as the antecedent condition for קֶצֶף and explains that punishment was involved as a retributive measure but the people disregarded the punishment. In the following reference, קָצַף is paralleled with פָּגַע.

25. Isa 64:4[5]

פָּגַעְתָּ אֶת־שָׂשׂ וְעֹשֵׂה צֶדֶק you entreat well those who rejoice and do right

בִּדְרָכֶיךָ יִזְכְּרוּךָ who remember you in your ways

הֵן־אַתָּה קָצַפְתָּ (But) behold! קָצַפְתָּ you were angry

וַנֶּחֱטָא בָּהֶם עוֹלָם because we continued to sin against them

וְנִוָּשֵׁעַ, How can we be saved?

This verse falls into the context of restoration of the Israelites as already stated in the preceding verses. In this specific verse, God assures the Israelites of his good deeds, that is, he intervenes in the course of history to help those who remember him but also to punish those who sin against him as stated in Isaiah 64:4[5] and 64:8[9]. This passage falls within a large corpus of Isaiah 63 and 64 which is an account of God's vengeance and redemption for the Israelites. In verse 4[5], the Israelites recall how God became קָצַף "angry" because they had sinned perennially (v. 5). In verse 8[9], they plead with God not to be קָצַף "angry" beyond measure. The author implies that whenever God would remember their continuous sins he would become קָצַף "angry." Sin, therefore, would make God קָצַף "angry."

This bicola is base-contrast parallelism,[360] contrasting the deeds of God in lines ab and the response from the people in lines cd. The main verb in line a is פָּגַעְתָּ "you entreat well" which is a gnomic perfective,[361] meaning this is the universal truth of God's character. This verb פָּגַע can mean to encounter with kindness, hostility or with a request.[362] In this context, it means "to encounter with kindness"[363] and that is the reason it is translated as "to entreat well." The object of the verb is marked by the definite object marker in this phrase

---

360. Wendland, *Analyzing the Psalms*, 74.
361. Gibson, *Davidson's Introductory Hebrew Grammar*, 57c.
362. BDB, 803b.
363. BDB, 803b.

אֶת־שָׂשׂ וְעֹשֵׂה צֶדֶק "those who rejoice and do right." The words שָׂשׂ וְעֹשֵׂה are both participles with a present time predicate function.[364] Those who rejoice and do right are further described as בִּדְרָכֶיךָ יִזְכְּרוּךָ "who remember you in your ways." The verb of this clause is יִזְכְּרוּךָ "who remember" which is a stative non-perfective,[365] meaning who never change in remembering the Lord's ways. The suffix in the phrase בִּדְרָכֶיךָ "in your ways" is a genitive of agency,[366] meaning the ways, commandments for living, which are given by God.[367]

This colon, line b, is contrasted with line c which begins with הֵן whose syntactical function is exclamation in the sense of calling to attention to what follows – God קָצַפְתָּ "was angry."[368] The personal pronoun אַתָּה is anaphoric referring to God who קָצַפְתָּ "was angry." The verb קָצַפְתָּ "you were angry" has a definite past perfective function[369] since it is referring to one specific occurrence in the past when God was angry as the Israelites continued to sin. The reason God was angry is because וַנֶּחֱטָא בָּהֶם עוֹלָם "we (the Israelites) continued to sin against 'them'" – meaning the ways of the Lord. The conjunction וְ has an adversative function,[370] hence its translation as "but" because it is contrasting what God did and how the Israelites responded instead. The verb וַנֶּחֱטָא "we (continued) to sin" has a constative perfective function,[371] denoting the inception and continuation of sinning. This constative perfective function is strengthened by the noun עוֹלָם "continuously" which is describing the manner in which they sinned. The sinning was בָּהֶם "against them" – referring to the ways of the Lord. This pronoun has preposition בְּ which has adversative function indicating a connection of disadvantage.[372] This colon ends with the verb וְנִוָּשֵׁעַ which is a non-perfective of deliberation,[373] denoting the speakers' meditation as to whether the action implied by the verb will take place or not. This understanding has led to its translation as a rhetorical question "and

---

364. Waltke and O'Connor, *Introduction to Biblical Hebrew*, 37.6e.
365. Waltke and O'Connor, 31.3c.
366. Van der Merwe, Naudé, and Kroeze, *Biblical Hebrew Reference Grammar*, 198.
367. BDB, 204a.
368. Arnold and Choi, *Guide to Biblical Hebrew*, 4.5.1a.
369. Waltke and O'Connor, *Introduction to Biblical Hebrew*, 30.5.1b.
370. Seow, *Grammar for Biblical Hebrew*, 284.
371. Waltke and O'Connor, *Introduction to Biblical Hebrew*, 30.1d.
372. Arnold and Choi, *Guide to Biblical Hebrew*, 4.1.5d.
373. Waltke and O'Connor, *Introduction to Biblical Hebrew*, 31.4f.

how can we be saved?" Although the verb has no interrogative particle, the idiomatic translation as a rhetorical question fits the context better since the verb is in the niphal stem, passive function.[374] The salvation in this context refers to deliverance from external evils,[375] probably referring to captivity.

In summary, line d makes sin the antecedent condition for God's קֶצֶף. Those who "do right" is paralleled with "those who continue to sin" while פָּגַעְתָּ "you entreat" is paralleled with קָצַפְתָּ "you were angry." The verb פָּגַעְתָּ "you entreat well" has a semantic usage as discussed earlier. It, therefore, definitely evokes a wider frame than its parallelism with קֶצֶף, hence it is part of the extrathematic frame. In a rejoinder, the Israelites implored God to relent in his קֶצֶף in the following verses of this chapter, Isaiah 64:8.

26. Isa 64:8[9]

אַל־תִּקְצֹף יְהוָה עַד־מְאֹד Do not be קֶצֶף "angry" exceedingly, O Lord

וְאַל־לָעַד תִּזְכֹּר עָוֺן Do not remember עָוֺן "iniquity" forever

הֵן הַבֶּט־נָא עַמְּךָ כֻלָּנוּ behold, look upon us, we are your people, all of us

The first two lines, line a and b, begin with a negation marker. These two lines are synonymous parallelism, base-amplification[376] since the second line adds "iniquity" as a significant detail explaining why God would be angry. The address is directed to יְהוָה "God" who is vocative nominative,[377] which is an address of plea. The main verb of line a is תִּקְצֹף "be angry" which is a jussive of request[378] since it is a plea to God that he should not be angry with them. The use of the prepositional phrase עַד־מְאֹד, which can be translated as "exceedingly" in the sense of "to the extreme,"[379] is paralleled with לָעַד "forever" in line b. That is, if the people continue to sin forever, then God will be exceedingly (continuously) angry. The main verb in the line b is תִּזְכֹּר "to remember" which like תִּקְצֹף "to be angry" is also a jussive of request asking God not to remember their sins. In this bicola, קֶצֶף is paralleled with

---

374. Seow, *Grammar for Biblical Hebrew*, 288.
375. BDB, 446b.
376. Wendland, *Analyzing the Psalms*, 71.
377. Waltke and O'Connor, *Introduction to Biblical Hebrew*, 8.3d.
378. Waltke and O'Connor, 34.3b.
379. Seow, *Grammar for Biblical Hebrew*, 74.

עָוֹן "iniquity." It implies that the remembrance of עָוֹן "iniquity" would be an antecedent of קָצַף. The grammatical equivalence of this passage is that of effect and cause, paralleling remembrance of how עָוֹן would result in God becoming קָצַף "angry." This appeal ends with הֵן הַבֶּט־נָא עַמְּךָ כֻלָּנוּ "behold, please look upon us, we are all your people." The particle הֵן "behold" has an exclamation of immediacy[380] which calls attention to their address to God, just the same way they called his attention by the use of the vocative at the beginning of the verse. The main verb of this clause is הַבֶּט־נָא "please look upon us" and has an imperative of request function.[381] This meaning is enhanced by the use of the נָא "please" particle by the fact that it is expressing a craving for a favorable consideration of a request.[382] The object of the verb is עַמְּךָ "your people," which has a genitival affix of relation.[383] The object is qualified further by כֻלָּנוּ "all of us," which has an emphatic function since it is grammatically in apposition to עַמְּךָ "your people."[384] This passage shows that iniquity, the antecedent condition, resulted in קָצַף.

Isaiah 64:8 brings to an end a series of parallelism of קֶצֶף/קָצַף within Isaiah's prophecies where the penalty was captivity. The last example, where קָצַף occurs in the poetic texts, is in Lamentations 5:21–22.

27. Lam 5:21–22

הֲשִׁיבֵנוּ יְהוָה אֵלֶיךָ וְנָשׁוּב return us to yourself, O Lord, that we may return

חַדֵּשׁ יָמֵינוּ כְּקֶדֶם renew our days of old

כִּי אִם־מָאֹס מְאַסְתָּנוּ Unless you have utterly מָאַס "rejected" us

קָצַפְתָּ עָלֵינוּ עַד־מְאֹד (unless you) are exceedingly קָצַף with us

The context of this verse is about the Israelites pleading with God to restore them to himself. The only hindrance to their plea is if God has utterly מָאַס "rejected" them or is exceedingly קָצַף "angry" with them. The author "implies that YHWH's anger is still standing in the way"[385] but hopes that God

---

380. Arnold and Choi, *Guide to Biblical Hebrew*, 4.5.1a.
381. Gesenius, *Gesenius' Hebrew Grammar*, 110b.
382. BDB, 609c.
383. Van der Merwe, Naudé, and Kroeze, *Biblical Hebrew Reference Grammar*, 198.
384. BDB, 481d.
385. Lee, *Singers of Lamentations*, 194.

will heed their plea for restoration. The implied message is that if God does not restore them, then he is still angry against them. The author therefore recognizes that God is the only one who can save them if he relents from being קָצַף "angry."

The relationship of lines ab with lines cd is that of synthetic parallelism, completive correlation, base-alternative.[386] The content in the first bicola, ab, is the plea to which the only impediment (detailed in lines cd) would be God's unrelenting anger.

The relationship of line a with line b is that of synonymous parallelism, base-amplification[387] because, although the content in the two lines is similar, line b is adding a minor detail to the content of line a. Line a begins with an imperative of request[388] הֲשִׁיבֵנוּ "return us" because it is an appeal from a junior to a superior. The double use of the verb שׁוּב in this verse has the sense of spiritual relations. The speaker expresses optimism that if the Lord returns him (and others) to himself in being shown favor,[389] then וְנָשׁוּב "we shall return" in the sense of turning to God and turning away from apostasy.[390] Other passages where שׁוּב is used with the above senses are Zechariah 1:3 and Malachi 3:7 among others. The appeal is to יְהוָה "O Lord" whose syntactical function is vocative[391] to return the Hebrews to himself.

In line b the speaker again makes an appeal using another imperative of request[392] חַדֵּשׁ "renew" in the sense of asking for a repair of the strained relationship.[393] The appeal in this colon is that God would renew יָמֵינוּ כְּקֶדֶם "our days of old." He prayed that their lives would be as they were in the former days – according to the context of this passage, the former is when they had no discord with God. As mentioned earlier, this bicola, ab, is parallel to the following bicola cd.

---

386. Wendland, *Analyzing the Psalms*, 95.
387. Wendland, 63.
388. Van der Merwe, Naudé, and Kroeze, *Biblical Hebrew Reference Grammar*, 151.
389. BDB, 997d–998a.
390. BDB, 997d.
391. Arnold and Choi, *Guide to Biblical Hebrew*, 2.1.1–4.
392. Gesenius, *Gesenius' Hebrew Grammar*, 110a.
393. BDB, 294a.

The relationship of line c and line d is that of synthetic parallelism, temporal correlation, base-simultaneous,[394] meaning the events are happening approximately at the same time. In this parallelism, קָצַף "to be angry" is paralleled with מָאַס "to reject" which means to disassociate with.[395] In this case, קָצַף "to be angry" and מָאַס "to reject" form an inverted parallelism since מָאַס ends in line c and קָצַף "to be angry" begins in line d. The imbedded message is that, rejection is the effect on the landmark, when Ego is קָצַף "angry."

The first colon, line c, begins with כִּי אִם, which has an exceptive function[396] because the context expresses hope of restoration unless God has rejected them. The infinitive מָאֹס is translated as "utterly" because it is an infinitive absolute of intensification of the root.[397] The verb is מְאַסְתָּנוּ "you have rejected us" is a present perfect[398] because it connotes a resulting state in the present time from a past time according to the speaker. However, the verb קָצַפְתָּ "you are angry" is a simple present perfective[399] since the speaker is wondering whether God is still angry at them at the time of speaking. In the second colon, line d, the verse ends with the construction עַד־מְאֹד "exceedingly" which can literally be translated as "until exceedingly." This construction has an intensifying effect,[400] intensifying the act of קָצַפְתָּ "you are angry." Poetically, עַד־מְאֹד "exceedingly" is paralleled with מָאֹס "utterly." However, the former עַד־מְאֹד connotes "abundance"[401] of קָצַף while מָאֹס has the idea of completeness of the action.[402] In this case, this passage sheds more light into the understanding of what קָצַף "to be angry" is, in that, to utterly reject someone meant God was exceedingly angry with that person. In the context of Lamentations, being the lament of Jeremiah over the destruction of Jerusalem, the antecedent condition for God being קָצַף "angry" was sin.

The different lexical items that are paralleled with קֶצֶף, as discussed in the section 3.1.3.2 above, form the extrathematic frame elements of קֶצֶף. As

---

394. Wendland, *Analyzing the Psalms*, 92.
395. BDB, 549c.
396. Arnold and Choi, *Guide to Biblical Hebrew*, 4.3.3m.
397. Waltke and O'Connor, *Introduction to Biblical Hebrew*, 35.3.li.
398. Waltke and O'Connor, 30.5.2b.
399. Chisholm, *From Exegesis to Exposition*, 87, 97–98.
400. Arnold and Choi, *Guide to Biblical Hebrew*, 4.2.12.
401. BDB, 547b.
402. BDB, 549c.

mentioned earlier, extrathematic frame elements are those elements which are related to the core frame elements of קצף frame, but they introduce a different frame. The relationship of צָפֹוק and the lexical items discussed in section 3.1.3.2 can be illustrated in the following diagram.

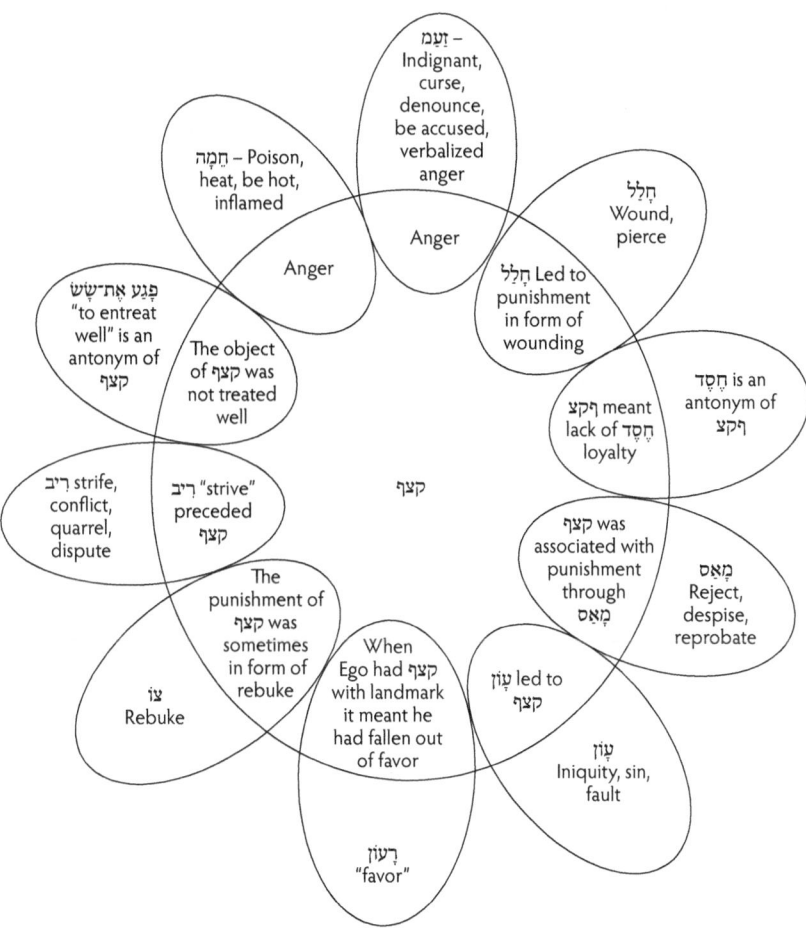

Chart 3

So far, section 3.1 has shown the core, peripheral and extrathematic frame elements of קצף. The following section examines the distinctive features of the קצף frame.

3.2 Distinctiveness of קצף Frame

The קצף frame has distinctive marks that are not shared by the other lexical items that have a sense of anger in the BHS. The following section highlights these distinctive marks.

3.2.1 The קצף Frame

From the קצף discussions analyzed so far, the main distinctive feature of קצף is its frame – which is not shared by the other Hebrew words that have the sense of anger. It has been demonstrated that, first, the קצף occurrences fit within a specific frame, named in this project as the קצף frame. The קצף frame, I argued, is characterized first of all by קֶצֶף being perceived as an abstract object[403] which comes/falls out of (comes/falls from) the Ego, the one experiencing קֶצֶף, and follows an abstract trajectory marked by the verb היה and rests on the landmark identified by the preposition עַל. Second, it has been demonstrated that this frame has a vertical relationship because of the syntactical function of the preposition עַל and that it is associated with punishment, either intended or achieved. Third, it is explained later that the קצף usage in the Aramaic texts fits within the קצף frame.

In addition to the information in the paragraph above, the following section gives other distinctive features of the קצף frame. First, the following section explains that קֶצֶף, with the sense of anger has a "vertical relational function." That is, it is experienced by a superior, either superiority of rank or superiority of military strength (mostly when experienced by a group), and directed to a subordinate. Second, when קֶצֶף was experienced by a subordinate, it did not necessarily have the sense of anger. Instead, it means that the subordinate is provoking the superior if קצף is in the hiphil stem, the subordinate is experiencing frustration if קצף is in the qal stem or the subordinate is expressing anger to a superior if קצף is in the hithpael stem. The following section explores these additional features in detail. The order of the study is as follows: the first discussion is on the קֶצֶף noun forms, beginning with God as the Ego and followed by human as the Ego. The second

---

403. Although קֶצֶף is an emotion and, therefore, a nontangible thing, it is idiomatically talked of in the BHS as if it is something tangible but invisible. This kind of perception by the Hebrews in antiquity has informed the use of "abstract object" when referring to קֶצֶף within its frame.

discussion is on the קָצַף verb forms, beginning with God as the Ego followed by human as the Ego.

3.2.2 The Noun Forms of קֶצֶף: God (Deity) Is the Ego (Superior to Subordinate)

Out of the twenty-eight times that קֶצֶף occurs in the BHS, in twenty-five of these, God is the Ego. Out of the twenty-five times in which God is the Ego, the Israelites are the landmarks eighteen times, while the other nations are the landmarks four times and individuals are the landmarks three times. In all the occurrences where God is the Ego of קֶצֶף, there is a punishment involved or intended. In addition to the punishment profile, the one effecting the punishment has authority/is superior over the subordinate. This superior-subordinate relationship is what is called in this research, "a vertical relational function" and complements the "syntactical vertical function" discussed earlier in section 3.1.1.2.

3.2.2.1 The Israelites Are the Landmarks

The first two occurrences of the trajector, קֶצֶף, in which the Israelites are the landmarks are in Numbers 1:53 and 17:11[16:46] and have already been discussed, though for a different focus. The third passage in which the Israelites are the landmark is in Deuteronomy 29:27[28]. There are two important features to note in this passage. First, there are three lexical items used together in the same verse as explained in this construction בְּאַף וּבְחֵמָה וּבְקֶצֶף. This construction is translated as "in anger (reddening of face), in anger (internal irritation), and בְּקֶצֶף 'in anger' (abstract object)." The translation of אַף as "reddening of face" is based on its usage especially when it is paired with חרה. For example, in Genesis 30:2, אַף is paired with חרה to mean that Jacob's face/nose was burning, an idiom meaning he was angry. This idiom of a burning face/nose is also used in Exodus 4:14, Numbers 25:4 and Isaiah 5:25 among other passages.[404] The translation of חמה as "internal irritation" is based on its association with poison or venom, and its figurative presentation as something which can be poured out (Isa 42:25) or put in a cup (Isa 51:17).[405] Zacharias Kotzé argues that חמה is the fluid released from the

---

404. Köhler and Baumgartner, "אַף," *HALOT*, 1:76.
405. Köhler and Baumgartner, "חמה," *HALOT*, 1:326.

gallbladder as already discussed in chapter 1, section 1.5.2. However, Ezekiel 16:38 notes that it can also be associated with blood, that is, דם חמה "blood of anger" probably meaning "hot blood." Due to its wide semantic range and uncertainty of its actual meaning, the term "internal irritation" is preferred in this research to m.ean חמה.

The reason for the above sequence is that the first two lexical items are functioning as emphatic adjectives[406] of the last lexical item. The second feature is the use of קֶצֶף גָּדוֹל "great anger." In the other passages, already discussed under sections 3.1 and 3.2, קֶצֶף occurs alone without the adjective. The observable feature common in most of the passages where קֶצֶף גָּדוֹל, as discussed in the following passages under this section (3.2.2.1), is used is that idol worship is the antecedent condition followed by judgment. The first reference to be considered is Deuteronomy 29:27[28].

28. Deut 29:27[28]

וַיִּתְּשֵׁם יְהוָה מֵעַל אַדְמָתָם בְּאַף וּבְחֵמָה וּבְקֶצֶף גָּדוֹל וַיַּשְׁלִכֵם אֶל־אֶרֶץ אַחֶרֶת כַּיּוֹם הַזֶּה:

The Lord uprooted them from their land in anger (reddening of face), in anger (internal irritation), and גָּדוֹל בְּקֶצֶף "in great anger" (abstract object), and cast them out into another land, until this day.

The context of this passage is that of a reminder to the Israelites of how their descendants will be taken into captivity because of their disobedience characterized by the worship of idols. This reminder in itself is remarkable when looked at from the standpoint of the future, since chronologically, it had not yet happened. The worship of idols was more than mere disobedience; it amounted to the breaking of their covenant with God (v. 25). As a result, they would be banished into exile, which was an execution of God's קֶצֶף. The intention of this reminder is to bring the current generation into a better relationship with God and avoid provoking God's קֶצֶף, which would lead to punishment.

This verse begins with וַיִּתְּשֵׁם "he uprooted" which is a telic perfective[407] meaning the audience then will see their current state as an end of the Lord's

---

406. Bullinger, *Figures of Speech*, 673.
407. Waltke and O'Connor, *Introduction to Biblical Hebrew*, 30.2.1d.

uprooting. The verb "uproot" is figurative, meaning "to be attacked." It is significant because this is the first time the Israelites were taken to a foreign land as captives. It is used elsewhere with the same meaning in Daniel 11:4.[408] The manner in which the Lord did this was בְּאַף וּבְחֵמָה וּבְקֶצֶף גָּדוֹל "in anger (reddening of face), in anger (internal irritation), and in great anger (abstract object)." All the three lexical items in the phrase above have a preposition בְּ, which has a realm function,[409] meaning the state of being angry. While in that state, God וַיִּתְּשֵׁם "uprooted" them. The use of the three lexical items, all with the sense of anger, is for emphasis since they are a hendriatris. Three nouns are used but only one thing is intended – to show the intensity of the emotion.[410]

What the Lord did in his anger was to וַיַּשְׁלִכֵם "cast them" which is a definite past perfective[411] because it is referring to a onetime occurrence at a given time. He cast them אֶל־אֶרֶץ אַחֶרֶת "into another land" which is a genitive object of the preposition. This verse demonstrates a vertical relational function in which the Ego is superior and the landmark is a subordinate. The context explains that the worship of idols was the antecedent condition and punishment/judgment in the form of captivity was the result.

The three lexical items, בְּאַף וּבְחֵמָה וּבְקֶצֶף גָּדוֹל, as used in this passage are also used together in the same order but with minor variations in three other references: Deuteronomy 9:19,[412] Jeremiah 21:5 and Jeremiah 37:32.

i.. Deut 9:19

כִּי יָגֹרְתִּי מִפְּנֵי הָאַף וְהַחֵמָה אֲשֶׁר קָצַף יְהוָה עֲלֵיכֶם לְהַשְׁמִיד אֶתְכֶם וַיִּשְׁמַע יְהוָה אֵלַי גַּם בַּפַּעַם הַהוּא

I was afraid because of the anger (reddening of face) and the anger (internal irritation), and because the Lord was קָצַף "angry" against you to destroy you, but once again the Lord listened to me.

---

408. BDB, 684c.
409. Köhler and Baumgartner, "בְּ," *HALOT*, 1:103–5.
410. Bullinger, *Figures of Speech*, 673.
411. Waltke and O'Connor, *Introduction to Biblical Hebrew*, 30.50.1b.
412. Although Deuteronomy 9:19 should chronologically be discussed before Deuteronomy 29:27(28), it is discussed at this point because the three lexical items with sense of anger appear together.

The context of the verse is a reminder to the Israelites about God being קָצַף "angry" because they made a golden calf and turned to idol worship. Moses was so shocked by the sight of the calf he threw the tablets down and broke them into pieces (vv. 16–17). He then fasted and prayed for forty days and forty nights interceding for the Israelites (vv. 18–19). Aaron too sinned and Moses interceded for him and he burned the golden calf they had made, crushed it and ground it into dust (vv. 20–21).

The verse begins with the כִּי particle, which has an evidential function[413] – the contents in this verse are the underlying motivation for Moses's prayer. It is therefore left untranslated and the focus is given to the content of the motivation. The speaker is Moses who says יָגֹרְתִּי "I was afraid," which is a definite past perfective[414] denoting a onetime experience Moses had at this time. The preposition מִפְּנֵי is translated as "because of" since it has a causal function[415] showing the cause of Moses's fear. The reason Moses feared was מִפְּנֵי הָאַף וְהַחֵמָה אֲשֶׁר קָצַף יְהוָה because of "the anger (reddening of face) and the anger (internal irritation), and because the Lord was קָצַף 'angry.'" The relative particle אֲשֶׁר in this clause is translated as "because" since contextually it has a conjunction's function,[416] and is in tandem with the preposition מִפְּנֵי, which also means "because." The first two lexical items הָאַף וְהַחֵמָה both have a definite article, which is associated with nouns in the imagination.[417] These two items are a hendiadys[418] since the same meaning is intended – to show intensity of the emotion. God's anger is directed against the עֲלֵיכֶם "you," Israelites. The preposition עַל has an adversative function,[419] showing that the action of the verb is directed against the landmark, hence its translation as "against." The effect of God being קָצַף "angry" is לְהַשְׁמִיד אֶתְכֶם "to destroy you." The verb לְהַשְׁמִיד is an infinitive construct, which is an object of the preposition לְ used to indicate a purpose clause,[420] to destroy.

---

413. Arnold and Choi, *Guide to Biblical Hebrew*, 4.3.4b.
414. Waltke and O'Connor, *Introduction to Biblical Hebrew*, 30.5.1b.
415. Arnold and Choi, *Guide to Biblical Hebrew*, 4.1.14b.
416. Seow, *Grammar for Biblical Hebrew*, 111.
417. Chisholm, *From Exegesis to Exposition*, 73.
418. Bullinger, *Figures of Speech*, 657.
419. Arnold and Choi, *Guide to Biblical Hebrew*, 4.1.16f.
420. Chisholm, *From Exegesis to Exposition*, 78.

Although this destruction is what was intended, it wasn't achieved because Moses pleaded for them as summarized in the last clause וַיִּשְׁמַע יְהוָה אֵלַי גַּם בַּפַּעַם הַהִוא "but once again the Lord listened to me." The וְ conjunction at the beginning of this clause has an adversative function[421] hence its translation as "but." The verb of this clause is וַיִּשְׁמַע "he listened," which is a telic perfective[422] since the speaker is looking at the action from the end of it. Moses asserted that the Lord was listening to him גַּם "again" because he had listened to him in the past, for example in Exodus 32:1–14. In addition, Moses noted that God listened to him בַּפַּעַם הַהִוא "at that time." The noun בַּפַּעַם "time" has a preposition בְּ prefix, which has a temporal function[423] denoting a point of time when something took place. This noun is accompanied by הַהִוא which has an attributive function[424] meaning "that." This verse explains that the landmark was the Israelites when God was the Ego. This is a vertical relational function since the Ego is superior to the landmark. In addition, it explains that punishment was intended. Just like the verse preceding this, the antecedent condition in this verse is idol worship (vv. 15–16, 21) and judgment/destruction was looming.

ii. Jer 21:5

וְנִלְחַמְתִּי אֲנִי אִתְּכֶם בְּיָד נְטוּיָה וּבִזְרוֹעַ חֲזָקָה וּבְאַף וּבְחֵמָה וּבְקֶצֶף גָּדוֹל:

And I myself will fight against you with an outstretched hand and mighty arm, in anger (reddening of face), in anger (internal irritation), and in great קֶצֶף anger (abstract object).

The context of this passage is about God handing over his people into the hands of the Babylonians during the reign of Zedekiah (vv. 1–3). Although God had been the defender of his people, he is now fighting against them using the Babylonians as his tool (v. 4).

This verse begins with וְנִלְחַמְתִּי אֲנִי "and I myself will fight." The personal pronoun אֲנִי "I" has an emphatic function[425] on the subject, hence the translation "I myself will fight." The manner in which God will fight them is

---

421. Seow, *Grammar for Biblical Hebrew*, 284.
422. Waltke and O'Connor, *Introduction to Biblical Hebrew*, 30.2.1d.
423. Arnold and Choi, *Guide to Biblical Hebrew*, 4.1.5b.
424. Seow, *Grammar for Biblical Hebrew*, 93.
425. Seow, 93.

בְּיָד נְטוּיָה וּבִזְרוֹעַ חֲזָקָה "with an outstretched hand and a mighty arm" which is a hendiadys.[426] Both the בְּיָד and the וּבִזְרוֹעַ have a בְּ preposition, which has an instrument function,[427] hence the translation "with." The hand and the arm are anthropomorphisms symbolizing the Babylonians whom the Lord will use. The state in which God will fight against them is וּבְאַף וּבְחֵמָה וּבְקֶצֶף "in anger (reddening of face), in anger (internal irritation), and in great קֶצֶף anger (abstract object)." Here is another example of hendiatris[428] giving an emphasis to how angry God was. Just as in Deuteronomy 29:27, all the lexical items in this quotation have a preposition בְּ which has a state function,[429] meaning he will fight them in the state of anger. The antecedent condition for God's anger in this passage is not stated. However, an examination of Jeremiah 32 where the same story is retold explains the evil that Zedekiah had done was the worship of idols (Jer 32:32–34). This situation supports the argument in this research that קֶצֶף גָּדוֹל is used in contexts that have idol worship as the antecedent condition. Similarly, the argument given for the use of the three lexical items above with the sense of anger is that they also occur together in contexts involving worship of idols and pronouncement of judgment, mainly captivity. The use of these words show emphasis of the great displeasure the Lord had against Judah at the time of the prophecy. Therefore, God, in his great anger, used the Babylonians to take to captivity (punish) his people. Since God is superior to the Israelites, this passage explains the vertical relational function as discussed earlier.

The use of the three words above with the sense of anger is repeated in Jeremiah 32:37. While in the former passage God is putting them to death in war, in this passage God is making a promise to gather them again – the survivors who will be taken to captivity. He reminds them that he had handed them over to captivity in בְּאַפִּי וּבַחֲמָתִי וּבְקֶצֶף גָּדוֹל "because of anger (reddening of face), because of anger (internal irritation), and because of great קֶצֶף anger (abstract object)." Below is the reference in Jeremiah 32:37.

---

426. Bullinger, *Figures of Speech*, 659.
427. Arnold and Choi, *Guide to Biblical Hebrew*, 4.1.5c.
428. Bullinger, *Figures of Speech*, 673.
429. Köhler and Baumgartner, "בְּ," *HALOT*, 1:104–5.

iii. Jer 32:37

הִנְנִי מְקַבְּצָם מִכָּל־הָאֲרָצוֹת אֲשֶׁר הִדַּחְתִּים שָׁם בְּאַפִּי וּבַחֲמָתִי וּבְקֶצֶף
גָּדוֹל וַהֲשִׁבֹתִים אֶל־הַמָּקוֹם הַזֶּה וְהֹשַׁבְתִּים לָבֶטַח׃

> See, I will gather them from all the lands where I was caused to banish them in my anger (reddening of face), in my anger (internal irritation) and in great anger (abstract object); I will bring them back to this place and settle them safely.

The context of this verse is about God's promise to gather his people from captivity, where he had banished them. Specifically, the verse above is about that promise. The events leading to the banishment to captivity concern the spread of idol worship in Israel during the reign of Zedekiah (Jer 32:30–36). However, God in his mercy did not allow the people to be held captives forever. He promised to deliver them.

This verse begins with הִנְנִי, which has an immediacy function[430] that points to immediacy of the participle that follows it, hence its translation as "see." The verb of the first clause is מְקַבְּצָם "I will gather them" which has a future function,[431] denoting that action will take place in the future but the duration is not specified. The action could be instantaneous, short or durative. The place from which the Lord will gather them is מִכָּל־הָאֲרָצוֹת "from all the lands." The construction מִכָּל "from all" – referring to the specific localities the people lived – demonstrates how thorough the gathering will be. The הָאֲרָצוֹת "the lands" noun has a definite article of a particular reference[432] since it is known in the context that they had been taken captive by the Babylonians.

These lands are further described in a relative clause introduced by אֲשֶׁר הִדַּחְתִּים שָׁם בְּאַפִּי וּבַחֲמָתִי וּבְקֶצֶף גָּדוֹל "where I (was caused to)[433] banish them because of my anger (reddening of face), my anger (internal irritation) and great anger (abstract object)," another example of hendiatris.[434] The verb הִדַּחְתִּים "I banished" is in the hiphil stem which contextually implies the intensity of the action. It also has a telic perfective function[435] since the

---

430. Arnold and Choi, *Guide to Biblical Hebrew*, 4.5.1b.
431. Waltke and O'Connor, *Introduction to Biblical Hebrew*, 37.6f.
432. Gibson, *Davidson's Introductory Hebrew Grammar*, 30a.
433. Through their evil deeds (vv. 30–35) the Israelites caused God to banish them.
434. Bullinger, *Figures of Speech*, 673.
435. Waltke and O'Connor, *Introduction to Biblical Hebrew*, 30.2.1d.

context implies the speaker is looking at the situation from the end. Unlike the other two verses where the three words with the sense of anger are used, the first two, בְּאַפִּי וּבַחֲמָתִי "in my anger and in my anger," have genitive affixes. These affixes have a genitive characteristic function,[436] although signifying temporal characteristics since he was not permanently in anger. The author adds the third lexical item קֶצֶף גָּדוֹל "great anger." The reminder pronounced in this passage explains that the antecedent condition was idol worship, and judgment had been effected.

Although the Lord had banished them, he makes a twofold promise that he will וַהֲשִׁבֹתִים אֶל־הַמָּקוֹם הַזֶּה וְהֹשַׁבְתִּים לָבֶטַח "I will bring them back to this place and let them live in safety." The verbs וַהֲשִׁבֹתִים "I will bring them back" is a specific future non-perfective,[437] meaning this will certainly happen in the future. The second promise is introduced by the וְהֹשַׁבְתִּים "settle them" which is taken to mean a specific future[438] since it will certainly happen. The manner in which they will live is לָבֶטַח "safely" which has a preposition לְ which has a manner function[439] explaining how their stay will be. According to the קֶצֶף frame, אַף and חֵמָה are both extrathematic frame elements of קֶצֶף. It is no surprise, therefore, that they are used in the same verse here to show the intensity of God's anger. Their usage in the same passages is illustrated in the following diagram.[440]

The section above has examined passages in which קֶצֶף occur in the same context with אַף and חֵמָה. The other verses in which the Israelites are the landmark is in Joshua 9:20, 2 Kings 3:27 and Zechariah 7:12 which have already been discussed. All the references in section 3.2.2.1 above concern the landmark of God's קֶצֶף, the Israelites. The following section discusses God's קֶצֶף on the nations. As will be explained below, the references concerning the nations can be found only in the prophetic literature of Isaiah, Jeremiah and Zechariah.

---

436. Van der Merwe, Naudé, and Kroeze, *Biblical Hebrew Reference Grammar*, 198.
437. Gibson, *Davidson's Introductory Hebrew Grammar*, 64a.
438. Gibson.
439. Arnold and Choi, *Guide to Biblical Hebrew*, 4.1.10j.
440. The meanings of אַף and חֵמָה that show how different they are from קֶצֶף are discussed in section 3.2.2.1. More detailed research on אַף and חֵמָה is beyond the limitations of this research.

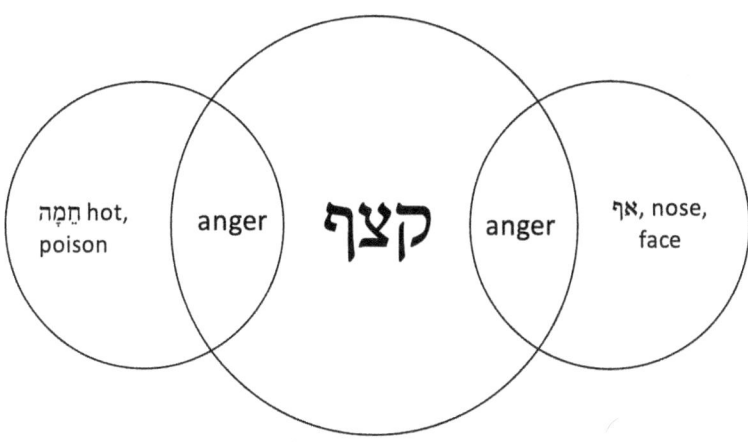

Chart 4

3.2.2.2 The Nations (Foreigners) Are the Landmarks

This is the second category in which יְהוָה "the Lord" is the Ego of קֶצֶף but the landmark is different, the nations. There are only two references to be examined; the first reference in Ezra 7:23 – which is in Aramaic – in which the nations are the landmark. There are two Aramaic passages only in the BHS, Ezra 7:23 and Daniel 2:12, in which the equivalent קצף occurs. The noun form is in Ezra while the verb form is in Daniel. As shown in the following reference, Ezra 7:23 supports the BHS's קֶצֶף frame.

3.2.2.2.1 King Artaxerxes and Family (Aramaic text)

29. Ezra 7:23

כָּל־דִּי מִן־טַעַם אֱלָהּ שְׁמַיָּא יִתְעֲבֵד אַדְרַזְדָּא לְבֵית אֱלָהּ שְׁמַיָּא דִּי־לְמָה
לֶהֱוֵא קְצַף עַל־מַלְכוּת מַלְכָּא וּבְנוֹהִי

Whatsoever is commanded by the God of heaven[441] let it be diligently done for the house of the God of heaven: for why should קְצַף come/fall on the realm of the king and his sons?

The Aramaic קְצַף is a noun related to the Hebrew קֶצֶף. This passage records the decree by King Artaxerxes concerning the rebuilding of the house of God

---

441. The analysis of קצף shows that it was also directed to non-Israelites – people who did not have a binding covenant with God.

by Ezra. He ordered that it should be done diligently lest God's קְצַף (related to the Hebrew קֶצֶף) will come/fall on the king and his sons. The use of "sons" is understood to be a synecdoche of the part for the whole,[442] referring to his successors – who may include his biological sons but not necessarily so. This understanding means he feared that God's קֶצֶף would fall on him and the entire Persian Empire.[443] This verse identifies קְצַף as the subject, which comes/falls on the landmark. Since the one speaking in this verse is King Artaxerxes, it is a sign that even foreigners recognized the anger of the God of the Israelites.[444] As in the Hebrew texts, this verse has the לֶהֱוֵא verb – third person imperfect of הוה meaning "to come/fall, become or exist," and the preposition עַל, identifying the trajectory and the landmark, respectively. In this context, the reason why God would be קְצַף angry with the king and his sons is due to lack of diligence in rebuilding God's house. In this case, the punishment is implied.

While this example from Ezra supports the core frame elements of the קצף frame, the example in Daniel 2:12 profiles different elements of the frame that show that קְצַף was associated with people in authority and is, also, associated with retribution.[445] Section 3.2 has shown that the Aramaic equivalent noun form of the Hebrew קֶצֶף fits within the core frame elements of קצף.

The second passage in which the landmark of קֶצֶף is a foreigner (other nations) is in Jeremiah 50:13.

3.2.2.2.2 The Babylonians

30. Jer 50:13

מִקֶּצֶף יְהוָה לֹא תֵשֵׁב Because of the Lord's קֶצֶף "anger" it shall not be inhabited

וְהָיְתָה שְׁמָמָה כֻּלָּהּ and will become a wasteland, all of it

כֹּל עֹבֵר עַל־בָּבֶל יִשֹּׁם everyone who passes by Babylon will be appalled

וְיִשְׁרֹק עַל־כָּל־מַכּוֹתֶיהָ and murmur at all its wounds

---

442. Bullinger, *Figures of Speech*, 640.
443. Batten, *Ezra and Nehemiah*, 313.
444. Davies, *Ezra and Nehemiah*, 47.
445. The passage from Daniel 2:12 is discussed later in this chapter in the section on the distinctive features of קצף.

This passage is about Jeremiah's prophecy concerning the Babylonians, who will be plundered (v. 10). The reason given for this plunder is that they rejoiced over the pillaging of the Israelites (v. 11). Therefore, Babylon will be completely destroyed and uninhabited (v. 13). The destruction of the Babylonians is therefore a result of God's קֶצֶף.

This verse begins מִקֶּצֶף יְהוָה "because of the anger of the Lord" with a preposition מִן prefixed to קֶצֶף which has a causal function,[446] hence its translation as "because of." The result of the קֶצֶף of God is לֹא תֵשֵׁב וְהָיְתָה שְׁמָמָה כֻלָּהּ "it shall not be inhabited and will become a wasteland." The verbs תֵשֵׁב "it shall (not) be inhabited" and וְהָיְתָה "will become" are both specific future non-perfective[447] denoting the certainty of this utterance. The construction שְׁמָמָה כֻלָּהּ "wasteland, all of it" are nouns in apposition, which is, the apposition of measure.[448] This means כֻלָּהּ "all of it" is a measure of the wasteland. Because of this terrible outcome, כֹּל עֹבֵר עַל־בָּבֶל יִשֹּׁם וְיִשְׁרֹק עַל־כָּל־מַכּוֹתֶיהָ "everyone who passes by Babylon will be appalled and murmur at all its wounds." The particle כֹּל "everyone" shows how the damage will be so conspicuous that it will be hard to miss the sight. This is followed by the particle עֹבֵר which has a substantive function[449] acting like a noun, hence its translation as "who passes." Anyone who passes by this place יִשֹּׁם וְיִשְׁרֹק "he will be appalled and will murmur." These verbs are both specific future,[450] meaning being appalled and murmuring will certainly happen. The object of these verbs is עַל־כָּל־מַכּוֹתֶיהָ "at all its wounds." The preposition עַל has an interest function meaning "at" which usually is the case when this preposition occurs with verbs of thought, mood or feeling.[451]

The section 3.2.2.2.2 above has examined God's קֶצֶף on the nations – those that he had used to punish the Israelites in the past but here he was punishing them for their wickedness. The following subsection concerns God's קֶצֶף on individuals.

---

446. Arnold and Choi, *Guide to Biblical Hebrew*, 4.1.13d.
447. Gibson, *Davidson's Introductory Hebrew Grammar*, 64.
448. Van der Merwe, Naudé, and Kroeze, *Biblical Hebrew Reference Grammar*, 230.
449. Seow, *Grammar for Biblical Hebrew*, 83.
450. Chisholm, *From Exegesis to Exposition*, 91–92.
451. Arnold and Choi, *Guide to Biblical Hebrew*, 4.1.16h.

3.2.2.2.3 Individuals Are the Landmarks

The passages in which individuals are the landmarks have already been discussed although under different subheadings. They are, however mentioned in this section but without discussion. God directed his קֶצֶף to King Jehoshaphat (2 Chr 19:2) and individual psalmists (Pss 38:2[1]; 102:10[11]).

The analysis done in the section above explains that קֶצֶף had a vertical relational function in which the Ego is superior. The analysis has also shown that קֶצֶף had an intention of retribution or retribution was effected. It also explains that קֶצֶף occurred among people who had an existing relationship: God and the Israelites, God and the nations which he had used before to punish the Israelites, and God and the individuals. The diagram below illustrates the details that have been discussed so far.

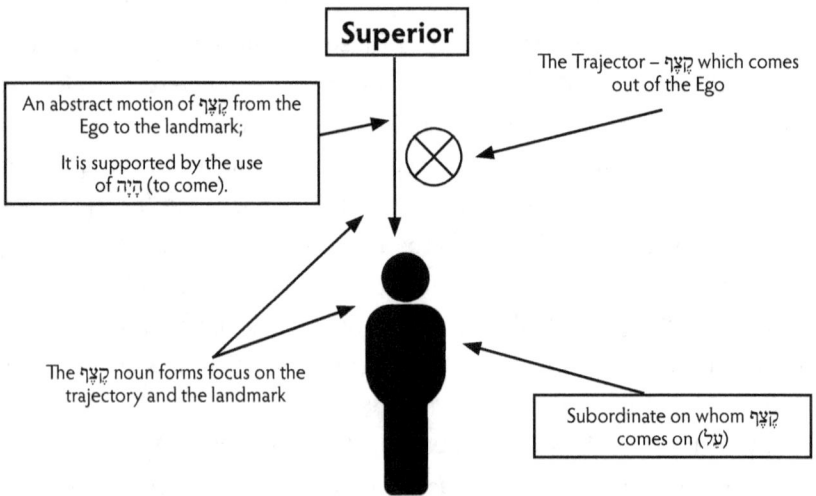

Chart 5

Having examined the passages in which God was the Ego of קֶצֶף, the following section examines passages where human is the Ego of קֶצֶף.

3.2.3 The Noun Forms of קֶצֶף: Human Is the Ego

In the passages where the Ego, the experiencer of קֶצֶף, is human, the focus of the passage is the Ego and the relationship of the Ego with the landmark is not stated. The argument in this section is that when קֶצֶף was experienced by a human being, the verb הָיָה and the preposition עַל are missing and the focus is on the experiencer of the emotion. Contextually, in these passages קֶצֶף can be translated as "frustration" although this does not falsify the translation of קֶצֶף in those passages as "anger." The cues in the contexts that are guiding the translation of קֶצֶף as "frustration" are two: first, the emotion of קֶצֶף is not directed to any object[452] unlike in the other passages where קֶצֶף is usually directed, and, second, the context contains other words or phrases that show emotional distress. What is apparent in the following examples is that the author changed focus from the relationship of the Ego and landmark to the experiencer of the emotion when a human is the Ego. The following examples illustrate this.

3.2.3.1 King(s) Officials as the Ego: An Expression of Frustration

The only reference in the BHS where it is implied that the officials of a king may experience קֶצֶף is in Esther 1:18.

31. Esth 1:18

וְהַיּוֹם הַזֶּה תֹּאמַרְנָה שָׂרוֹת פָּרַס־וּמָדַי אֲשֶׁר שָׁמְעוּ אֶת־דְּבַר הַמַּלְכָּה לְכֹל שָׂרֵי הַמֶּלֶךְ וּכְדַי בִּזָּיוֹן וָקָצֶף׃

When this day the Persian and Median noblewomen hear of the queen's conduct and say (the same things) to all the king's officials, (there will be) a lot of contempt and קֶצֶף "anger/frustration."

The context of this verse concerns King Xerxes who gave a banquet for all his officials in all the 127 provinces he ruled over (vv. 1–3). This banquet lasted 180 days after which he gave another banquet in his palace lasting 7 days (vv. 4–8). His wife, Queen Vashti, also gave a banquet for the women in the palace (v. 9). On the seventh day, the last day, of the banquet in the palace, the king commanded his seven eunuchs to bring Queen Vashti before him but she refused (vv. 10–12). After this the king consulted his experts in matters of law and justice, among them was Memucan (vv. 13–14). The content recorded in verses 16 to verse 20 is the response and advice Memucan gave the king. Therefore, the words in verse 18 are Memucan's to King Xerxes

---

452. The author of this research acknowledges that anger can be experienced and not directed. The context therefore remains a key factor in determining the meaning of the word.

expressing concern that if this kind of behavior was allowed to continue, then disrespect of wives against their husbands would continue and the king and his nobles, and probably all who would receive the news, would continually be provoked to קֶצֶף.[453]

This verse begins with וְהַיּוֹם הַזֶּה "this day" with a conjunction וְ, which has a circumstantial function fitting the translation "when."[454] The noun הַיּוֹם "the day" has a definite article of a particular reference[455] since Memucan was referring to a specific day. The near demonstrative הַזֶּה "this" has an attributive adjectival function,[456] hence its translation as "this day." The verbs תֹּאמַרְנָה "say" and שָׁמְעוּ "hear" complement each other since what is said is what is heard. Both verbs are present perfectives[457] since they denote a situation that can extend from the present into the future. The object of שָׁמְעוּ "hear" is אֶת־דְּבַר הַמַּלְכָּה "the matter of the queen." The construction דְּבַר הַמַּלְכָּה is a genitive of product,[458] meaning the action[459] of the queen. The result of this would be וּכְדַי בִּזָּיוֹן וָקָצֶף "(Therefore), to all the king's officials, (will have) enough contempt and קֶצֶף 'anger/frustration.'" The construction בִּזָּיוֹן וָקָצֶף "contempt and anger/frustration" is hendiadys[460] since they both show the annoyance the king's officials would have. The word בִּזָּיוֹן is used in this context to mean disregard[461] in the sense of being useless, meaning the action of the women would make their husbands to be despised, treated in a demeaning manner. Its verbal form זָאַב is used with the same sense in Malachi 1:7. In this case, both בִּזָּיוֹן and קֶצֶף are used together to show emotional distress. In addition, the focus of the author, demonstrated by the absence of the verb הָיָה and the preposition עַל, is on the experience of the Ego. Therefore, the noun קֶצֶף in this verse can be translated as "frustration"[462] since the context shows the ill

---

453. Paton, *Book of Esther*, 156.
454. Seow, *Grammar for Biblical Hebrew*, 285.
455. Gesenius, *Gesenius' Hebrew Grammar*, 126d.
456. Seow, *Grammar for Biblical Hebrew*, 104.
457. Waltke and O'Connor, *Introduction to Biblical Hebrew*, 9.5.1e.
458. Waltke and O'Connor, 9.5.1e.
459. BDB, 183c.
460. Bullinger, *Figures of Speech*, 671.
461. BDB, 102c.
462. Clines, "קצף," *DCH*, 7:283–84.

feeling of the Ego.[463] The other passage in which the focus of קֶצֶף is a human being and the context demonstrates his ill feeling is in Ecclesiastes 5:16(17).

3.2.3.2 An Ordinary Man (Person) as the Ego of קֶצֶף: An expression of Frustration

32. Eccl 5:16 [17]

גַּם כָּל־יָמָיו בַּחֹשֶׁךְ יֹאכֵל וְכָעַס הַרְבֵּה וְחָלְיוֹ וָקָצֶף׃

Moreover, all his days he eats in darkness, much sorrowing, sickness and קֶצֶף "anger/frustration."

The narrator of this passage talks about a man who is in pursuit of worldly wealth but is never satisfied (vv. 10–14). The problem of pursuing wealth is compounded by the fact that man comes from God naked and he takes with him nothing when he departs (v. 15). This forms the background of Ecclesiastes 5:16 [17].

This verse begins with the גַּם particle, which has an additional function,[464] meaning "moreover," since the contents of this verse are an addition to the troubles mentioned in the preceding verse. This particle is followed by the construction כָּל־יָמָיו "all his days" which has the כָּל noun which has a hyperbole function,[465] meaning "most of his days." The use of "a man" is generic, not referring to any specific person but to anyone who pursues wealth as her/his ultimate goal in life. This construction is followed by a noun, which figuratively describes the man's state. It says בַּחֹשֶׁךְ "in the gloom" which literally means "in the darkness." This is a metonymy of adjunct, the sign for the thing signified.[466] In this case, "darkness" signifies "gloom" in the sense of distress.[467] The preposition בְּ has a "state" function, meaning the environment within his state of gloom or frustration. This noun, בַּחֹשֶׁךְ, also has a definite article of nouns in the imagination[468] because the context, in the preceding verses, is about the futility of pursuing wealth as the ultimate goal. The verb

---

463. Köhler and Baumgartner, "קצף," *HALOT*, 2:1125.
464. Arnold and Choi, *Guide to Biblical Hebrew*, 4.2.5a.
465. Bullinger, *Figures of Speech*, 423.
466. Bullinger, 603.
467. BDB, 365a.
468. Chisholm, *From Exegesis to Exposition*, 73.

of the first part of the verse is יֹאכֵל "he eats" which is a stative non-perfective, meaning this is the state of such a man (person). The use of the verb "to eat" is a metonymy of adjunct, a sign for the thing signified[469] meaning "eat"' signifies consequences of his action.[470]

The author adds that this man will eat וְכָעַס הַרְבֵּה וְחָלְיוֹ וָקָצֶף "in much sorrowing, sickness and קֶצֶף 'frustration,'" an expression which shows emotional distress. This phrase begins with a conjunction וְ , which has a circumstantial function,[471] hence its translation as "in" meaning the circumstances within which he eats. The verb כָעַס "sorrowing" has a progressive non-perfective function,[472] meaning the state of the subject began in the past and is still continuingin the present. Since this verb is polysemous, as explained in the table at the beginning of this chapter, the context of the chapter dictates that it be translated as "sorrow." Another passage in which כָעַס has the sense of sorrowing is Ecclesiastes 2:23. The sorrowing of this man is qualified further by the adverb הַרְבֵּה "much." In addition to sorrowing, he is in a state of וְחָלְיוֹ "affliction" and קֶצֶף "frustration,"[473] expressing an ill feeling[474] because of his unmet expectations. As with the reference in Esther 1:18, this passage too does not have the verb הָיָה and the preposition עַל which are characteristics of the קצף frame vertical relationship. Additionally, there is no grammatical cue showing to whom the emotion was directed. Instead, the focus is on the Ego, the experiencer of the emotion. The context of this verse shows a state of emotional distress and קֶצֶף is translated as "frustration" since it fits well within the emotional distress context.

In this example, the Ego of קֶצֶף is an ordinary person. The argument in this section is that when קֶצֶף was experienced by a human being, the verb הָיָה and the preposition עַל are missing and the focus is on the experiencer of the emotion. Contextually, in these passages קֶצֶף can be translated as "frustration" instead of "anger" since the emotion of קֶצֶף is not directed to any object. While the section 3.2.3 above examined the קֶצֶף noun forms, the following section is on the קָצַף verbal forms.

---

469. Bullinger, *Figures of Speech*, 603.
470. BDB, 37c.
471. Arnold and Choi, *Guide to Biblical Hebrew*, 4.3.3e.
472. Waltke and O'Connor, *Introduction to Biblical Hebrew*, 31.3b.
473. Clines, "קצף," *DCH*, 7:283–84.
474. Köhler and Baumgartner, "קצף," *HALOT*, 2:1125.

3.2.4 The Verbal Form of קָצַף: God Is the Ego

This section examines verses in which the קָצַף verbal forms occur as found in Genesis 40:2; 41:10; Exodus 16:20; Leviticus 10:6, 16; Numbers 16:22; 31:14; Deuteronomy 1:34; 9:7–8, 19, 22; Joshua 22:18; 1 Samuel 29:4; 2 Kings 5:11; 13:19; Esther 8:21; Isaiah 47:6; 54:9; 57:17 (used twice); 64:5[4], 9[8]; Jeremiah 37:15; Lamentations 5:22; and Zechariah 1:2, 15 (used twice); 8:14. The discussion in this section will be divided into two main categories: passages in which God is the Ego and others where human is the Ego. In the passages where God is the Ego, the references are further divided into the qal stem and the hiphil stem. The reason for this categorization is that the profiled elements in the two stems are different. The profiled element in the qal stem is the Ego, who, as in the noun forms, is superior to the landmark. These verbs, in which God is the Ego, in the qal stem are in Leviticus 10:6; Deuteronomy 1:34; Joshua 22:18; Ecclesiastes 5:5(6); and Zechariah 1:2, 15. On the contrary, in the hiphil stem, the profiled elements are the antecedent conditions in which a subordinate provokes a superior. As it will be explained, the verbs in the hiphil stem have a causative function and God is the affected object. The verbs in the hiphil stem are found in Deuteronomy 9:7, 8, 22; Psalm 106:32; and Zechariah 8:14. One uniqueness of these references is that, in three (Deut 9:7, 8, 22) out of the five references, God is identified with the direct object marker, אֵת, while in the other two references the direct marker is missing but God is the implied object.

One of the key prepositions in the קָצַף verbal forms is עַל. Unlike the use of this preposition in the nouns forms of קֶצֶף, in which it is translated as "on," in the verbal forms it has an adversative sense (since it is not accompanied by a motion verb as in the noun form) and should be translated either as "with" or "against." This understanding justifies the use of אֶל (to) in Joshua 22:18, which is the only clause where that preposition occurs with קצף. As Arnold and Choi note, the preposition אֶל can have a terminative function in which it marks the end "when the goal of the movement is reached."[475] Other passages in which the preposition אֶל is used to show movement, and translated as "to," are in Exodus 2:11; Deuteronomy 17:14; and 2 Samuel 11:10. Therefore, the translation of the preposition אֶל as "against" in Joshua 22:18 complements the use of the preposition עַל as discussed in this research. This research,

---

475. Arnold and Choi, *Guide to Biblical Hebrew*, 4.1.2a.

therefore, holds a contrary view to that of Salzburg Reiterer who says that the use of אֶל in Joshua 22:18 is a mistake.[476] The first section to be considered is on the qal stem in which God is the Ego.

3.2.4.1 *In the Qal Stem* קָצַף *God Is the Focus: Superior to Subordinate*

33. Lev 10:6

וַיֹּאמֶר מֹשֶׁה אֶל־אַהֲרֹן וּלְאֶלְעָזָר וּלְאִיתָמָר בָּנָיו רָאשֵׁיכֶם אַל־תִּפְרָעוּ וּבִגְדֵיכֶם לֹא־תִפְרֹמוּ וְלֹא תָמֻתוּ וְעַל כָּל־הָעֵדָה יִקְצֹף וַאֲחֵיכֶם כָּל־בֵּית יִשְׂרָאֵל יִבְכּוּ אֶת־הַשְּׂרֵפָה אֲשֶׁר שָׂרַף יְהוָה:

Then Moses said to Aaron and, Eleazar and Ithamar, his sons, "do not let your hair become unkempt and do not tear your clothes, so that you will not die and (the Lord) will not be angry with the whole community. But your relatives, all the Israelites, may mourn for those whom the Lord's fire has burned up."

The context of this verse is about Moses warning Aaron and his sons, Eleazar and Ithamar, against keeping their hair unkempt or tearing their clothes. Mark Rooker notes that "according to Rabbinic tradition, the high priest was to have his hair cut once a week and an ordinary priest once a month."[477] Keeping tidy hair and being neat was one of the signs of moral purity (Lev 21:10) that the priests had to maintain. The tearing of clothes in this passage is necessitated by the mourning of the deaths of Nadab and Abihu, the brothers of Eleazar and Ithamar. The tearing of clothes elsewhere is associated with grief and not necessarily death (Gen 37:29, 34; 44:13). Although Aaron and his remaining sons were mourning, they "were not to let anything interrupt their service of the living God at the tabernacle"[478] by violating the Levitical codes. If they did, then God would become קָצַף "angry" with not only them but also the whole community and the penalty would be death (vv. 1–2, 7).

This verse begins with a specific address by Moses to Aaron and his remaining sons. The address of his speech was אֶל־אַהֲרֹן וּלְאֶלְעָזָר וּלְאִיתָמָר בָּנָיו "to Aaron, and Eleazar and Ithamar, his sons" who are objects of a speech

---

476. Reiterer, "קצף," *Theological Dictionary of the Old Testament*.
477. Rooker, *Leviticus*, 159.
478. Rooker, 159.

and are marked by the preposition אֶל whose function is declarative.[479] The content of Moses's address, in this verse (because it extends to the following verse), can be divided into three parts.

The first part of the address is רָאשֵׁיכֶם אַל־תִּפְרָעוּ וּבִגְדֵיכֶם לֹא־תִפְרֹמוּ "do not let your hair become unkempt and do not tear your clothes." This clause has two sections, each with a prohibitive word. The verb of the first prohibition is תִּפְרָעוּ "you let loose," which is translated as "unkempt," a jussive of prohibition,[480] meaning Aaron and his two remaining sons must obey. The object of this verb is רָאשֵׁיכֶם "your head" which is a synecdoche of the whole for one of its parts,[481] referring to the hair but mentioning the head. The verb of the second prohibition is תִפְרֹמוּ "(do not) you tear" which is also a jussive of prohibition.[482] The object is the noun, clothes, in this construction וּבִגְדֵיכֶם and the pronoun is a possessive genitive.[483]

The reason for these prohibitions is that, וְלֹא תָמֻתוּ וְעַל כָּל־הָעֵדָה יִקְצֹף "so that you will not die and (the Lord) will not be angry with the whole congregation." This clause begins with a conjunction וְ which has a conjunctive result function,[484] hence its translation as "so that." The two verbs of this clause תָמֻתוּ "you will (not) die" and יִקְצֹף "he will (not) be angry" are both specific future non-perfectives,[485] meaning they will surely happen if Moses's prohibition is not heeded. The subject of the second verb is not explicitly stated but from the context, it is clear that it is "the Lord." The Lord is angry וְעַל כָּל־הָעֵדָה "with the whole community" since the preposition עַל has an adversative function.[486] The noun הָעֵדָה "the community" has a definite article of a particular reference[487] since it is used in this chapter interchangeably with "the people" (v. 3).

The last part of Moses's address concerns the whole community. He said: וַאֲחֵיכֶם כָּל־בֵּית יִשְׂרָאֵל יִבְכּוּ אֶת־הַשְּׂרֵפָה אֲשֶׁר שָׂרַף יְהוָה "but your brothers, all the Israelites, may mourn the burning which the Lord has burned up." This

---

479. Arnold and Choi, *Guide to Biblical Hebrew*, 4.1.2c.
480. Van der Merwe, Naudé, and Kroeze, *Biblical Hebrew Reference Grammar*, 152.
481. Bullinger, *Figures of Speech*, 637.
482. Arnold and Choi, *Guide to Biblical Hebrew*, 3.3.1a.
483. Joüon and Muraoka, *Grammar of Biblical Hebrew*, 129d.
484. Seow, *Grammar for Biblical Hebrew*, 285.
485. Waltke and O'Connor, *Introduction to Biblical Hebrew*, 31.4e.
486. Arnold and Choi, *Guide to Biblical Hebrew*, 4.1.16f.
487. Gesenius, *Gesenius' Hebrew Grammar*, 126d.

last clause begins with a conjunction וְ which has an adversative function,[488] hence its translation as "but" because it contrasts what Aaron and his two remaining sons should not do and what the Israelites should do. The content of this clause begins by identifying the subjects of the verb, who are וַאֲחֵיכֶם כָּל־בֵּית יִשְׂרָאֵל "your brothers, all the Israelites." The use of brothers is a synecdoche of the part for the whole, meaning all Israelites who are also called כָּל־בֵּית יִשְׂרָאֵל "all the house of Israel." The use of "house" is a metonymy of the subject for the adjunct,[489] meaning household in the sense of a nation.

This passage bears the warning by Moses against the failure to heed God's instructions, which would mean that he would be קָצַף "angry" with them. The Ego is superior to the landmark and therefore supports that argument advanced in this research that קָצַף "to be angry" was experienced by a superior. The vertical relational function is therefore demonstrated in the contents of this verse. Another passage in which God is the Ego of קָצַף verb in its qal stem is in Numbers 16:22.

34. Num 16:22

וַיִּפְּלוּ עַל־פְּנֵיהֶם וַיֹּאמְרוּ אֵל אֱלֹהֵי הָרוּחֹת לְכָל־בָּשָׂר הָאִישׁ אֶחָד יֶחֱטָא וְעַל כָּל־הָעֵדָה תִּקְצֹף

> But they fell prostrate and exclaimed, "O God, God of the spirits of all living creatures, if one man sins will you be angry with the whole community?"

The context of this passage is about the prayer of Moses and Aaron for the Israelites so that God would spare them from imminent destruction. The sin of the Israelites was that of opposing the leadership of Moses (v. 2). Numbers 16:22 is specifically about Moses and Aaron falling prostrate in prayer, with the larger portion of the verse bearing the content of the prayer. Their prayer is to God whom they address in appositional title – אֵל אֱלֹהֵי הָרוּחֹת לְכָל־בָּשָׂר "O God, God of the spirits of all living creatures." The genitive אֱלֹהֵי הָרוּחֹת "God of the spirits" is a genitive of source,[490] meaning God is the one who gives spirit (life). The beneficiary of this life is לְכָל־בָּשָׂר "of all flesh." This prayer and the appeal to God who gives life is a fitting prayer in the face of

---

488. Seow, *Grammar for Biblical Hebrew*, 284.
489. Bullinger, *Figures of Speech*, 573.
490. Van der Merwe, Naudé, and Kroeze, *Biblical Hebrew Reference Grammar*, 229.

imminent death. Dennis Cole notes that Moses acknowledges that God is the giver and sustainer of life.[491]

After crying out to God, he addresses God using a rhetorical question הָאִישׁ אֶחָד יֶחֱטָא וְעַל כָּל־הָעֵדָה תִּקְצֹף "if one man sins will you be angry with the whole community?" Moses and Aaron were concerned about whether the act of sin יֶחֱטָא of one man would make God תִּקְצֹף "angry" with the entire community. In this passage, קָצַף is an anterior future[492] since for God to be angry is dependent on the people sinning. The implication of this passage is that the effects of God being קָצַף "angry" are so severe that they are intended against the entire community. However, Moses's concern is God's anger should not be against the entire community since the sin is not communal. The effect of this sin was death (v. 21, vv. 31–36).

This passage shows that the קָצַף in the qal stem had a vertical relationship of a superior against a subordinate. Another passage in which God is the Ego of the קָצַף verb in its qal stem is in Deuteronomy 1:34.

35. Deut 1:34

וַיִּשְׁמַע יְהוָה אֶת־קוֹל דִּבְרֵיכֶם וַיִּקְצֹף וַיִּשָּׁבַע לֵאמֹר׃

When the Lord heard what you said, he was angry, and took an oath.

The context of this verse is about God who had become קָצַף "angry" because of the grumbling of the Israelites in their tents. The content of their grumbling is recorded in Deuteronomy 1:27–28 which says: "The LORD hates us; so he brought us out of Egypt to deliver us into the hands of the Amorites to destroy us. Where can we go? Our brothers have made our hearts melt in fear. They say, 'The people are stronger and taller than we are; the cities are large, with walls up to the sky. We even saw the Anakites there'" (NIV). However, the content of verse 34 indicates that the sin of the Israelites was more than just grumbling. It is part of rebellion not to obey God's commands (v. 26). In verse 34, קָצַף is accompanied by swearing, a commitment that he will punish them. The punishment is that they would not enter the promised land (v. 35). Their act, therefore, impelled the Lord to react in anger.

---

491. Cole, *Numbers*, 266.
492. Arnold and Choi, *Guide to Biblical Hebrew*, 3.2.2a.

This verse begins with a conjunction וְ, which has a circumstantial function,[493] hence its translation as "when." The first verb of this verse is וַיִּשְׁמַע "he heard" which is a definite past perfective,[494] meaning the Lord heard their conversation from the beginning to the end. The content of their grumbling was their complaint concerning taking possession of the land (vv. 23–26). The effect of their words was that וַיִּקְצֹף וַיִּשָּׁבַע "he (God) became angry and took an oath." The verb וַיִּשָּׁבַע "he took an oath" is an ingressive perfective[495] because the verb that follows לֵאמֹר "saying" introduces the content of the oath. The content of the oath is in verse 35 that says, "no one from this evil generation shall see the good land I swore to give your ancestors" (NIV). This is the only instance in which קָצַף is executed through an oath. The reason for this occurrence of swearing in this passage is based on the fact that God had sworn (Gen 22:16; Exod 13:11; Deut 1:8) to give the Israelites the land they were now getting possession of. The effect of God being קָצַף "angry" was that they did not enter the promised land (v. 35).

Again, the focus of this verb is the Ego, God, who became קָצַף "angry" and is superior to the landmark, therefore supporting the argument that קָצַף with sense of anger had a vertical relational function. The next verse to consider is Joshua 22:18, in which Ego is the focus in the use of קָצַף in its qal stem.

36. Josh 22:18

וְאַתֶּם תָּשֻׁבוּ הַיּוֹם מֵאַחֲרֵי יְהוָה וְהָיָה אַתֶּם תִּמְרְדוּ הַיּוֹם בַּיהוָה וּמָחָר אֶל־כָּל־עֲדַת יִשְׂרָאֵל יִקְצֹף׃

> If today you turn away from following the Lord, and it happens, you become rebellious against him, then tomorrow he will be angry against the whole community of Israel.

The context of this verse is about a warning by a delegation led by Phinehas to Reuben, Gad and the half tribe of Manasseh concerning their mistaken apostasy (vv. 10–23). They warned that if they rebelled against God by turning to idols as they did in Peor (v. 17; cf. Num 25), he would be קָצַף "angry" with the whole community. This delegation explains how quickly God would become קָצַף "angry" with them by insisting that if they would rebel against

---

493. Seow, *Grammar for Biblical Hebrew*, 284.
494. Waltke and O'Connor, *Introduction to Biblical Hebrew*, 30.5.1b.
495. Waltke and O'Connor, 30.2.1b.

the Lord that day, he would be קָצַף "angry" with them the following day – figuratively meaning soon after the offence was done. The rebellion would have been the building of an altar other than that of the Lord, as Lewis Hawk has noted, "the land west of the Jordan is YHWH's land, the site of YHWH's tabernacle. In addition, by implication, only those inhabiting the land are the people. By refusing to live in Canaan, the two and one-half tribes (in their view) demonstrated their intent to be other-than-Israel. Thus, when the easterners constructed the altar, they seemed to confirm this point of view, for the altar at the Jordan represented an alternative to the altar."[496] Therefore, they were allowed to construct their altar as long as it was not an altar for the worship of idols.

This verse begins with a conjunction וְ, which is introducing a conditional clause[497] hence its translation as "if." The first part, the protasis, is as follows: וְאַתֶּם תָּשֻׁבוּ הַיּוֹם מֵאַחֲרֵי יְהוָה וְהָיָה אַתֶּם תִּמְרְדוּ הַיּוֹם בַּיהוָה "If today you turn away from following the Lord, by becoming rebellious against him." The first verb of this clause is תָּשֻׁבוּ "turn away" which is an ingressive perfective,[498] warning them against starting to turn away from the Lord. The verb שׁוּב is used in this verse to mean to apostatize, that is, abandoning their spiritual relationship with God.[499] The independent personal pronoun אַתֶּם "you" has an emphatic function,[500] emphasizing the subject, since its syntactical function of being the subject is already represented by the affix attached to תָּשֻׁבוּ. This conditional clause captures the period of the beginning of this action by stating that הַיּוֹם "today" is a metonymy of the adjunct, a sign for the thing signified.[501] In this case, "today" signifies "soon," that is, as soon as they turn away from the Lord, then the Lord will be angry with them. The turning away is complemented by the preposition מֵאַחֲרֵי "from following" which carries the force of the two combined prepositions[502] to show that they stopped their allegiance to God. The means through which this can happen is by the means of אַתֶּם תִּמְרְדוּ הַיּוֹם בַּיהוָה, "you become rebellious against him." The

---

496. Hawk, *Joshua*, 240.
497. Arnold and Choi, *Guide to Biblical Hebrew*, 4.3.3f.
498. Gibson, *Davidson's Introductory Hebrew Grammar*, 57 Rem. 2.
499. BDB, 997d.
500. Seow, *Grammar for Biblical Hebrew*, 93.
501. Bullinger, *Figures of Speech*, 603.
502. Arnold and Choi, *Guide to Biblical Hebrew*, 4.1.13i.

verb תִּמְרְדוּ "you become rebellious" is an incipient present non-perfective which is a warning against beginning and continuing to be rebellious. The noun הַיּוֹם "today" is left untranslated, for idiomatic purposes, since its sense in the verse is already contained in its first usage in the verse although it is repeated with an emphatic function – meaning as soon as the sin is committed then punishment will follow. The rebellion is בַּיהוָה "against the Lord." In this case, the preposition בְּ, is used, which has an adversative function,[503] meaning "against."

The apodosis is וּמָחָר אֶל־כָּל־עֲדַת יִשְׂרָאֵל יִקְצֹף "then tomorrow he will be angry against the whole community of Israel." The ו conjunction has a conjunctive sequence function[504] hence its translation as "then." The verb of this last clause is יִקְצֹף "he will be angry" which is a specific future non-perfective[505] since it has certainty that it will happen. The Lord's anger is directed אֶל־כָּל־עֲדַת יִשְׂרָאֵל "against all the community of Israel" which is marked by the preposition אֶל. This preposition has an estimative function of disadvantage[506] since they will be objects of God's anger. The effect of God being קָצַף "angry" would have been death (v. 20).

In this verse, the focus of the קָצַף verb in its qal stem is the Ego who is superior to the landmark. A reminder of what happened during Achan's sin (v. 20) is an indication that if they turned away from God then punishment would be imminent. The next example considered in this category in which the focus of קָצַף is the Ego is in Ecclesiastes 5:5[6].

37. Eccl 5:5[6]

אַל־תִּתֵּן אֶת־פִּיךָ לַחֲטִיא אֶת־בְּשָׂרֶךָ וְאַל־תֹּאמַר לִפְנֵי הַמַּלְאָךְ כִּי שְׁגָגָה הִיא לָמָּה יִקְצֹף הָאֱלֹהִים עַל־קוֹלֶךָ וְחִבֵּל אֶת־מַעֲשֵׂה יָדֶיךָ:

Do not let your speech cause you to sin, and do not say in the presence of his messenger, "it was a mistake." Why should God be angry because of your words and destroy the works of your hands?

---

503. Arnold and Choi, 4.1.5d.
504. Seow, *Grammar for Biblical Hebrew*, 285.
505. Gibson, *Davidson's Introductory Hebrew Grammar*, 64a.
506. Arnold and Choi, *Guide to Biblical Hebrew*, 4.1.1b.

The author in this passage gives advice to anyone who would like to make a vow to God. Such a person should be careful to honor whatever she/he vows to God. Failure to honor it would cause God to become קָצַף "angry" and destroy the work of their hands – which is a focus on the retributive result of קצף (in both its verbal and noun forms) as earlier stated. Such an act of vowing and not fulfilling one's vows is seen as a mockery to God who values truth. That act "could never pass by with impunity."[507] Breaking of a vow made the vow maker guilty of sin (Num 30:2; 30:1–16; Deut 23:21–23).

This verse begins with אַל־תִּתֵּן אֶת־פִּיךָ לַחֲטִיא "do not let your speech cause you to sin," which is a jussive of prohibition.[508] The object of the verb is אֶת־פִּיךָ "your speech" although its literal translation is "your mouth." However, it is a metonymy of cause representing an instrument for the thing effected by it,[509] meaning "your speech" since the speech comes from the mouth. The reason for this exhortation on speech is so that it will not lead the one making a vow לַחֲטִיא "to sin." It has a causative function[510] because it is in the hiphil stem. The object of the infinitive אֶת־בְּשָׂרֶךָ "your flesh" is a synecdoche of the part for the whole,[511] meaning the whole person.

In addition to heeding this vow, the vow maker had to pay attention to the second prohibition: וְאַל־תֹּאמַר לִפְנֵי הַמַּלְאָךְ כִּי שְׁגָגָה הִיא "and do not say in the presence of his messenger it (was) a mistake." The construction וְאַל־תֹּאמַר "do not say" is used to forbid a specific action – what should not be said. The manner of this prohibition is that it should not be said לִפְנֵי הַמַּלְאָךְ "in the presence of the messenger" who has a definite article of a well-known person[512] – probably the priest since the setting is in the house of God (v. 1). The vow maker is warned against saying that כִּי שְׁגָגָה הִיא "it (was) a mistake." The כִּי in this phrase is introducing direct speech.[513]

After these prohibitive statements, the author ends the verse with a rhetorical question: לָמָּה יִקְצֹף הָאֱלֹהִים עַל־קוֹלֶךָ וְחִבֵּל אֶת־מַעֲשֵׂה יָדֶיךָ "Why should God become angry because of your words and destroy the works of your

---

507. Bridges, *Book of Ecclesiastes*, 109.
508. Van der Merwe, Naudé, and Kroeze, *Biblical Hebrew Reference Grammar*, 152.
509. Bullinger, *Figures of Speech*, 545.
510. Seow, *Grammar for Biblical Hebrew*, 181.
511. Bullinger, *Figures of Speech*, 640.
512. Gesenius, *Gesenius' Hebrew Grammar*, 126d.
513. Seow, *Grammar for Biblical Hebrew*, 332.

hands?" The first verb of this rhetorical question יִקְצֹף "become angry" is an incipient present non-perfective,[514] denoting the beginning and continuation of an action. The reason why God would became angry is עַל־קוֹלֶךָ "because of your words," marked by a preposition עַל, which has a causal function.[515] If this happens and God becomes קָצַף "angry," the result would be to וְחִבֵּל אֶת־מַעֲשֵׂה יָדֶיךָ "and destroy the work of your hands." The verb of this clause is חִבֵּל "destroy," is incipient present non-perfective[516] just like the verb קָצַף mentioned above. The object of the verb is "work" in this phrase אֶת־מַעֲשֵׂה יָדֶיךָ "the work of your hands" while "of hands" is a genitive of product, meaning the work which is a product of your efforts.[517] Of course, "hands" is a synecdoche of the part for the whole, meaning the whole person.[518]

This verse has explained that the focus of the קָצַף verb in the qal stem is the Ego who is superior to the landmark. In addition, the details of this verse affirm an argument in this research that קָצַף and קֶצֶף have a retributive effect, whether actualized or intended. The other passage where God is the Ego and the Israelites are the landmark of קָצַף is in Zechariah 1:2.

38. Zech 1:2

קָצַף יְהוָה עַל־אֲבוֹתֵיכֶם קָצֶף׃

The Lord was very angry (angry with anger) with your ancestors.

The context of this verse is a reminder to the Israelites of how God was קָצַף "angry" and handed over their forefathers to the exile (2 Chr 36:15–21) and allowed the Babylonians to destroy Jerusalem in 586 BC. The aim of this reminder is so that the postexilic Hebrews might return to their God (v. 3) and be different from their ancestors (v. 4) who had mocked God's messengers, despised their words and scoffed at the prophets (2 Chr 36:15–16). As a result, God sent the Babylonians who killed scores and took others to captivity (2 Chr 36:17). By implication, if they were to follow the example of their ancestors, the same fate would befall them.

---

514. Waltke and O'Connor, *Introduction to Biblical Hebrew*, 31.3d.
515. Waltke and O'Connor, 31.3d.
516. Chisholm, *From Exegesis to Exposition*, 92–93.
517. Van der Merwe, Naudé, and Kroeze, *Biblical Hebrew Reference Grammar*, 199.
518. Bullinger, *Figures of Speech*, 640.

Zechariah 1:2 begins with קָצַף "angry" which is a definite past perfective denoting an action that took place in the past.[519] The object of this verb is קֶצֶף "anger" which is a cognate internal accusative,[520] meaning "I was angry with anger" hence its translation as "very angry." This usage shows how strong the emotion was since cognate internal accusatives sometimes are used to show how strong (intensity) the action of the verb is.[521] For example, in Psalm 14:5, the phrase פָּחֲדוּ פָחַד "they dreaded with dread" can be translated as "were overwhelmed with dread."[522] This anger was directed toward עַל־אֲבוֹתֵיכֶם "your forefathers." This construction has the preposition עַל which has an adversative function[523] and identifies the landmark as discussed at the opening paragraphs of this chapter. The next verse in which the nations are the landmarks is in Zechariah 1:15.

39. Zech 1:15

וְקֶצֶף גָּדוֹל אֲנִי קֹצֵף עַל־הַגּוֹיִם הַשַּׁאֲנַנִּים אֲשֶׁר אֲנִי קָצַפְתִּי מְעָט וְהֵמָּה עָזְרוּ לְרָעָה:

But I am קֹצֵף "being angry" with great קֶצֶף "anger" with the complacent nations; when I was only a little קָצַף angry, they compounded the disaster.

The message in Zechariah 1:15 is in contrast with the content in verse 14 in which God says he is jealous for Jerusalem and Zion. As for the nations, God was very angry קצף with them citing that they felt secure – which was a security based on being used in the past by God as his agents to punish the Israelites for their sins. Their false sense of security was based on the failure to realize that they too had sinned against God and their time of judgment is coming. The result of God's קצף on the nations would be a military defeat and destruction (vv. 18–21).

Just like the reference in Jeremiah 50:13, this verse begins in a non-conventional way, not in the verb-subject-object form. The construction וְקֶצֶף גָּדוֹל אֲנִי קֹצֵף can be translated as "I am angry with great anger." The

---

519. Waltke and O'Connor, *Introduction to Biblical Hebrew*, 30.5.1b.
520. Gibson, *Davidson's Introductory Hebrew Grammar*, 93.
521. Van der Merwe, Naudé, and Kroeze, *Biblical Hebrew Reference Grammar*, 45.
522. Waltke and O'Connor, *Introduction to Biblical Hebrew*, 10.2.1g.
523. Arnold and Choi, *Guide to Biblical Hebrew*, 4.1.16f.

קֹצֵף "angry" participle has a verbal function[524] with the personal pronoun אֲנִי "I" being the subject, hence the translation "I am angry." The noun קֶצֶף is a cognate internal accusative[525] which means "I am exceedingly angry." This understanding means that the entire phrase וְקֶצֶף גָּדוֹל אֲנִי קֹצֵף "I am exceedingly angry" has the subject and the verb is complemented by the prepositional phrase עַל־הַגּוֹיִם הַשַּׁאֲנַנִּים "with the complacent nations." The preposition עַל has an adversative function,[526] meaning this anger is directed against the object הַגּוֹיִם "the nations." The reason why God is וְקֶצֶף גָּדוֹל אֲנִי קֹצֵף "exceedingly angry" is explained in the last clause of the verse.

The last clause says אֲשֶׁר אֲנִי קָצַפְתִּי מְּעָט וְהֵמָּה עָזְרוּ לְרָעָה "when I was only a little angry, they [the nations] compounded the punishment." The verb of the first part of this clause is קָצַפְתִּי "I was angry" which is a definite past perfective[527] denoting an action that took place once in the past. This anger is qualified further by the מְעָט, "little" referring to the degree of the emotion[528] that is functioning like an adverb, meaning "a little angry." In this verse, the phrase "a little angry" is contrasted with "I was exceedingly angry" as mentioned at the beginning of the verse. The adverb מְעָט indicates that קֶצֶף was a strong emotion but with varying degrees. In both phrases, the personal pronoun אֲנִי is the subject, which is anaphoric referring to God (v. 14). The author uses it here presumably because he is introducing a different characteristic of God, being a little angry, as opposed to the preceding phrase where God is exceedingly angry.

The next phrase begins with the subject personal pronoun וְהֵמָּה "they." The personal pronoun is used for emphatic purposes,[529] emphasizing the subject, since its sense is captured in the affix in the verb עָזְרוּ "they compounded" which is a telic perfective, meaning God is looking at the end of their actions which are making punishment severe. They made it severe by oppressing the Israelites (Jer 25:8–9, 12–13; 50:11, 31–32). This is the only reference in which וְקֶצֶף גָּדוֹל "great anger" is used with the landmark being the nations. While

---

524. Seow, *Grammar for Biblical Hebrew*, 81.
525. Gibson, *Davidson's Introductory Hebrew Grammar*, 93.
526. Arnold and Choi, *Guide to Biblical Hebrew*, 4.1.16f.
527. Waltke and O'Connor, *Introduction to Biblical Hebrew*, 30.1d.
528. BDB, 590a.
529. Seow, *Grammar for Biblical Hebrew*, 93.

וְקֶצֶף גָּדוֹל] against the Israelites was caused by idolatry, in this reference it was caused by undue oppression against God's people.

The section 3.2.4.1 above has examined the verses in which God is the subject of the קָצַף verbal forms in the qal stem. This section has ascertained the vertical relationship of Ego and landmark since the Ego is a superior and was קָצַף "angry" against a subordinate. The following section deals with the hiphil stem of קָצַף. The meaning of the קָצַף changes with the stem. While in the qal stem the usage was a superior being angry against a subordinate, in the hiphil stem it is a subordinate provoking a superior. The following examples demonstrate this argument.

3.2.4.2 In the Hiphil Stem of קָצַף God Is the Affected Object: Inferior Provoking Superior

Here are the examples that show that קָצַף in the hiphil stem means that a subordinate is provoking a superior. In the examples given, God is the affected object of the verb. The first example to be considered is in Deuteronomy 9:7.

40. Deut 9:7

זְכֹר אַל־תִּשְׁכַּח אֵת אֲשֶׁר־הִקְצַפְתָּ אֶת־יְהוָה אֱלֹהֶיךָ בַּמִּדְבָּר לְמִן־הַיּוֹם אֲשֶׁר־יָצָאתָ מֵאֶרֶץ מִצְרַיִם עַד־בֹּאֲכֶם עַד־הַמָּקוֹם הַזֶּה מַמְרִים הֱיִיתֶם עִם־יְהוָה׃

> Remember and do not forget how you provoked to anger, הִקְ־צַפְתָּ, the Lord, your God, in the wilderness. Because from the day when you left the land of Egypt until you came to this place you have been rebellious against the Lord.

The context of this verse is about the instructions that God was giving the Israelites before they crossed the River Jordan to enter Canaan (v. 1). God promised them that he would go ahead of them and subdue the enemy (v. 3). He then reminded them that he was not giving them the land because of their righteousness but because the nations he was driving out were wicked (vv. 4–6). In verse 7, the Israelites had angered God before.

Deuteronomy 9:7 begins with the verb זְכֹר "remember" which is an imperative of command[530] since the context indicates that God did not want

---

530. Van der Merwe, Naudé, and Kroeze, *Biblical Hebrew Reference Grammar*, 151.

a repeat of the sin. The second verb that follows is אַל־תִּשְׁכַּח "do not forget" which is an exhortation[531] to the Israelites not to forget what happened in the past.

The object of these two verbs is אֵת אֲשֶׁר־הִקְצַפְתָּ "how you provoked to anger, הִקְצַפְתָּ." With this translation, the focus is not on the Lord but on the action, which leads to the Lord being provoked. The verb הִקְצַפְתָּ "you provoked to anger" has a causative function[532] and has a definite past perfective function[533] since it took place in the past, in the wilderness. The object of this verb is אֶת־יְהוָה אֱלֹהֶיךָ "the Lord your God" which is a direct object accusative[534] since it is already marked by a direct object marker. The result of this provocation was intended retribution (v. 8). Since God is the object of קצף, the Ego, the subject (Israelites) in this case is an inferior provoking a superior. The argument in this research is that when קצף is in the hiphil stem, its usage shows an inferior provoking a superior. This provocation happened while they were בַּמִּדְבָּר "in the wilderness." This word has a preposition בְּ, which has a spatial function[535] indicating the locality in which the action of the verb took place.

In the last clause of this sentence, the author clearly demonstrates that his main focus is on the Israelites' rebellious attitude and sinfulness as he reminded them that לְמִן־הַיּוֹם אֲשֶׁר־יָצָאתָ מֵאֶרֶץ מִצְרַיִם עַד־בֹּאֲכֶם עַד־הַמָּקוֹם הַזֶּה מַמְרִים הֱיִיתֶם עִם־יְהוָה: "because, from the day when you left the land of Egypt until you came to this place, you have been rebellious toward the Lord." Throughout their journey, their rebellious attitude persisted as the author notes עַד־בֹּאֲכֶם עַד־הַמָּקוֹם הַזֶּה "until you came to this place." The construction עַד־בֹּאֲכֶם "until you came" is an infinite construct with a temporal use,[536] indicating lapse of time. The destination, at the time of speaking, of their movement is עַד־הַמָּקוֹם הַזֶּה "to this place" which can literally be translated as "as far as this place." While in the first construction the preposition עַד is understood to mean "until," in this second usage it has the sense of "as far

---

531. Waltke and O'Connor, *Introduction to Biblical Hebrew*, 34.3b.
532. Seow, *Grammar for Biblical Hebrew*, 181.
533. Waltke and O'Connor, *Introduction to Biblical Hebrew*, 30.5.1b.
534. Chisholm, *From Exegesis to Exposition*, 64.
535. Arnold and Choi, *Guide to Biblical Hebrew*, 4.1.5a.
536. Chisholm, *From Exegesis to Exposition*, 78.

as" which has guided its translation as simple "to" because it has a locative function indicating the extent of the movement.⁵³⁷

During the period of the entire journey, the author describes the Israelites' negative character by saying מַמְרִים הֱיִיתֶם עִם־יְהוָה "you have been rebellious against the Lord." The participle מַמְרִים "rebellious" has a predicate function.⁵³⁸ The verb הֱיִיתֶם "you have been" is a persistent perfective,⁵³⁹ meaning the rebellion started in the past and has continued to the present. The rebellion is עִם־יְהוָה "against the Lord" with the preposition עִם which has a meaning of "against."⁵⁴⁰ The way this verse ends further affirms the position taken at the beginning of this verse, which stated that the focus of the author by the use of the הִקְצַפְתָּ hiphil form draws the reader to focus on the action of provocation. The second example in which the same hiphil form is used is in Deuteronomy 9:8.

41. Deut 9:8

וּבְחֹרֵב הִקְצַפְתֶּם אֶת־יְהוָה וַיִּתְאַנַּף יְהוָה בָּכֶם לְהַשְׁמִיד אֶתְכֶם׃

Also at Horeb you so provoked to anger the Lord and he became angry with you to destroy you (to the extent of destroying you).

This verse is in the same context as the previous one, and it serves to remind the Israelites about their sinfulness. This verse begins with וּבְחֹרֵב "also, at Horeb" which has a ו which is translated as "also" since the verse is subordinate⁵⁴¹ to the previous one, verse 7. The preposition בְ, which is prefixed to this noun, has a spatial function indicating locality⁵⁴² hence its translation as "at." The verb of this first clause is הִקְצַפְתֶּם "you provoked to anger the Lord." This verb, as the one discussed in the previous verse, is in the hiphil stem with a causative function.⁵⁴³ The affected object is God as indicated by a direct object marker אֶת־יְהוָה "the Lord."⁵⁴⁴

---

537. Arnold and Choi, *Guide to Biblical Hebrew*, 4.1.15a.
538. Waltke and O'Connor, *Introduction to Biblical Hebrew*, 37.6b.
539. Waltke and O'Connor, 30.5.1c.
540. Clines, "עִם," *DCH*, 6:459.
541. BDB, 253a.
542. Arnold and Choi, *Guide to Biblical Hebrew*, 4.1.5a.
543. Seow, *Grammar for Biblical Hebrew*, 181.
544. Chisholm, *From Exegesis to Exposition*, 64.

After explaining about the provocation, the author uses another Hebrew word, which has a sense of anger, וַיִּתְאַנַּף "and he became angry." This verb is in the hithpael stem with a factive function[545] since the author is indicating the state that God was in – angry. This understanding is supported by the already mentioned meaning of אָנַף in section 3.1.1, which can mean "reddening of face," hence a visible characteristic of anger. The author further adds לְהַשְׁמִיד אֶתְכֶם "to destroy you," which is an object of the לְ preposition and was the intended retribution. The next occurrence in which the hiphil stem is used is in Deuteronomy 9:22.

42. Deut 9:22

וּבְתַבְעֵרָה וּבְמַסָּה וּבְקִבְרֹת הַתַּאֲוָה מַקְצִפִים הֱיִיתֶם אֶת־יְהוָה׃

Likewise at Taberah, at Massah, and at Kibroth-hattaavah you were the ones provoking to anger the Lord.

The message of reminding the Israelites is maintained throughout this chapter. In Deuteronomy 9:22, the author gives a summary of places which mark specific areas in which they provoked their God. He gives a list of three places: וּבְתַבְעֵרָה וּבְמַסָּה וּבְקִבְרֹת הַתַּאֲוָה "At Taberah, at Massah, and at Kibroth-hattaavah." Each of these places has a conjunction וְ which has an inclusive function,[546] hence its translation as "likewise" at the beginning. Although the understanding is that all those conjunctions have the same sense, only the first one is translated for the purposes of maintaining an idiomatic translation. Equally, they all have a preposition בְ which has a spatial function[547] indicating the locality, hence its translation as "at." At Taberah they complained about hardships in the desert (Num 11:1), at Massah they questioned if God was still with them (Deut 6:16; 33:8; Exod 17:7) and at Kibroth-hattaayah they complained about manna and craved for other kinds of food (Num 11:4, 20). The first verb of this verse is מַקְצִפִים "the ones provoking" which, like the previously discussed forms, has a causative function.[548] The addition of הֱיִיתֶם "you were" after the above participle has an emphatic effect – drawing the attention of the reader to the culprit – on the doer, the one who did the

---

545. Waltke and O'Connor, *Introduction to Biblical Hebrew*, 26.2b.
546. Köhler and Baumgartner, "וְ," *HALOT*, 1:258.
547. Arnold and Choi, *Guide to Biblical Hebrew*, 4.1.5a.
548. Seow, *Grammar for Biblical Hebrew*, 181.

provoking. The object of this verb is אֶת־יְהוָה "the Lord" who is the accusative of the direct of object.[549] The result of this provocation was punishment by death (Num 11:34). Like the passages already discussed above, the focus in this verse is the antecedent entity – the one provoking. Another passage in which קָצַף is used in the hiphil stem is Psalm 106:32.

43. Ps 106:32

וַיַּקְצִיפוּ עַל־מֵי מְרִיבָה They provoked to anger (the Lord) at the waters of Meribah

לְמֹשֶׁה בַּעֲבוּרָם וַיֵּרַע and Moses was offended for their sake.

This verse is a reminder of how the Israelites sinned against their God at the waters of Meribah. At this place, they grumbled against the Lord and questioned his presence in their midst (Num 20:1–13). In the immediate context of verse 32, we find several verbs in the hiphil stem, which have a causative sense placing the blame for God's action on the Israelites. For example in verse 29 the psalmist said, וַיַּכְעִיסוּ בְּמַעַלְלֵיהֶם וַתִּפְרָץ־בָּם מַגֵּפָה "they provoked to anger (the Lord) by their wicked deeds, and a plague broke out among them." And in verse 33 he said, כִּי־הִמְרוּ אֶת־רוּחוֹ וַיְבַטֵּא בִּשְׂפָתָיו "because they provoked God's Spirit and Moses spoke recklessly with his lips." Just as in Deuteronomy 9, the focus in this psalm is on the evil deeds of the Israelites.

The verb of the first clause in Psalm 106:32 is וַיַּקְצִיפוּ "they provoked to anger," which has a causative function.[550] It also is a definite past perfective[551] since it took place in the past. The object of the verb is not stated in the verse but according to the context, the object is "the Lord." The author further explains where this took place עַל־מֵי מְרִיבָה "at the waters of Meribah." In addition to provoking the Lord, their action also affected Moses as is explained in the second clause.

The second clause states that וַיֵּרַע לְמֹשֶׁה בַּעֲבוּרָם "and Moses was offended for their sake." The verb of this clause וַיֵּרַע "was offended" is a definite past perfective, denoting an action that took place once in the past. The cause of Moses's trouble was the constant grumbling of the Israelites. This cause is captured in the word בַּעֲבוּרָם "for their sake" which has a preposition בְּ which

---

549. Chisholm, *From Exegesis to Exposition*, 64.
550. Seow, *Grammar for Biblical Hebrew*, 181.
551. Waltke and O'Connor, *Introduction to Biblical Hebrew*, 30.5.1b.

has a causal function.⁵⁵² This causal function has a sense of "disadvantage" meaning since the noun עֲבוּר has the sense of "on account of uncleanness."⁵⁵³ The noun עֲבוּר is used with this same meaning in Psalm 132:10. The result of this provocation was that Moses beat the rock instead of talking to it and as a result he died, and Aaron too (Num 20:24; 27:12–14).

The last reference in which קָצַף is used in the hiphil stem is Zechariah 8:14.

44. Zech 8:14

כִּי כֹה אָמַר יְהוָה צְבָאוֹת כַּאֲשֶׁר זָמַמְתִּי לְהָרַע לָכֶם בְּהַקְצִיף אֲבֹתֵיכֶם אֹתִי אָמַר יְהוָה צְבָאוֹת וְלֹא נִחָמְתִּי׃

> This is what the Lord of hosts says: "Just as I had determined to injure you when your ancestors angered me," says the Lord of hosts, and I had no compassion.

The context of this passage is that of a reminder to the Israelites that God showed no pity to their ancestors when they angered him, by implied sin, and the consequence was life in captivity (Jer 50:17–18; 51:8; Isa 21:9). This verse precedes an assurance in verse 15 about God doing good and restoring the Israelites. The main message in this passage is the assurance of God's certainty in doing that which he has intended to do. That is, the certainty with which God's judgment happened in the past, by bringing disaster to the Israelites when they angered him, is the same certainty with which he guarantees the fulfillment of his promise of restoring them.⁵⁵⁴

This verse begins with the conjunction כִּי which has an evidential function,⁵⁵⁵ hence its translation as "this is" because it is drawing attention to the evidence of the content of the preceding verse, which has an assurance of their restoration. This evidential function of כִּי is supported by the phrase אָמַר יְהוָה צְבָאוֹת "the Lord of hosts says." The syntactical function of this phrase has been discussed before in section 3.1.1.1 (4) although it is worth noting that it is used twice in this verse. The content of what the Lord is saying is introduced by a relative clause כַּאֲשֶׁר "just as" because it is comparing what the Lord says in this verse and what he says in the next, verse 15, which is

---

552. Köhler and Baumgartner, *HALOT*, 1:104.
553. BDB, 721a.
554. Smith, *Micah–Malachi*, 237.
555. Arnold and Choi, *Guide to Biblical Hebrew*, 4.3.4b.

an assurance that he will be favorable to them. The first verb of the relative clause is זָמַמְתִּי "I had determined" which is a past perfective[556] denoting a past action antecedent to another past action, which is discussed in the following paragraph. What the Lord had determined to do was לְהָרַע לָכֶם "to injure you," which is an object of the לְ preposition.

The time when the Lord had determined to do this was בְּהַקְצִיף אֲבֹתֵיכֶם אֹתִי "when your ancestors angered me." This clause begins with a preposition בְּ, which has a temporal function,[557] indicating a time when something took place and hence its translation as "when." The verb of this clause is הַקְצִיף "angered," which is a hiphil infinitive construct, which, because of the preposition בְּ, has a temporal clause function.[558] The object of the verb is אֹתִי "me," which accords with other usages under section 3.2.4.2 showing that the verb קָצַף "angry" in its hiphil stem, takes God as the object. To prove that when the Lord was קָצַף "angry" his anger led to retribution, he added וְלֹא נִחָמְתִּי "and I had no compassion" which is definite past perfective,[559] meaning God punished them. In this passage, just like the others discussed above, the focus is the antecedent entity – the provoking ones.

The passages discussed in this category are in the hiphil stem with God as the direct object of the verb. The discussions so far have explained that קָצַף "to be angry" when used with an inferior and being directed to a superior, meant the inferior is provoking the superior. In addition, the focus of the hiphil stem has been the antecedent element, identifying what caused Ego to be קָצַף "angry." The diagram below illustrates this.

---

556. Gibson, *Davidson's Introductory Hebrew Grammar*, 58a.
557. Arnold and Choi, *Guide to Biblical Hebrew*, 4.1.5b.
558. Waltke and O'Connor, *Introduction to Biblical Hebrew*, 36.2.3d.
559. Waltke and O'Connor, 30.5.1b.

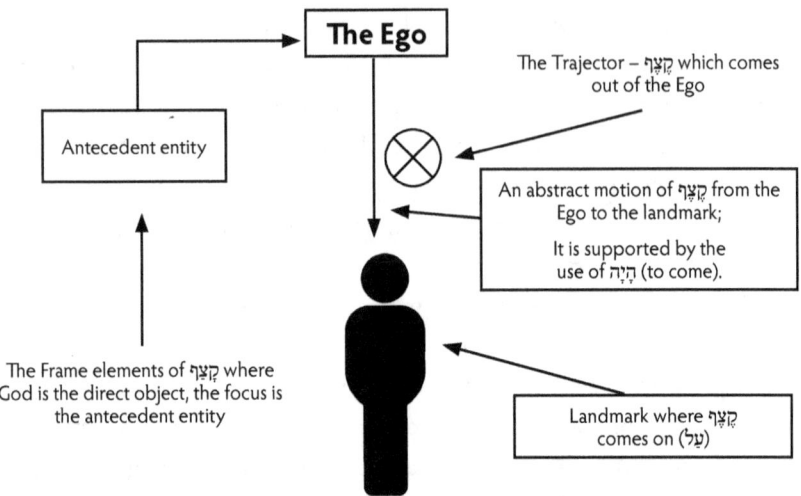

Chart 6

The following section focuses on the verbal forms of קָצַף in the qal stem in references where human is the Ego. The discussion in the following passages demonstrates that the one being קָצַף "angry" was a superior to a subordinate and, therefore, supports the argument that קָצַף has a vertical relation function.

3.2.5 The Verbal Form of קָצַף: Human Is the Ego

This section examines the passages where קָצַף occurs in its verbal form with humans as the Ego. The section is divided into three main categories: Individuals (superior to landmark) as the Ego, individuals (inferior to landmark) as the Ego and groups as the Ego. The first category below is on individuals as the Ego of קָצַף, a superior to a subordinate.

3.2.5.1 Individuals as the Ego of קָצַף: Superior to Subordinate

The individuals discussed in this subsection are Pharaoh, Moses, Elisha and King Xerxes. The examples examined in this subsection will show that, first, קָצַף in the qal stem shows a vertical relationship of a superior being angry at a subordinate (Gen 40:2; 41:10; Exod 16:20; Lev 10:16; Num 31:14; 2 Kgs 13:19; Esth 1:12). Second, קָצַף in the qal stem without contextual and grammatical cues distinguishing who is superior or subordinate has the meaning of frustration (2 Kgs 5:11). Third, קָצַף in the hithpael stem indicates that a subordinate is angry with a superior. The only occurrence in which a subordinate is angry with a superior can be found in Isaiah 8:21. The following section begins with the examination of קָצַף in the qal stem showing the vertical relationship. The first reference concerns Pharaoh.

3.2.5.1.1 Pharaoh as the Ego

Pharaoh is mentioned as the Ego who was קָצַף "angry" in two verses. The two references are as follows:

45. Gen 40:2

וַיִּקְצֹף פַּרְעֹה עַל שְׁנֵי סָרִיסָיו עַל שַׂר הַמַּשְׁקִים וְעַל שַׂר הָאוֹפִים:

Pharaoh became angry with his two officials, the chief cupbearer and the chief baker.

Twice Pharaoh is the Ego of קָצַף as recorded in Genesis 40:2 and Genesis 41:10. In these two occurrences of קָצַף, the servants of Pharaoh, the cupbearer and the baker, are the landmarks. Acting out of being קָצַף Pharaoh sent both of them to prison. Their crime is unspecified; only the consequence of the Pharaoh's anger is mentioned. The leadership role of Pharaoh is made manifest by the use of "the king of Egypt" as indicated in Genesis 40:1, which says, "Some time later, the cupbearer and the baker of the king of Egypt offended their master, the king of Egypt" (NIV). Keeping with the same choice of words, the writer uses the titles "cupbearer" and "baker" instead of their real names. This choice of words puts focus on the professions of the characters in this story. Taking note of this usage, Claus Westermann says, "It is obviously deliberate on the part of the writer when he twice uses 'king of Egypt' instead of 'pharaoh' and calls the officials simply 'cupbearer' and 'baker.'"[560] This passage presents a scenario in which a superior is being קָצַף "angry" with his servants.

The verb of this verse is וַיִּקְצֹף "he became angry" which is an ingressive perfective[561] denoting the beginning of the action. This understanding is informed by verse 1, which talks about the servants offending the king. The people offending the king are identified by the prepositional phrase עַל שְׁנֵי סָרִיסָיו "with his two officials" which literally means "two of officials of

---

560. Westermann, *Genesis 37–50*, 73.
561. Gibson, *Davidson's Introductory Hebrew Grammar*, 57 Rem. 2.

him." The construction שְׁנֵי סָרִיסָי "two of his officials" is a genitive measure[562] since they socially relate as master and servant. The two officials are explained further as עַל שַׂר הַמַּשְׁקִים וְעַל שַׂר הָאוֹפִים "with the chief cupbearer and the chief baker." Although the object of the verb has already been identified with the preposition עַל, each of the servants is again identified by the same preposition and is left untranslated. The construction has two genitives and both are genitives of characteristic,[563] meaning the cupbearer and the baker bear the characteristics of being chiefs.

In the second example, which is found in Genesis 41:10, Pharaoh is again the Ego of being קָצַף "angry."

46. Gen 41:10

פַּרְעֹה קָצַף עַל־עֲבָדָיו וַיִּתֵּן אֹתִי בְּמִשְׁמַר בֵּית שַׂר הַטַּבָּחִים אֹתִי וְאֵת שַׂר הָאֹפִים:

Pharaoh was (once) angry with his servants; he put me in custody in the house of the chief steward, me and the chief baker.

This verse begins with the subject of the verb, פַּרְעֹה "Pharaoh." The verb of the first part of the sentence is קָצַף, which is a simple past perfective.[564] The adverb "once" is added in translation since it is a reference to Genesis 40:2. The persons to whom the anger of Pharaoh is directed are marked by a prepositional phrase עַל־עֲבָדָיו "with his servants" which has a preposition עַל which has an adversative function[565] and is translated as "with."

Because he was קָצַף "angry," he וַיִּתֵּן "put" his servants into custody. The verb וַיִּתֵּן "he put" is a telic perfective[566] since its focus is on the result of his anger. The object of this verb is אֹתִי "me" which contextually refers to the cupbearer (v. 9). He goes further to describe the place he was confined in בְּמִשְׁמַר בֵּית שַׂר הַטַּבָּחִים "in custody in the house of the chief steward." This phrase has a preposition בְּ, which has a spatial function[567] denoting the locality. That is why it is translated as "in." The locality was בֵּית "house of" which

---

562. Arnold and Choi, *Guide to Biblical Hebrew*, 2.2.11.
563. Arnold and Choi, 2.2.11.
564. Chisholm, *From Exegesis to Exposition*, 86, 95.
565. Arnold and Choi, *Guide to Biblical Hebrew*, 4.1.16f.
566. Waltke and O'Connor, *Introduction to Biblical Hebrew*, 30.2.1d.
567. Arnold and Choi, *Guide to Biblical Hebrew*, 4.1.5a.

belonged to the chief steward. The הַטַּבָּחִים "the chief steward" has a definite article of a unique referent.[568] The last clause repeats the object, אֹתִי "me," for anaphoric referring to chief butler[569] but the וְאֵת שַׂר הָאֹפִים "chief baker" is introduced for the first time in this verse.

These two verses – Genesis 40:2 and Genesis 41:10 (and the latter is referring back to Genesis 40:2) – are the only references in which Pharaoh is the Ego who was קָצַף "angry," and both demonstrate a vertical relational function in which the Ego is superior to the landmark. In addition, the punishment by imprisonment was involved. The following verses concern Moses as the Ego.

3.2.5.1.2 Moses as the Ego

Three times Moses is mentioned as the Ego who was קָצַף "angry": Exodus 16:20, Leviticus 10:16 and Numbers 31:14.

47. Exod 16:20

וְלֹא־שָׁמְעוּ אֶל־מֹשֶׁה וַיּוֹתִרוּ אֲנָשִׁים מִמֶּנּוּ עַד־בֹּקֶר וַיָּרֻם תּוֹלָעִים וַיִּבְאַשׁ וַיִּקְצֹף עֲלֵהֶם מֹשֶׁה׃

But they did not obey Moses, instead (some) people kept a part of it over until morning, and it became wormy and stank. Therefore, Moses was angry with them.

In this passage, Moses was provoked by the Israelites and he became קָצַף "angry" because the Israelites disobeyed him and gathered more food than they needed, keeping it for the following day. In the morning, it had maggots and it was stinking. This manna was a one-day meal, which had to be eaten the day it was gathered; otherwise, it became rotten and infested with worms. The manna was to be gathered in the morning before the sun warmed it enough to melt it (Exod 16:21). Because of the disobedience, Moses was קָצַף "angry."

What the Israelites did instead of obeying Moses was וַיּוֹתִרוּ אֲנָשִׁים מִמֶּנּוּ עַד־בֹּקֶר "instead (some) people kept a part of it over until morning." The conjunction וְ has a motive function[570] hence the translation "instead." The verb in this clause is וַיּוֹתִרוּ "they kept" which is a definite past perfective[571] since the

---

568. Gesenius, *Gesenius' Hebrew Grammar*, 126d–e.
569. Seow, *Grammar for Biblical Hebrew*, 93.
570. Köhler and Baumgartner, "וְ," *HALOT*, 1:510.
571. Waltke and O'Connor, *Introduction to Biblical Hebrew*, 30.5.1b.

context explains that the keeping lasted until the following day. The subject of the verb is אֲנָשִׁים "(some) people."[572] These people kept part of the manna since the compound preposition מִמֶּנּוּ "some of it" has a partitive function.[573] The last construction of this clause complements the verb וַיּוֹתִרוּ "they kept" in that it tells us for how long the keeping was. It was עַד־בֹּקֶר "until morning" because the preposition עַד has a temporal function[574] indicating the duration. After keeping the manna overnight, וַיָּרֻם תּוֹלָעִים וַיִּבְאַשׁ [it] "became wormy and stank."

This kind of act resulted in Moses being קָצַף "angry." The last clause of this verse says וַיִּקְצֹף עֲלֵהֶם מֹשֶׁה "therefore Moses became angry with them." The conjunction וְ is introducing a consequence[575] hence its translation as "therefore." The verb in this clause is וַיִּקְצֹף "he became angry" which is an ingressive perfective, meaning Moses began to be angry after he discovered that they had disobeyed him. The antecedent condition in this passage was disobedience of Moses by the Israelites and by extension, they disobeyed God who had given Moses the instructions (vv. 4–5). The consequence of this disobedience was that the manna went bad (v. 20). In essence, God whom they disobeyed through Moses punished them by allowing the manna to go bad except on the sixth day when they collected enough for the Sabbath.[576] The Ego of קָצַף in this passage is superior to the landmark and therefore supports the argument that קָצַף has a vertical relation function. The second passage where it is recorded that Moses is the Ego who was קָצַף "angry" is in Leviticus 10:16.

48. Lev 10:16

וְאֵת ׀ שְׂעִיר הַחַטָּאת דָּרֹשׁ דָּרַשׁ מֹשֶׁה וְהִנֵּה שֹׂרָף וַיִּקְצֹף עַל־אֶלְעָזָר וְעַל־אִיתָמָר בְּנֵי אַהֲרֹן הַנּוֹתָרִם לֵאמֹר׃

---

572. The translation reads "some people" because the context implies that not everybody disobeyed Moses (v. 27).

573. Seow, *Grammar for Biblical Hebrew*, 74.

574. Arnold and Choi, *Guide to Biblical Hebrew*, 4.1.15a.

575. BDB, 254c.

576. The fact that the manna collected on the sixth day could last until the following day shows it had the potential of not getting bad. The Israelites even kept some for the future generations (v. 13). When it went bad during the other days, it shows that it became inedible as a form of punishment.

When Moses inquired closely about the goat of the purification and behold, he discovered that it had all been burned, he therefore קָצַף "became angry" with the Eleazar and Ithamar, the surviving sons of Aaron, saying...

In this passage, Moses was provoked by Eleazar and Ithamar, and became קָצַף "angry" because they burned the goat of the purification. This goat was supposed to be eaten in the sanctuary area and its blood sprinkled in the holy place (vv. 17–18), instead, it was burned up. However, Aaron explained the offering by Eleazar and Ithamar, and Moses was satisfied (vv. 19–10). The implied penalty for breaking this Levitical code concerning offerings was death (vv. 1–2).

This verse begins with a conjunction וְ which has a circumstantial function,[577] hence its translation as "when." The verb of the first part of this verse is דָּרֹשׁ "inquired" which is complemented by the infinitive דָּרַשׁ "to inquire." Since the infinitive has an intensifying function[578] the two verbs are translated as "inquired carefully." What Moses inquired about was וְאֵת שְׂעִיר הַחַטָּאת "the goat of the purification." The construction שְׂעִיר הַחַטָּאת "goat of the purification" is a genitive of purpose,[579] meaning it is a goat for the purpose of purification.

After the enquiry, Moses made a discovery concerning the status of the offering. The narrator says, וְהִנֵּה שֹׂרָף וַיִּקְצֹף עַל־אֶלְעָזָר וְעַל־אִיתָמָר בְּנֵי אַהֲרֹן הַנּוֹתָרִם "and behold, he discovered that it had all been burned," therefore, he קָצַף "became angry" with Eleazar and Ithamar, "the surviving sons of Aaron." This clause begins with וְהִנֵּה "and behold." The particle הִנֵּה is understood in this research to have an exclamatory function of calling the attention[580] of the readers to the content of Moses's discovery, which was the burned offering. The first verb in this clause is שֹׂרָף "it had been burned" which is a pluperfect perfective denoting a past state of the offering. The result was Moses became וַיִּקְצֹף "angry." This verb has a conjunction וְ, which introduces a consequence,[581] hence its translation as "therefore." In addition, the verb is an ingressive

---

577. Seow, *Grammar for Biblical Hebrew*, 284.
578. Waltke and O'Connor, *Introduction to Biblical Hebrew*, 35.3.1i.
579. Gesenius, *Gesenius' Hebrew Grammar*, 126q.
580. Arnold and Choi, *Guide to Biblical Hebrew*, 4.5.1a.
581. BDB, 254c.

perfective[582] denoting the beginning of the emotion. The people to whom the emotion is directed against is marked by the prepositional phrase עַל־אֶלְעָזָר וְעַל־אִיתָמָר בְּנֵי אַהֲרֹן הַנּוֹתָרִם "with Eleazar and Ithamar, the surviving sons of Aaron." The sons, Eleazar and Ithamar, are the objects of the preposition[583] and are further described as "the surviving sons of Aaron."

This verse explains that the Ego who was קָצַף "angry" is superior to the landmark and, therefore, supports the argument that קָצַף meaning "angry" was associated with superiors. The third passage in which Moses is the Ego of being קָצַף "angry" is in Numbers 31:14.

49. Num 31:14

וַיִּקְצֹף מֹשֶׁה עַל פְּקוּדֵי הֶחָיִל שָׂרֵי הָאֲלָפִים וְשָׂרֵי הַמֵּאוֹת הַבָּאִים מִצְּבָא הַמִּלְחָמָה׃

Moses became angry with the officers of the army, the commanders of thousands and the commanders of hundreds, who were returning from the battle.

In the context of this passage, Moses became קָצַף "angry" because the army officers spared women of the Midianites. These women were not supposed to live because they were the reason the Israelites had turned away from the Lord at Peor (v. 16). It was at Peor that the Israelites abandoned their true God and worshiped idols (Num 25:6–16). The Israelite men engaged in sexual immorality with the Midianite women who in turn invited them to offer sacrifice and worship their gods. For this reason, it was unfathomable for Moses that his army had allowed the same women to live. The penalty was that Moses ordered the killing of all the women (except virgins) and boys (v. 15).

This verse begins with וַיִּקְצֹף "he became angry" which is an ingressive perfective[584] denoting the beginning of the action of the verb. Moses is קָצַף "angry" עַל פְּקוּדֵי הֶחָיִל "with the officers of the army." This construction has the preposition עַל which has an adversative function,[585] hence its translation as "with." These officers are described further as שָׂרֵי הָאֲלָפִים וְשָׂרֵי הַמֵּאוֹת "the commanders of thousands and the commanders of hundreds." This

---

582. Gibson, *Davidson's Introductory Hebrew Grammar*, 5 Rem. 2.
583. Gesenius, *Gesenius' Hebrew Grammar*, 129.
584. Gibson, *Davidson's Introductory Hebrew Grammar*, 57 Rem. 2.
585. Gesenius, *Gesenius' Hebrew Grammar*, 129.

construction has two sets of genitive, which are both genitives of extent[586] since they show the different levels of stipulated ranks.

The narrator of this story suggests that Moses וַיִּקְצֹף "became angry" when these officers הַבָּאִים מִצְּבָא הַמִּלְחָמָה "were returning from the battle." The verb of this clause is הַבָּאִים "who were returning" which is a participle with a predicate function.[587] The subject of this clause is מִצְּבָא הַמִּלְחָמָה, which literally means "from army of the battle." The prefixed מִן preposition has a source function[588] identifying their locality of departure. The rest of the construction is a genitive of purpose[589] meaning that the purpose of the army was to fight.

In the three stated cases of Moses above, Moses was the Ego of being קָצַף "angry" and he was superior to the landmark. The three occurrences support the proposition that the קצף frame, which is complemented by the קָצַף "angry" verbal form, is associated with people in authority over their subordinates. Another example supporting this proposition is Elisha as mentioned in 2 Kings 13:19.

3.2.5.1.3 Elisha as the Ego

50. 2 Kgs. 13:19

וַיִּקְצֹף עָלָיו אִישׁ הָאֱלֹהִים וַיֹּאמֶר לְהַכּוֹת חָמֵשׁ אוֹ־שֵׁשׁ פְּעָמִים אָז הִכִּיתָ אֶת־אֲרָם עַד־כַּלֵּה וְעַתָּה שָׁלֹשׁ פְּעָמִים תַּכֶּה אֶת־אֲרָם׃

The man of God became angry with him and said, "you should have struck five or six times, then you would have beaten Aram until you finished him. But now you will beat Aram only three times."

The context of this verse is about Elisha who וַיִּקְצֹף "was angry" against Jehoash, the king of Israel because he didn't strike the ground as many times as Elisha wanted – five or six times. Robert Bergen points out that "the Lord's true prophets were conduits through which the divine word came to kings. These prophets were in a functionally superior position to royalty. Royal power would have divinely set limits, and the Lord's prophets would define

---

586. Waltke and O'Connor, *Introduction to Biblical Hebrew*, 9.5.3f.
587. Seow, *Grammar for Biblical Hebrew*, 81.
588. Arnold and Choi, *Guide to Biblical Hebrew*, 4.1.13a.
589. Gesenius, *Gesenius' Hebrew Grammar*, 128q.

those limits."⁵⁹⁰ According to Elisha, since the king only struck the ground three times, it meant he would only defeat the Arameans three times. The effect of Elisha becoming וַיִּקְצֹף "angry" was the pronunciation of the partial defeat of the Arameans.

This passage begins with וַיִּקְצֹף "he became angry" which is an ingressive perfective,⁵⁹¹ stating the beginning of the emotion. Elisha וַיִּקְצֹף "he became angry" עָלָיו "with him" which has the preposition עַל whose function is adversative,⁵⁹² hence the translation "with." Because of Elisha being קָצַף "angry," he spoke to the king and the content of his speech is introduced by the verb וַיֹּאמֶר "and he said" and can be divided into three sections. First, Elisha's response was לְהַכּוֹת חָמֵשׁ אוֹ־שֵׁשׁ פְּעָמִים "you should have struck five or six times." The verb in this clause is לְהַכּוֹת "you should have struck" which has a modality of obligation function,⁵⁹³ meaning the king had the obligation to strike more times. Elisha's expectation was that he would have struck five or six times, which is an accusative of measure⁵⁹⁴ specifying the extent to which an action was to be performed.

The second part of Elisha's message was אָז הִכִּיתָ אֶת־אֲרָם עַד־כַּלֵּה "then you would have beaten Aram until you finished him." The main verb of this clause is הִכִּיתָ "you would have beaten," which is a future perfective,⁵⁹⁵ meaning the result would happen in the future but the speaker speaks as if it is in the past. The effect of the main verb is עַד־כַּלֵּה "until you finish him." This construction has a temporal function⁵⁹⁶ of the preposition עַד indicating the extent of the action.

The third and last part of Elisha's speech is: וְעַתָּה שָׁלֹשׁ פְּעָמִים תַּכֶּה אֶת־אֲרָם "but now you will beat Aram only three times." The conjunction וְ at the beginning of this verse has an adversative function,⁵⁹⁷ hence its translation as "but" because it is contrasting the expectation (possibility) of completely destroying Aram with the שָׁלֹשׁ פְּעָמִים "three times" that he will defeat him.

---

590. Bergen, *1, 2 Samuel*, 128.
591. Gibson, *Davidson's Introductory Hebrew Grammar*, 57 Rem. 2.
592. Arnold and Choi, *Guide to Biblical Hebrew*, 4.1.16f.
593. Waltke and O'Connor, *Introduction to Biblical Hebrew*, 36.2.3f.
594. Joüon and Muraoka, *Grammar of Biblical Hebrew*, 126j.
595. Gesenius, *Gesenius' Hebrew Grammar*, 106o.
596. Arnold and Choi, *Guide to Biblical Hebrew*, 4.1.15b.
597. Seow, *Grammar for Biblical Hebrew*, 284.

The verb in this last clause is תַּכֶּה "you will beat" which is a specific future non-perfective[598] denoting the certainty of the verb. Again, this is an example of the Ego who is being קָצַף "angry" and is in a superior position to the landmark. The following passage is about another leader, King Xerxes, an Ego, who was קָצַף "angry."

3.2.5.1.4 King Xerxes as the Ego

The story of King Xerxes and the refusal by his wife to appear before him and his guests is recorded in Esther 1. He sent seven eunuchs to bring his wife Vashti so that he would display her beauty before his guests, but she refused (vv. 10–12). As a result, he became קָצַף "angry."

51. Esth 1:12

וַתְּמָאֵן הַמַּלְכָּה וַשְׁתִּי לָבוֹא בִּדְבַר הַמֶּלֶךְ אֲשֶׁר בְּיַד הַסָּרִיסִים וַיִּקְצֹף הַמֶּלֶךְ מְאֹד וַחֲמָתוֹ בָּעֲרָה בוֹ:

But Queen Vashti refused to come at the king's order which he issued through the eunuchs. Therefore, the king וַיִּקְצֹף "became very angry" and his anger burned in him.

This verse begins with a conjunction וְ which has an adversative function,[599] hence the translation "but," because this verse contrasts the command of the king in the preceding passage and her refusal to comply. The first clause of this verse is וַתְּמָאֵן הַמַּלְכָּה וַשְׁתִּי לָבוֹא בִּדְבַר הַמֶּלֶךְ "but Queen Vashti refused to come at the king's order." The main verb of this clause is וַתְּמָאֵן "but she refused" which is contextually a recent act perfective[600] since she had just been summoned. The order that the king had issued is explained as אֲשֶׁר בְּיַד הַסָּרִיסִים "which he issued through the eunuchs." The clause is verbless and the verb "issued" is supplied as guided by the context. The construction בְּיַד הַסָּרִיסִים "through the eunuchs" has a preposition בְּ which has an agentive function,[601] hence its translation as "through."

The result of this refusal by Vashti is introduced by the conjunction וְ which is introducing a consequence[602] and so its translation as "therefore." This last

---

598. Gibson, *Davidson's Introductory Hebrew Grammar*, 64a.
599. Seow, *Grammar for Biblical Hebrew*, 284.
600. Waltke and O'Connor, *Introduction to Biblical Hebrew*, 30.5.1b.
601. Waltke and O'Connor, 11.2.5d.
602. BDB, 254c.

clause is וַיִּקְצֹף הַמֶּלֶךְ מְאֹד וַחֲמָתוֹ בָּעֲרָה בוֹ "therefore, the king וַיִּקְצֹף 'became very angry' and his anger burned in him." The verb וַיִּקְצֹף "he became very angry" is an ingressive perfective,[603] denoting the start of experiencing the emotion. This anger is further qualified by the adverb מְאֹד "very" which has an intensive function[604] – which further shows that קָצַף had varying degrees of strong emotion. The narrator adds that וַחֲמָתוֹ בָּעֲרָה בוֹ "and his anger burned in him." The affix genitive וַחֲמָתוֹ "his anger" has attributive genitive sense, meaning the king possessed the characteristics of being angry. This genitive is supported by the verb בָּעֲרָה בוֹ "burned in him." The noun חֵמָה has been highlighted before to mean "internal irritation" and the use of the phrase "his anger burned in him" is in line with that definition. This last clause "and his anger burned in him" is contextually explaining further the verb וַיִּקְצֹף "he became very angry." This understanding is in agreement with the argument discussed earlier in section 3.1.3 that חֵמָה, when used in the same contexts with קֶצֶף/קָצַף is an extrathematic frame element.

In this passage, the Ego who was קָצַף "angry" is a husband who directed his anger to his wife. The effect of the king being קָצַף "angry" was that he dethroned the queen from her royal position (vv. 20–21). At the same time, Ego is a king directing his anger to his queen who is a subordinate. Therefore, this passage supports the argument that when קָצַף is used in the sense of "angry," the Ego is superior to the landmark. The vertical relational function is maintained in this verse as in others discussed above.

In the following passage, the Ego of קָצַף is an inferior and it is contextually explained that although קָ can still mean "angry," the fitting translation is "frustration." This research argues that when קָצַף was experienced by an inferior, it did not necessarily carry the meaning of "anger."

3.2.5.2 Individuals as the Ego of קָצַף

The individual who was קָצַף "frustrated" is Naaman. Prior to coming to Israel, he was suffering from leprosy and his maidservant advised him to visit Israel for healing. In his encounter with Elisha, the instructions he was given concerning what to do did not match his expectation. This story is in 2 Kings chapter 5 but the specific focus for this research is verse 11.

---

603. Gibson, *Davidson's Introductory Hebrew Grammar*, 57 Rem. 2.
604. Arnold and Choi, *Guide to Biblical Hebrew*, 4.2.12.

3.2.5.2.1 Naaman as the Ego: An Expression of Frustration Starts Here

52. 2 Kgs 5:11

וַיִּקְצֹף נַעֲמָן וַיֵּלַךְ וַיֹּאמֶר הִנֵּה אָמַרְתִּי אֵלַי יֵצֵא יָצוֹא וְעָמַד וְקָרָא בְּשֵׁם־יְהוָה אֱלֹהָיו וְהֵנִיף יָדוֹ אֶל־הַמָּקוֹם וְאָסַף הַמְּצֹרָע:

But Naaman וַיִּקְצֹף "was frustrated" and he went away saying/thinking, "Surely, I thought that he would surely come out to me and stand there to call on the name of the Lord his God, and would stretch his hand over the place, and thus cure the leprous spot."

The context of verse 11 is on Naaman who became קָצַף "frustrated" because of the ritual that Elisha prescribed for his healing. Naaman hoped that Elisha would come out of his house and meet him, pray over him, wave his hand over his leprosy and cure him. On the other hand, Elisha asked him to go and wash himself seven times in the River Jordan. This unmet expectation וַיִּקְצֹף "frustrated" Naaman. The attention that the author draws the reader to is Naaman as the Ego of the emotion. Grammatically and contextually, the focus is on how Naaman felt without projecting the emotion. Other passages where קָצַף has the same focus and meaning in its noun form are in Esther 1:18 and Ecclesiastes 5:16[17]. Below is the analysis of 2 Kings 5:11 in more detail.

Verse 11 of chapter 5 in 2 Kings begins with the וַיִּקְצֹף "but he became frustrated," which is an ingressive perfective,[605] denoting the beginning of his disappointment. The conjunction וְ at the beginning of this verse has an adversative function,[606] meaning "but" because it is contrasting Naaman's positive attitude and different expectation when he came to Elisha (vv. 1–9) and his current attitude, of being קָצַף "frustrated" in verse 11. While he was still in this state, he went away וַיֹּאמֶר "saying/thinking"[607] to himself, since this passage implies that this was in the imagination, since he was not addressing anyone. The expression discussed in the following paragraph shows the emotional distress Naaman was going through and supports the argument in

---

605. Gibson, *Davidson's Introductory Hebrew Grammar*, 57 Rem. 2.
606. Seow, *Grammar for Biblical Hebrew*, 284.
607. BDB, 56b.

this research that when קצף is used with words or phrases that show emotional distress, the context implies קצף can be translated as "frustration."

In his thoughts, Naaman hoped that Elisha אֵלַי יֵצֵא יָצוֹא וְעָמַד וְקָרָא בְשֵׁם־יְהוָה אֱלֹהָיו "would surely come out to me and stand there to call on the name of the Lord his God." The first verb in this clause is יֵצֵא "come out" which is a historical future[608] because he is talking of the future from the standpoint of the past. This verb, יֵצֵא "come out," is understood in the context of the infinitive absolute יָצוֹא "to come," which has an affirmation function,[609] hence its translation as "surely." Upon coming out he would וְעָמַד וְקָרָא "and stand and call" which are both historical future[610] because they denote the future from the standpoint of the past. The object of his calling is בְשֵׁם־יְהוָה אֱלֹהָיו "on the name of the Lord his God" and he is expressing his frustration since he hoped Elisha would הַמְצֹרָע וְהֵנִיף יָדוֹ אֶל־הַמָּקוֹם וְאָסַף "wave his hand over the place, and thus cure the leprous spot." As with יֵצֵא "come out," the verbs וְהֵנִיף "to wave" and וְאָסַף "to heal" are historical future non-perfectives[611] since Naaman is denoting the future from the standpoint of the past. This phrase on the emotional distress, guide the translation of קצף as "frustration."

What is clear in this verse is that when קצף, both the noun and the verbal form, focuses on the Ego without the projection of the emotion to a third party, then קצף carries the meaning of frustration rather than anger.[612] While passages given between sections 3.2.5.1 to 3.2.5.2.1 have examined the qal stem of קָצַף, the following passage is on the hithpael stem of קָצַף. It is shown that the Ego of קָצַף in the hithpael stem is an inferior expressing the emotion to a superior.

---

608. Chisholm, *From Exegesis to Exposition*, 94.
609. Van der Merwe, Naudé, and Kroeze, *Biblical Hebrew Reference Grammar*, 158.
610. Waltke and O'Connor, *Introduction to Biblical Hebrew Syntax*, 31.6.2c.
611. Waltke and O'Connor, 31.6.2c.
612. This does not mean that an inferior cannot experience the emotion of anger, rather, the context implies the translation of קצף as "frustration" fits better in that context. Even with the possible meaning of קצף as "anger," the focus in the context is the inferior experiencing it and not projecting it, meaning the advanced vertical frame of קצף in this research is not reversed when an inferior was angered by a superior.

3.2.5.2.2 The Ungodly as the Ego: An Inferior Being Angry against a Superior in the Hithpael Stem

53. Isa 8:21

וְעָבַר בָּהּ נִקְשֶׁה וְרָעֵב וְהָיָה כִי־יִרְעַב וְהִתְקַצַּף וְקִלֵּל בְּמַלְכּוֹ וּבֵאלֹהָיו וּפָנָה לְמָעְלָה׃

He will pass through the land hard-pressed and hungry; and it will come to pass, when hungry, they shall become קָצַף "angry," and looking up they will curse their king and their God.

This verse demonstrates that the subject קָצַף in the hithpael stem is an inferior who is angry against a superior – this is the only reference in which קָצַף occurs in the hithpael stem. The context of this verse is about the ungodly who put their hope in mediums and spirits, and consult the dead (v. 19). Because of their dislike and abhorrence of God's word, their state is that of hopelessness (v. 20). In this state, they will subsequently blame/curse their God (v. 21). John H. Hayes and Stuart A. Irvine note that the context of Isaiah 8:21–22 is "thought to describe the oppressive conditions prevailing in the land, either in Israel following the Assyrian campaigns of Jerusalem in 734–732 or in Judah after the Babylonian destruction of Jerusalem in 586."[613] Regardless of the historical setting, the context depicts suffering and hard times for people who had despised their God. The presumed hard life in captivity was the antecedent condition to their experience of קָצַף "angry."

This verse begins with the וְעָבַר "he (they) will pass." Although this and many other verbs in this verse have the subject in the third masculine singular, the context preceding and following this verse has a plural subject. This occasions no surprise since "singular suffixes can have a collective reference"[614] and therefore can be translated in the plural. The translation, therefore, is more in agreement with the context than the literal wording of the verbs. The verb וְעָבַר "he (they) will pass" has a specific future non-perfective function[615] expressing the certainty of its occurrence. The manner in which they will live is explained in that they will be נִקְשֶׁה וְרָעֵב "hard-pressed and hungry."

---

613. Hayes and Irvine, *Isaiah*, 171.
614. Waltke and O'Connor, *Introduction to Biblical Hebrew*, 16.4b.
615. Gibson, *Davidson's Introductory Hebrew Grammar*, 64a.

These two words, a participle and an adjective, have substantive functions[616] acting like nouns.

The author continues to note that this will be a state that will persist by the use of the verb וְהָיָה "and it will come to pass" which has a specific future function[617] meaning it will come to pass without fail. What will happen is that כִּי־יִרְעַב וְהִתְקַצַּף וְקִלֵּל בְּמַלְכּוֹ וּבֵאלֹהָיו וּפָנָה לְמָעְלָה "when hungry, they shall be קָצַף 'angry' and looking up they will curse their king and their God." This sentence is a temporal clause[618] introduced by a כִּי particle, hence its translation as "when." This temporal clause prepares the reader to know what will happen when the subjects become יִרְעַב "hungry." The outcome is וְהִתְקַצַּף "they shall be angry" which is a specific future[619] stating the certainty of its fulfillment. The complexity of this passage obscures the meaning of the verb הִתְקַצַּף. The difficulty it poses is highlighted by Clines who notes that it can mean "be emaciated"[620] when the root קצף is taken as a homonym. Koehler and Baumgartner have taken note of the same possibility of קצף meaning "emaciated"[621] and have added that in that usage it is close to the Arabic *qaḍuba*. However, they prefer translating it as "fallen into a rage"[622] since the former is less plausible. Hans Wildberger says that קצף in this context means "that deep anger which wells up within a human being who knows that he or she has been cheated and betrayed."[623] Another scholar, Edward Young, says, "The people will work themselves into frenzy, exciting themselves to anger, and this anger will burst out in cursing."[624] According to this quote, Young's understanding of קצף is that it means "anger." Nonetheless, he adds, "Desperation has gripped the people, and they are willing to take leave of God, in wrath uttering curses against him. All they can do is to look upward in complete desperation."[625] These words by Young are echoed by Joseph

---

616. Seow, *Grammar for Biblical Hebrew*, 72, 83.
617. Gibson, *Davidson's Introductory Hebrew Grammar*, 64a.
618. Seow, *Grammar for Biblical Hebrew*, 332.
619. Arnold and Choi, *Guide to Biblical Hebrew*, 3.2.2a.
620. Clines, "קצף," *DCH*, 7:283.
621. Köhler and Baumgartner, "קצף," *HALOT*, 2:1124.
622. Köhler and Baumgartner, 2:1124.
623. Wildberger, *Isaiah 1–12*, 380.
624. Young, *Book of Isaiah*, 321.
625. Young, 321.

Alexander although in different terms. Alexander translates קָצַף as "anger" but while examining the subjects' act of cursing their king and God, he notes that both clauses on anger and curse are closely connected and that "together must be understood as indicating utter perplexity and absolute despair of help from God or man, from heaven or earth, from above or below."[626] The position of this research is that קָצַף means "angry," and being in the hithpael form, it was an inferior projecting his anger to a superior.

While the people were angry, they would וְקִלֵּל "begin to curse" which is a specific future.[627] The object of this verb is בְּמַלְכּוֹ וּבֵאלֹהָיו "their king and their God." While they would be cursing their king and their God, they would do so while וּפָנָה לְמָעְלָה "looking up," perhaps symbolizing the direction of their curses to the perceived place of God. This would be supported by the Septuagint's translation of looking up as ἀναβλέψονται εἰς τὸν οὐρανὸν ἄνω "looking up to the heaven above."

The following reference is on an Aramaic text and shows that the Aramaic קְצַף in the BHS fits within the same frame as קָצַף in Hebrew.

3.2.5.2.3 Nebuchadnezzar's Anger upon the Wise Men (Aramaic Text)

As it has been said in chapter 3 section 3.0, the Aramaic texts where קְצַף occurs fit within the קָצַף frame. The verbal form of קְצַף occurs in only one reference in Aramaic, Daniel 2:12.

> 54. Dan 2:12
>
> כָּל־קֳבֵל דְּנָה מַלְכָּא בְּנַס וּקְצַף שַׂגִּיא וַאֲמַר לְהוֹבָדָה לְכֹל חַכִּימֵי בָבֶל
>
> At this the king became furious and very angry, and ordered all the wise men of Babylon to be killed.

The context of this verse is about a dream that King Nebuchadnezzar had. He gathered the magicians, enchanters, sorcerers and astrologers to interpret the dream for him but there was none who could. He warned them that if they did not interpret his dream, then that meant they had conspired to mislead him (v. 9). Because of their failure to interpret his dream, the king became קְצַף angry.

---

626. Alexander, *Prophecies of Isaiah*, 195.
627. Gibson, *Davidson's Introductory Hebrew Grammar*, 64a.

The adjective דְּנָה points to the failure of all the magicians, enchanters, sorcerers and astrologers to interpret Nebuchadnezzar's dream (vv. 10–11). In this case, the provoking situation is the failure to tell what the dream was and to interpret it (v. 6). The result of this failure was that מַלְכָּא בְּנַס וּקְצַף שַׂגִּיא "the king became furious and very angry." This phrase has a hendiadys[628] of בְּנַס וּקְצַף שַׂגִּיא "furious and very angry" which are used to show intensity of the emotion. In his anger, he ordered the execution of all the wise men of Babylon. The genitive חַכִּימֵי בָבֶל "wise men of Babylon" is a genitive of location[629] meaning those who lived in Babylon, since Daniel and his fellows were supposed to be executed too (v. 13), although originally, they were from Jerusalem. However, since Daniel and his friends were not part of the wise men who appeared before the king (vv. 2–11), their execution was by implication.[630] This scenario is in line with the קצף frame in that it has a vertical relationship, experienced by a superior against a subordinate, and that it has a retributive effect in that in this passage, it is the intended killing of all the wise men.

The examples examined so far concern individuals who were the Egos of קָצַף. The following passages concern groups of individuals that are collective Egos of קָצַף. As it will be explained, one of the key characteristics of groups as Egos of קָצַף is that the groups had military might over the landmark.

3.2.5.3 Group as the Ego of קָצַף: Characterized by Military Might

This section has three references: 1 Samuel 29:4, Esther 2:21 and Jeremiah 37:15. In all the references, the Ego of קָצַף had numerical strength (since it is a group) and military might advantage over the landmark. The superiority is, therefore, that of military strength as opposed to relational superiority.

3.2.5.3.1 Philistine Chiefs as the Ego

55. 1 Sam 29:4

וַיִּקְצְפוּ עָלָיו שָׂרֵי פְלִשְׁתִּים וַיֹּאמְרוּ לוֹ שָׂרֵי פְלִשְׁתִּים הָשֵׁב אֶת־הָאִישׁ וְיָשֹׁב אֶל־מְקוֹמוֹ אֲשֶׁר הִפְקַדְתּוֹ שָׁם וְלֹא־יֵרֵד עִמָּנוּ בַּמִּלְחָמָה

---

628. Bullinger, *Figures of Speech*, 659.
629. Van der Merwe, Naudé, and Kroeze, *Biblical Hebrew Reference Grammar*, 199.
630. Irwin and Meadowcroft, *Book of Daniel*, 43.

וְלֹא־יִהְיֶה־לָּנוּ לְשָׂטָן בַּמִּלְחָמָה וּבַמֶּה יִתְרַצֶּה זֶה אֶל־אֲדֹנָיו הֲלוֹא בְּרָאשֵׁי הָאֲנָשִׁים הָהֵם:

> But the Philistine commanders became angry at him and said to him: "make this man return! Let him return to the place you picked out for him. Let him not go down into battle with us because during the battle he might become our enemy. For how else can he win back his master's favor, if not with the heads of our own men?"

The context of this verse concerns the Philistine commanders who became קָצַף "angry" because of the presence of David as a possible Hebrew spy in their army, and the result of their anger was the command that David (the perceived spy) should leave their camp (v. 4). They were afraid that, since he was an Israelite, he would betray them in their war against Saul. Such a betrayal had happened before at Gibeah (1 Sam 14:15–23) during which the Israelites who were in the company of the Philistines abandoned them and joined the Israelites in the war. As a result, the Philistines lost the battle. Following the command by the commanders, "Achish called David and said to him, 'as surely as the LORD lives, you have been reliable, and I would be pleased to have you serve with me in the army. From the day you came to me until today, I have found no fault in you, but the rulers don't approve of you. Now turn back and go in peace; do nothing to displease the Philistine rulers'" (1 Sam 29:6–7). Their address to Achish is in two parts.

In the first address, the first verb of the verse is וַיִּקְצְפוּ "they became angry" which is an ingressive perfective denoting the beginning of the action. This verb has a conjunction וְ which has an adversative function,[631] since it is contrasting Achish's favorable attitude toward David and the the Philistine chiefs' dislike of David, hence its translation as "but." The subject of the verb is שָׂרֵי פְלִשְׁתִּים "Philistine commanders." In this construction, the commanders are characterized by being Philistines, hence it is an attributive genitive.[632] The phrase שָׂרֵי פְלִשְׁתִּים "Philistine commanders" is repeated twice in this verse. This repetition is a case of dittography since it has no exegetical significance and it is notably omitted in the earlier translations: the old Greek, Syriac

---

631. Seow, *Grammar for Biblical Hebrew*, 284.
632. Chisholm, *From Exegesis to Exposition*, 63.

and the Vulgate. These earlier translations must have attempted to correct what was in their view a mistake. These commanders were angry עָלָיו "with him or at it" which has a preposition עַל which has an adversative function, and which can be translated as either "with" or "at"[633] depending on one's understanding of the affix יו "him/it." This affix is ambiguous since it is not clear who the referent is. According to this verse, the first option is that it can be referring to Achish so that the personal pronouns can be replaced and read as, "but the Philistine commanders became angry with Achish and said to him (Achish) . . ." Second, it can also be referring to David, meaning the verse can be rewritten as, "but the Philistine commanders became angry with David and said to him (Achish) . . ." Third, it can refer to the situation – when taken to mean "at it,"[634] the presence of a Hebrew, in their camp. With this option, the verse can read as "but the Philistine commanders became angry at this and said to Achish . . ."

Out of the three options, the position taken in this research is that עָלָיו refers to Achish since the context shows he was immediately addressed, that is, "and said to Achish." In 1 Samuel 27:2, Achish is mentioned as the son of Maoch, king of Gath (1 Sam 27:2), and therefore superior to the army generals. However, this passage presents us with a case of a "situational authority," meaning that under ordinary circumstances the Philistine commanders would not have authority over their king but in this case, they had a military authority and strength of numbers – it is a group being קָצַף "angry."

The exercise of authority over Achish is demonstrated in the use of the imperative of command[635] הָשֵׁב "make this man return!" The imperative form is usually of command if the speaker is a superior addressing a subordinate. Although it can be an imperative of request,[636] a subordinate addressing a superior, the context does not show that Achish had a choice to either accept or reject their request, as shown in the verse that follows. Instead, he obeyed. This is the reason this imperative is taken as command. Achish followed this command to the letter as written in 1 Samuel 29:6–7: "So Achish called David and said to him, 'As surely as the Lord lives, you have been reliable,

---

633. Arnold and Choi, *Guide to Biblical Hebrew*, 4.1.16f.
634. Seow, *Grammar for Biblical Hebrew*, 97–99.
635. Van der Merwe, Naudé, and Kroeze, *Biblical Hebrew Reference Grammar*, 151.
636. Van der Merwe, Naudé, and Kroeze, 151.

and I would be pleased to have you serve with me in the army. From the day you came to me until today, I have found no fault in you, but the rulers do not approve of you. Now turn back and go in peace; do nothing to displease the Philistine rulers'" (NIV). In the explanation Achish was giving to David, he made it clear that it was not his choice but that of the Philistine rulers. In essence, he was carrying out their instructions.

The second part of the Philistine commanders' address to Achish was אֶל־מְקוֹמוֹ אֲשֶׁר הִפְקַדְתּוֹ שָׁם "let him return to the place you picked out for him." The first verb of this clause is וְיָשֹׁב "let him return" which is a jussive of exhortation,[637] meaning Achish was to urge David to return. The place David was to return to is marked by the object of the preposition אֶל־מְקוֹמוֹ "to the place" and the preposition אֶל has a terminative function[638] identifying the end goal of movement. This place is explained further as אֲשֶׁר הִפְקַדְתּוֹ שָׁם "which you picked for him." The verb of this phrase הִפְקַדְתּוֹ "you picked for him" is a simple past.[639] The adverb שָׁם "there" is left untranslated since it is usually omitted when it is preceded by the relative particle אֲשֶׁר.[640] This second part of the Philistine rulers' order explains that Achish had no choice but to carry out the order given.

The Philistine commanders gave a reason why they wanted David sent back. The reason was וְלֹא־יֵרֵד עִמָּנוּ בַּמִּלְחָמָה וְלֹא־יִהְיֶה־לָּנוּ לְשָׂטָן בַּמִּלְחָמָה "he will not go down into battle with us because during the battle he might become our enemy." The first verb of this clause is וְלֹא־יֵרֵד "he will not go down" which is a non-perfective of injunction,[641] again, showing that the rulers were not giving Achish any choice. Their fear was that during the battle he might become their enemy.

This fear is replicated in their rhetorical question: וּבַמֶּה יִתְרַצֶּה זֶה אֶל־אֲדֹנָיו הֲלוֹא בְּרָאשֵׁי הָאֲנָשִׁים הָהֵם "for how else can he reconcile himself back to his master, if not with the heads of our own men?" The first verb of this clause יִתְרַצֶּה is translated as "reconcile himself back" because it has a reflexive function.[642] The near demonstrative זֶה "this one" is anaphoric referring to

---

637. Waltke and O'Connor, *Introduction to Biblical Hebrew*, 34.3b.
638. Arnold and Choi, *Guide to Biblical Hebrew*, 4.1.2a.
639. Chisholm, *From Exegesis to Exposition*, 86, 95.
640. BDB, 1027b.
641. Arnold and Choi, *Guide to Biblical Hebrew*, 3.2.2(d.4).
642. Seow, *Grammar for Biblical Hebrew*, 298.

David and is serving an emphatic function to mean, "he – this one."[643] Since in the English translation the focus is retained without the emphatic use of the demonstrative, it is left untranslated and the message is not altered. The reconciliation of David was אֶל־אֲדֹנָיו "to his master" which has the preposition אֶל, which has a terminative function identifying the goal of David's suspected movement.[644] The means through which the Philistines suspected he would reconcile himself to his master was הֲלוֹא בְּרָאשֵׁי הָאֲנָשִׁים הָהֵם "if not with the heads of our own men?" This is an idiom meaning betrayal. The effect of the commanders being קָצַף "angry" was that they ordered the leaving of David (v. 4).

The discussions on this verse show that the Ego of קָצַף "angry" was a group and had a military advantage over the landmark. The next verse in which Ego is both a group with a military advantage and is קָצַף "angry" is found in Esther 2.21.

3.2.5.3.2 King's Officers: Bigthan and Teresh as the Ego

This section is about two of the king's officials, Bigthan and Teresh, who became קָצַף "angry" with the king as recorded in Esther 2:21. As with the example in 1 Samuel 29:4, the antecedent entity for קָצַף is not clear in the context.

> 56. Esth 2:21
>
> בַּיָּמִים הָהֵם וּמָרְדֳּכַי יֹשֵׁב בְּשַׁעַר־הַמֶּלֶךְ קָצַף בִּגְתָן וָתֶרֶשׁ שְׁנֵי־סָרִיסֵי הַמֶּלֶךְ מִשֹּׁמְרֵי הַסַּף וַיְבַקְשׁוּ לִשְׁלֹחַ יָד בַּמֶּלֶךְ אֲחַשְׁוֵרֹשׁ׃
>
> During those days when Mordecai was sitting at the king's gate, Bigthan and Teresh, two of the king's eunuchs who were guarding the entrance, became angry and plotted to assassinate King Ahasuerus.

The context of this passage is about a conspiracy to kill the king that was unveiled by Mordecai. The reason the guards became קָצַף "angry" is not specified. The information reached the king through Queen Esther with whom Mordecai had maintained contact (vv. 19–22). The king ordered investigations which ascertained Mordecai's claim to be true and the two officers were killed.

---

643. Seow, 105.

644. Arnold and Choi, *Guide to Biblical Hebrew*, 4.1.2a.

Esther 2:21 begins with a description of the period, that is, בַּיָּמִים הָהֵם וּמָרְדֳּכַי יֹשֵׁב בְּשַׁעַר־הַמֶּלֶךְ "during those days when Mordecai was sitting at the king's gate." The preposition בְּ attached to בַּיָּמִים has a temporal function[645] hence its translation as "during." The "days" בַּיָּמִים have a definite article of a well-known thing[646] since it was a known period. The pronoun הָהֵם has an emphatic function[647] emphasizing "days," hence its translation as an adjective "those days." This period is further qualified as that time during which Mordecai sat at the king's gate. This translation is informed by the understanding of the conjunction ו as having a circumstantial function,[648] hence its translation as "when." The verb of this clause is יֹשֵׁב "sitting" which has a past time predicate function[649] giving a durative aspect of the action. The place they were sitting is marked by a prepositional phrase בְּשַׁעַר־הַמֶּלֶךְ "at the king's gate." This construction has a preposition בְּ which has a spatial function[650] identifying the locality, hence its translation as "at."

During that time Bigthan and Teresh, two of the king's eunuchs, who were guarding the entrance, became angry and plotted to kill King Ahasuerus. The first verb of this clause is קָצַף "he (they) became angry" which is an ingressive perfective denoting the beginning of the experience of the emotion. The verse gives us more details on these men saying they were שְׁנֵי־סָרִיסֵי הַמֶּלֶךְ "two of the king's eunuchs" which is a genitive of measure[651] and of relation,[652] respectively. Their role was מִשֹּׁמְרֵי הַסַּף "guarding the entrance." The construction סָרִיסֵי הַמֶּלֶךְ "guarding the entrance" is an objective genitive[653] since the entrance is the object of the verbal action. In addition to their role of guarding the entrance, they had another agenda – to kill the king. The last clause of this verse says: וַיְבַקְשׁוּ לִשְׁלֹחַ יָד בַּמֶּלֶךְ אֲחַשְׁוֵרֹשׁ "they plotted to kill King Ahasuerus" which is literally translated as "and they sought to lay a hand on the king, Ahasuerus." What they conspired to do is introduced by an infinite

---

645. Arnold and Choi, *Guide to Biblical Hebrew*, 4.1.5b.
646. Gesenius, *Gesenius' Hebrew Grammar*, 126d.
647. Seow, *Grammar for Biblical Hebrew*, 93.
648. Seow, 284.
649. Joüon and Muraoka, *Grammar of Biblical Hebrew*, 121f.
650. Arnold and Choi, *Guide to Biblical Hebrew*, 4.1.5a.
651. Waltke and O'Connor, *Introduction to Biblical Hebrew*, 9.5.3f.
652. Van der Merwe, Naudé, and Kroeze, *Biblical Hebrew Reference Grammar*, 198.
653. Chisholm, *From Exegesis to Exposition*, 62.

construct לִשְׁלֹחַ יָד "to lay a hand" which is an idiom meaning "to kill," hence the translation given above. The prepositional phrase בַּמֶּלֶךְ אֲחַשְׁוֵרֹשׁ "on King Ahasuerus," has a preposition בְּ which has a spatial function[654] indicating the object of the intended action. This construction is that of nouns in apposition, a proper noun in apposition to an office.[655]

It is not clear in this passage why the two eunuchs of the king קָצַף "became angry," or what had angered them and why the king was the target of the schemes. What is clear is that although they were not superior to the king, they had a guarding role "military might," which gave them an advantaged oversight role over their master. Their intention to kill the king supports an argument in this research that the קצף frame (which includes both the noun and the verbal forms) had a retributive intention. The next category in which the Ego of קָצַף is a group with a military might is in Jeremiah 37:15.

3.2.5.3.3 Judean Officials as the Ego

The group in this passage is the Judean officials. Unlike in the last two examples, it is clear in this passage why the officials were angered because Jeremiah resisted being taken to Babylon (Jer 37:14). Since they were Judean officials in the government of the day, they technically had administrative authority over Jeremiah. The result of their anger was that they imprisoned Jeremiah (v. 15). The primary verse in focus is Jeremiah 37:15.

> 57. Jer 37:15
>
> וַיִּקְצְפוּ הַשָּׂרִים עַל־יִרְמְיָהוּ וְהִכּוּ אֹתוֹ וְנָתְנוּ אוֹתוֹ בֵּית הָאֵסוּר בֵּית
> יְהוֹנָתָן הַסֹּפֵר כִּי־אֹתוֹ עָשׂוּ לְבֵית הַכֶּלֶא׃
>
> The officials וַיִּקְצְפוּ "became angry" with Jeremiah and had him beaten and imprisoned in the house of Jonathan the scribe, for they were using it as a jail.

This verse begins with וַיִּקְצְפוּ "became angry" which has an ingressive perfective[656] function, meaning they started to experience the emotion. The subject of the verb is הַשָּׂרִים "the princes" who have a definite article of a

---

654. Arnold and Choi, *Guide to Biblical Hebrew*, 4.1.5a.
655. Arnold and Choi, 2.4.5.
656. Gibson, *Davidson's Introductory Hebrew Grammar*, 57 Rem. 2.

well-known person.⁶⁵⁷ The prepositional phrase עַל־יִרְמְיָהוּ "with Jeremiah" has preposition עַל, which has an adversative function,⁶⁵⁸ hence its translation as "with."

Out of their emotion of being קָצַף "angry," they made a decision in which they וְהִכּוּ אֹתוֹ וְנָתְנוּ אוֹתוֹ בֵּית הָאֵסוּר בֵּית יְהוֹנָתָן הַסֹּפֵר "had him beaten and imprisoned in the house of Jonathan the scribe." This clause has two main verbs, the first is וְהִכּוּ "they had (him) beaten" which has a causative function, meaning they were not the ones who beat him, since it is in the hiphil stem.⁶⁵⁹ In addition to the beating, they also had him וְנָתְנוּ אוֹתוֹ בֵּית הָאֵסוּר בֵּית יְהוֹנָתָן הַסֹּפֵר "imprisoned in the house of Jonathan the scribe." The place of imprisonment בֵּית הָאֵסוּר בֵּית יְהוֹנָתָן "the house of prison and the house of Jonathan" is a phrase in apposition of function to a proper noun⁶⁶⁰ because the house is the prison hence its translation as just "imprisoned in the house of Jonathan." The first construction בֵּית הָאֵסוּר "house of prison" is a genitive of purpose⁶⁶¹ while the second construction בֵּית יְהוֹנָתָן "house of Jonathan" is a possessive genitive.⁶⁶² In this last construction, Jonathan is further described as הַסֹּפֵר "the scribe" which is in apposition to Jonathan, and its function is apposition to a proper noun.⁶⁶³

The reason for putting Jeremiah in Jonathan's house is given in the last clause which is introduced by a כִּי clause saying כִּי־אֹתוֹ עָשׂוּ לְבֵית הַכֶּלֶא "for they were using it as a jail." This last clause supports the above-mentioned hendiadys concerning this house. This passage shows that the Ego of קָצַף was a group with a military advantage over the landmark.

This chapter so far has discussed the קצף frame and ascertained its frame, which consists of the core frame elements, the peripheral frame elements and the extrathematic frame elements. In addition, this chapter has demonstrated the distinctive frame elements that are unique to קצף and that are foundational for the comparative study in this research. The distinctive קצף features discussed showed that, first, קצף is used within a frame (קצף frame).

---

657. Gesenius, *Gesenius' Hebrew Grammar*, 126d.
658. Arnold and Choi, *Guide to Biblical Hebrew*, 4.1.16f.
659. Seow, *Grammar for Biblical Hebrew*, 181.
660. Van der Merwe, Naudé, and Kroeze, *Biblical Hebrew Reference Grammar*, 229.
661. Chisholm, *From Exegesis to Exposition*, 63.
662. Van der Merwe, Naudé, and Kroeze, *Biblical Hebrew Reference Grammar*, 198.
663. Waltke and O'Connor, *Introduction to Biblical Hebrew*, 12.3e.

180 A Cross-Cultural Conceptual Study of the Emotion of קצף in the Hebrew Bible

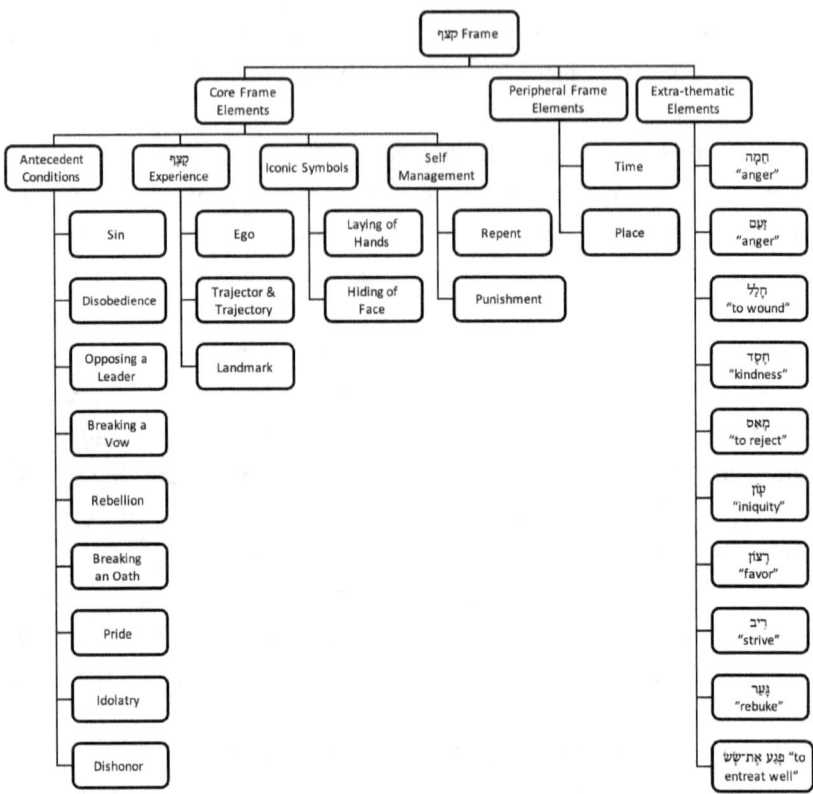

Chart 7

The details of this frame are that קֶצֶף is an abstract object which comes out (comes from) the Ego, the one experiencing קֶצֶף, and follows an abstract trajectory marked by the verb היה and rests on the landmark identified by the preposition עַל. Second, this chapter has also explained that the קצף usage in the Aramaic texts fit within the קצף frame. Third, it has been explained that קצף has distinctive features. These features carry the sense of "anger" when experienced by a superior against a subordinate. Fourth, קָצַף/קֶצֶף means "frustration" when it is experienced by an inferior and is not projected, or "provocation" when קָצַף is in the hiphil stem and is projected by an inferior to a superior. Lastly, when קָצַף/קֶצֶף was experienced by a group, the group had a military might (superior advantage over the target) and that קָצַף/קֶצֶף is associated with punishment either actualized or intended but averted. The diagram below illustrates the קצף frame in light of the discussions in this chapter.

3.3 The Homonyms of קצף

This section now examines the homonyms of קצף with the aim of highlighting how different they are from the meaning advanced in the argument for the קצף frame. The first occurrence of קצף as a homonym is if one takes it to mean "to be emaciated"[664] in Isaiah 54:8. Although this is not the position held in this research, it is highlighted in chart 7 to show that the author of this research is aware of this possibility. The position held in this research is discussed in detail in section 3.2.5.2.2 number 56.

The second occurrence in which קצף has a different sense other than anger is in Hosea 10:7. This passage reads as follows: נִדְמֶה שֹׁמְרוֹן מַלְכָּהּ כְּקֶצֶף עַל־פְּנֵי־מָיִם "Samaria [and] her king will be cut off, like a splinter upon the waters." The context of this passage is about the destruction of Samaria and her king. The main verb of this verse is נִדְמֶה which means to "be destroyed, cut off"[665] and has a future instantaneous[666] function, meaning it will certainly happen. Other passages where this verb is used with the same sense of destruction are Isaiah 6:5; 15:1 and Ezekiel 32:2. Perhaps an additional passage that supports the translation of קצף as "twig" is Joel 1:7 which says שָׂם גַּפְנִי לְשַׁמָּה וּתְאֵנָתִי לִקְצָפָה חָשֹׂף חֲשָׂפָהּ וְהִשְׁלִיךְ הִלְבִּינוּ שָׂרִיגֶיהָ "It has stripped bare my vines, splintered my fig tree, Shearing off its bark and throwing it away, until its branches turn white" (NAB). Duane Garrett says, "This is the only place קֶצֶף is translated as 'twig' or the like in the Bible. Elsewhere it always means 'wrath' and generally refers to God's wrath. But, 'like wrath on the surface of water' leaves the reader entirely at a loss."[667] James Mays adds that Samaria "will be swept away by the Assyrian forces as a branch broken from a tree is carried in a flood."[668] Douglas Stuart supports the translation of קֶצֶף as a "twig." He says that the king of Samaria "will be carried off, powerless to resist, like a twig or chip of wood is born along on water."[669] These scholars, among other scholars, find the translation of קֶצֶף as a "twig" fitting in the context.

---

664. Clines, "קצף," *DCH*, 7: 283.
665. Clines, "דמה," *DCH*, 2:448.
666. Joüon and Muraoka, *Grammar of Biblical Hebrew*, 121e.
667. Garrett, *Hosea, Joel*, 211.
668. Mays, *Hosea: A Commentary*, 143.
669. Stuart, *Hosea–Jonah*, 163.

The subjects of the verb are Samaria and the king. The noun מַלְכָּהּ has a feminine affix (of her), which is a genitive of relation.[670] The fate of the king is likened to a "snapped-off twig,"[671] "splinter, chip [or] foam"[672] on the surface of the water. Scholars are divided as to whether קֶצֶף, in this passage, means "twig" or means "foam." The scholars who hold the view that קֶצֶף means foam in Hosea 10:7 are already mentioned and their thoughts captured in chapter 1 section 1.5.1. This research has not taken a position on what קצף means in Hosea 10:7 since it is clearly a homonym and goes beyond the limit of this study.

---

670. Van der Merwe, Naudé, and Kroeze, *Biblical Hebrew Reference Grammar*, 198.
671. Köhler and Baumgartner, "קצף," *HALOT*, 2:1125.
672. Clines, "קצף" *DCH*, 7:284.

CHAPTER 4

The Akamba Folk Theory of *Ngoò* "Anger"

The analysis that is discussed below forms the backdrop for the cross-cultural comparison of *ngoò* and קֶצֶף. As a prelude to this folk theory analysis, the following sections focus on the basic details of the Akamba people, followed by a grammatical orientation of the Kĩkamba language.

The people whose folk theory of anger is presented here are "known as Akamba; one person is a Mukamba, their language is Kĩkamba, and their country Ukambani (or Ukamba)."[1] The word "country" as used by Mbiti in the quotation above refers to the region where they live in Kenya. According to the last national census done in 2009, the Akamba population is close to three million, which means they are the fifth largest community in Kenya. They occupy the Machakos, Makũenĩ and Kĩtui counties, although some live in other areas but their numbers are not significantly high.

4.1 The Akamba Origin

According to the Akamba tales of their origin, they migrated from the Democratic Republic of Congo, and then passed through what is now Uganda and Tanzania before they entered the territory that is now Kenya. In Kenya, they first settled in the Nzaũĩ Hills and later dispersed to the present localities.

---

1. Mbiti, *Akamba Stories*, 3.

It is believed that even today, the Akamba are still found in the Democratic Republic of Congo, and in Uganda and Tanzania.[2]

In this chapter, I will present the Kenya Akamba folk theory of *ngoò* "anger." According to the Kĩkamba-English Dictionary published in 2003, there are only three words that are defined as anger: *ũthatu* and its cognates: *thata, ũthatyo, thilĩ* and its verbal form – *ũthilĩku*, and *ngoò*.[3] My research also will show that *ngoò* "anger" is a reference to *ngoo* "heart" which is the body organ where the event of anger occurs according to the Akamba folk theory. The correlation of *ngoò* "anger" and *ngoo* "heart" makes the folk theory of *ngoò* "anger" central in its usage and worthy of investigation to determine how all the other words fit together within a single taxonomy.

In my analysis of this folk theory, all the examples will be done in Kĩkamba followed by a translation in English. It is therefore necessary to highlight some elements of Kĩkamba grammar, which will be useful in understanding the examples that will be given later in this chapter.

4.2 The Kĩkamba Language

The Kĩkamba language has a developed orthography in the category of E55 placed in Bantu zone E.[4] Like many Bantu languages, Kĩkamba is syntactically a subject-verb-object (SVO) language. In this section, I will only analyze the basic verbal forms of Kĩkamba that are necessary for understanding the examples that will be used later in the chapter. I will focus on the tenses, infinitive forms, negation of clauses and aspect only, since they are the relevant ones for the examples that will later follow.

The verbal forms comprise a verb root with prefixes, infixes and suffixes. Most of the prefixes are either a focus or a person marker designating either the agent of the verb, if it is active, or the patient, if the verb is passive. These two are the common prefixes that are usually attached to the verb. Concerning suffixes, most but not all of the Kĩkamba verbs have a final vowel (FV) after the suffix. The FV is marked by either -as, -a or -e. The mood is marked by

---

2. My informant for this was David Kitavi who was eighty years old (at the time of interview) and was one of the community elders in Yathui region, lower parts of Machakos.

3. Mũtĩsya and Ndũnda, *Kĩkamba-English Dictionary*, 126, 156, 186.

4. Guthrie, *Bantu Languages*, 42–43.

infixes; -i- for perfect marker and -a- or -ete- for imperfect.[5] I will begin by looking at the Kĩkamba tenses, starting with the present tense.[6]

The present tense is marked by -kũ- prefix:

1. *Nĩngũya*
Nĩ.n.**kũ**.ya
FOC[7].1sg.PRT[8].eat
"I am eating"

The next item is the past tense. Kĩkamba has four past tenses, the immediate past (PST_a) represented by the -ná[9]- prefix, the near past (PST_b) represented by the -nĩ- prefix, the distant past (PST_c) represented by the -nâ- prefix and the remote past (PST_d) represented by the -â- prefix. Here are some examples to demonstrate this:

2. *Nĩnaya*
Nĩ.**ná**.ya
1sg.PST_a.eat.
"I have eaten" (immediate past)

3. *Nĩnĩĩye*
Nĩ.**nĩ**.ĩ.ye
1sg.PST_b.PERF.ate
"I ate" (near past)

4. *Nĩnaaĩye*
Nĩ.**nâ**. ĩ.ye
1sg.PST_c.PERF.ate
"I ate" (distant past)

---

5. Guthrie, 25.

6. The prefix changes with the tense, mood, voice, person and number of the verb, as well as the case and number of the noun (the subject or object) it goes with.

7. The term "focus" is used in this example, and the others that follow, to mean the main participant in the phrase and to whom the utterer wants to draw the attention of the readers/listeners.

8. The abbreviation "PRT" is a shortened form of "present tense". The page on the list of abbreviations at the beginning of this document has more forms.

9. This accent marks high tone.

5. *Nâiye*
Nĩ.â.ĩ.ye
1sg.PST$_d$.PERF.ate
"I ate" (remote past)

The last tense to be considered is the future tense. Kĩkamba has three future tenses. It has the prefix -kã- for the immediate future (FUT$_a$), the prefix -ka- for the distant future (FUT$_b$) and the prefix -ká-[10] for the remote future (FUT$_c$). This tense pattern is illustrated by the following examples:

6. *Nĩngũya*
Nĩ.n.**kũ**[11].ya
FOC.1sg.FUT$_a$.eat
"I will eat" (immediate future)

7. *Ngaya*
N.**ka**.ya
1sg.FUT$_b$.eat
"I shall eat" (distant future)

8. *Nĩngaya*
Nĩ.n.**ká**.ya (remote future)
FOC.1sg.FUTc.eat
"I shall eat" (remote future)

Having looked at the tenses, the following example is on the infinitive form. The infinitive in Kĩkamba is marked by -kũ- prefix as explained in the following example:

9. *kũya*
kũ.ya
INF.eat
"to eat"

---

10. The difference in these future tenses is the tone which begins with a low tone for the immediate future and ends with high tone for the remote future.

11 The 1sg marker "n" prefix is combined, in speech, with the "kũ" of the immediate future and the "k" phonetically sounds like "g", both giving the "ng" sound. Although the -ng- is originally -nk-, in pronunciation Kĩkamba does not have the high pitched -nk- sound, it instead has the -ng- sound. Since the main difference in the future markers is the tone as mentioned in footnote 8 above, the -kã- is so low it is pronounced as ũ, hence *nĩngũya*.

The following examples focus on negation of verbs. The Kĩkamba clauses are negated by the prefix -ndi- in the 1st person, -ndũ- in the 2nd person and -nde- in the 3rd person. Examples to illustrate these are:

10. *Ndiya*
Ndi.ya
NEG.1sg.eat
"Not-eat"
"(I will) not eat"

11. *Ndũkaye*
Ndũ.ka.ye
NEG. 2sg.eat
"Not.you.eat"
"Don't eat" (this is functioning like a negated imperative)

12. Ndeya
Nde.ya
NEG.eat
"She/he will not eat"

The last item I am considering is the aspect of a Kĩkamba verb. The verbal forms in Kĩkamba show a difference between perfect (completed) and imperfect (incomplete) aspects. The perfect is marked by the suffix -ie- or the prefix -i- while the imperfect is marked by the suffix -a- when it is habitual (HAB) or the suffix -ete- when it is progressive (PRG). Below are some examples:

13. *Nĩnĩĩe*
Nĩ.nĩ.ĩ.ye
FOC.1sg.PERF.eat
"I ate"

14. *Nĩnĩnaĩye*
Nĩ.nĩ.na.ĩe[12].ye
FOC.1sg.PST$_b$.PERF.ate
"I ate" (near past)

---

12. The "ie" contracts to "ĩ."

15. *Nĩnĩĩsaá*
Nĩ.nĩ.ĩ.ĩsa[13].á
FOC.1pl.eat.HAB.FV
"I eat"

16. *Nĩnĩĩte*
Nĩ.nĩ.ĩ.ete.e
FOC.1sg.eat.PRG.FV
"I am eating"

The review offered above is designed to help the reader understand the subsequent examples used in this chapter. Since the focus of this chapter is the folk theory of *ngoò* "anger," a good grasp of the Akamba emotional structure in general is also a useful tool.

4.3 The Akamba Emotional Category

There is no specific word for "emotion" in Kĩkamba. When the Akamba talk of an emotion, mainly they use *ĩw'a* "feel" in its infinitive form *kwĩw'a* "to feel" for good emotions and *kũlikwa* "to be entered" in its passive form for bad emotions. The Akamba determine whether emotions are good or bad depending on how they perceive the emotions' effect in the society. Bad emotions consist of hate, envy and jealousy among others, and are associated with evil since they destroy the society. The good emotions are associated with goodness in the society in that they contribute to the well-being of the society. The verbal description of bad emotions implies that those emotions are external "objects" that are not intrinsic within the human body while the good emotions are within the body system. These sentences describing the bad emotions are normally constructed in the passive form. For example:

17. Ego *alikilwe ni kĩmena*
Ego *a.likilwe*   nĩ   kĩmena
Ego 3sg.enter   by   hate
"Ego has hatred. Literally, Ego has been entered by hate"

---

13. The "ya" root changes to "to" in the Imperfect. Take note of example 16 also.

To illustrate this further I will use a quote from a story of a young girl and a bull that is written by Mwīkali Kīeti in her book: *Barking, you'll be eaten*.[14] In this story, there was a man who had several sons who were single. When the youngest of all got married to a beautiful girl, the rest of his brothers became envious. In the story it says:

> 18. *Anaaniny'a   ī,   malikwa   nī   kīwīu*
> *Ana.a.niny'a   ma.lika.w.a*
>   3pl-enter-PASS-FV
> Sons.of.mother idiophone were entered   by envy
> "The brothers became envious. Literally, the sons of the same mother were entered by envy"

In this sentence, the verb *malikwa* "were entered" is in the passive form, which demonstrates the Akamba thinking that this feeling is not part of the body system of the person experiencing it.

For the good emotions like love, there is no single reference I know or have heard in which love entered Ego. All the references are about Ego feeling love or having love, literally Ego *eīw'a wendo*, "Ego feels love" or *ena wendo*, "Ego owns love." Since the focus of this chapter is anger, which is a good emotion[15] and therefore is felt and owned, I will analyze the polysemous element of *īw'a* "feel":

> 19. *kwīw'a*
> *kū.īw'a*
> INF.feel
> "To feel"

The Akamba make a difference between emotional feelings like love and sensory feelings like that of touch. In expressions describing sensory feelings, *kwīw'a* "to feel" is accompanied by *kwata* "touch or *sama* "taste" but is never used on its own. For example, if a parent wants to touch her child's forehead to feel the body heat, one will have to say *kwata* "touch" and *īw'a* "feel," that is, touch and feel the body heat. A mother who is preparing food will *sama* "taste" and *īw'a* "feel," that is, taste and feel whether the food is ready to be served.

---

14. Kieti and Coughlin, *Kamba Oral Literature*, 51.
15. It is explained later in section 5.2 as to how anger is a good emotion.

In addition to *īw'a* "feel," there are three other usages of *īw'a*: *īw'a* "hear/listen," *īw'a* "ripen" and *īw'a* "obey" as demonstrated in the examples below:

20. *Nīngw'a   nzaa*
    Nī.nkū.īw'a
    FOC-1sg-feel
    Feel   1sg   hunger
    "I feel hungry"

21. *kweew'a   kana   īw'a*
    kū.īw'a   IMPER
    INF.hear   listen
    "Listen/hear   or   Listen"

22. *kwīw'a   kana   īw'a*
    kū.īw'a   IMPER
    INF.ripen   or   ripen
    "To.ripen"

23. *kwīw'a   kana   īw'a*
    kū.īw'a   or   IMPER
    INF.obey
    "To obey   or   obey"

When the Akamba verbally express their emotions, they associate the emotion with either *nthakame* "blood," *thayū* "soul" or *ngoo* "heart" such as:

24. *Nthakame   yakwa   ndī   kw'īw'ana   na   yake*
    Blood   of me   not   agree   with   his
    "My blood does not agree with his/hers"
    "We are not friends"

25. *Nthakame   yakwa   nī   īkwendete*
    Nthakame   yakwa   nī   ī.kū.enda.ete
    Blood   of me   is   3sg.INF.love. PRG
    "My blood loves (progressively) you"
    "I love you"

26. *Nthakame*   *yakwa*   *nī*   *īkūmenete*
Nthakame   *yakwa*   *nī*   *ī.kū.mena.ete*
Blood   of me   is   3sg.INF.hate. PRG
"My blood hates (progressively) you"
"I hate you"

The word *nthakame* "blood" in the three sentences above can be replaced with the word *thayū*-soul or *ngoo* "heart" and still mean the same. For example:

27. *Thayū*   *wakwa*   *nī*   *ūkūmenete*
                                Ū.kū.mena.ete
Soul   of me   is   3sg.INF.hate. PRG
"I hate (progressively) you"

28. *Ngoo*   *yakwa*   *nī*   *īkūmenete*
                                Ī.kū.mena.ete
Heart   of me   is   3sg.INF.hate. PRG
"My heart hates (progressively) you"

This interchangeable usage is based on the Akamba understanding that the soul is located in the blood.[16] When Ego dies, they believe that the soul of Ego left his blood, his heart is not pumping and therefore there is no blood flowing in Ego's veins. These three: *thayū* "soul," *nthakame* "blood" and *ngoo* "heart" feature prominently in Akamba expressions of emotions.

Therefore, based on the above examples and the analysis that I will do later in this chapter, my findings will demonstrate that the Akamba emotion of *ngoò* "anger" is in the soul which is located in the blood. Once this *ngoò* "anger" is triggered, it is carried by the blood to the *ngoo*-heart, which is the body organ in which the *ngoò* "anger" event occurs. My findings are supported by data which I collected and analyzed using the following methods.

---

16. This is an invisible element. If Ego is cut and bleeds, Akamba do not see that as a way of losing their soul. However, the same way water can be drained and leave toads without a place to live and hence die, the same is true with the soul. If Ego bleeds a lot, the soul will be like a toad whose pond has run dry and therefore dies (leaves the body).

4.4 The Akamba Folk Theory of *Ngoò* "Anger"

The Akamba have several words for anger: *ūthatu* (anger), *ūthilīku* (anger which sometimes involves cursing), *ngoo* (anger; but the word *ngoo* also has other meanings, that is, "heart," "nausea," "desire" and "banana flower"), *woo* (anger, pain), and *nzika* (anger; but *nzika* also means "doubt" in some regions of Ūkambanī). They have many other words, which they use to imply anger but which in themselves do not mean anger. These include: *kūng'athia*[17] (an expression of being stiff from intense anger), *ūū* (bitter), *ūlalako* (irritation, a hot feeling that people get when they eat hot pepper), *ūkaatu* (unpalatable taste), *kūtangwa* (to be choked) and *kwīw'a makindi* (to feel as if there are internal lumps that are making you bulge). The Akamba anger word analyzed here is *ngoò* "anger." The choice of *ngoò* "anger" is informed by my findings that it is a reference to the central organ where the Akamba believe that the emotion takes place.

4.4.1 Analysis of the *Ngoò* "Anger" Scenario

The evaluation and testing of Fessler's model in the methodology[18] section 2.3 has explained the usefulness of his model in the analysis of Akamba emotions. However, in situations where Ego is not the one violating a norm as discussed above, but is the one being violated, Fessler's model will need some adjustments to accommodate this twist. This is the case with the Akamba *ngoò* "anger" where in my analysis Ego is the one experiencing it. I propose a five-point logic as follows:

1. Ego perceives that X has done something displeasing to Ego.
   Nīwangosea
   nī.wa.ngose.a
   FOC-2sg-wrong-FV
   "You have wronged me"

---

17. *kūng'athia* has the same root as '*kwīng'athīlīlya* which means "to harden/stiffen self." When Ego is angry, she/he stiffens her/his face and other parts of the body. This can also be explained from the example of a small beetle, locally available in ūkambanī, which becomes stiff pretending to be dead when it senses danger. Its native name is *kīng'athū* which means the "rigid one," a name coined from its behavior of stiffness.

18. This method is discussed in depth in the methodology section.

2. This hurts Ego's soul which is in the blood.

   Ego　nīwathūkya thayū wakwa

   Ego　nī.wa.thūkia.a　　　　thayū　wakwa

   Ego　FOC-1sg-spoil-FV　　soul　　of me

   Ego　"has spoiled/disturbed my soul"

Although I indicated above that *nthakame* "blood" and *thayū* "soul" are used interchangeably in examples 25 and 26, in this sentence the phrase *nthakame* "blood" would not fit. Instead, the Akamba say that their souls are disturbed and add that:

   i. *nthakame yakwa nīsamūkīte*

   nthakame　　*yakwa*　　*nī.samūka.e*[19]*te*[20]

   Blood　　　　mine　　　FOC-boil-PRG

   "I am about to get angry." Literally, "my blood is heating up (progressively)"

Or,

   ii. *nthakame yakwa nīsembete*

   nthakame　　*yakwa*　　*nī.sembet.e*

   Blood　　　　mine　　　FOC-run-FV

   "I am almost getting angry." Literally, "my blood is running"

These two idioms suggest that Ego is about to get angry. Literally, "my blood is boiling or running." These idioms suggest that the body of the offended person is responding to the displeasing activity and that the offended person is aware of the response. This body response is that of a fast flow of blood within the offended person's system. Since some of my informants were illiterate, they could not tell what comes first between a fast flow of blood and a heart that is beating fast. Their understanding is that a hurt soul makes the heart beat faster and thus the blood flows fast and that fast flow continues for the period Ego is experiencing *ngoò* "anger."

---

19. The "ae" contracts to form ī.
20. *kūsamūka* is a borrowed word from Swahili *kūchemka* which means "boiling."

iii. The blood carries the hurting soul to Ego's heart.

nthakame yumaa ngoonĩ

nthakame	*yĩ.uma.a*	*ngoo.nĩ*
Blood	FOC.come.HAB	heart.in

"The blood comes from the heart"

The Akamba never talk of blood going into the heart, they only say it comes from the heart. However, the following expression explains that the disturbed soul, which makes the blood run fast (according to the folk theory) eventually affects the heart.

iv. This makes the Ego's heart beat fast but they say they have a "heavy heart"[21] instead.

This expression of a "heavy heart" prompts the following expressions.

Ena ngoo ngito

e.ena	*ngoo*	*ngito*
3sg-has	heart	heavy

"He has a heavy heart"

Another expression is that of a heart that is tying a knot.

Ena ngoo yĩkundĩkĩte

e-ena	*ngoo*	*yĩ.kundĩkĩt.e*
3sg-has	heart	FOC.tied.a.knot.FV

"He is in a bad mood (she/he is unhappy)." Literally, "his heart has tied a knot"

---

21. This expression of a "heavy heart" represents the fast beating of the heart. The reason for this idiom is because the literal expression of saying that the heart is beating fast is associated with a heart disease. If anyone says that her/his heart is beating fast, she/he would be wishing a bad thing on herself/himself. However, when Ego says that she/he has a heavy heart, the listener can infer that it is the heart that is literally beating fast as a result of an offence committed. In rare occasions, some people still say their hearts are beating fast.

v. Ego experiences *ngoò* "anger."

    eīw'a   *ngoò*

    e.īw'a   ngoò[22]

    3sg.feel   anger

    "He is angry." Literally, "he is feeling the heart"

At this level when Ego says: *nī īw'a ngoò*, X can infer from the context that Ego is angry. The context in this case is important because the phrase *nī īw'a ngoo* (without intonation) means that Ego is nauseated. That is:

  29. *Nī.īw'a*   *ngoo*

      Isg.feel   nausea

      "I feel nauseated"

Or,

  30. *Nī.īw'a*   *ngoò*

      Isg.feel   anger

      "I am angry"

Since according to the analysis above *ngoò* "anger" is experienced in the heart, then the following *anger* expressions are common in the day-to-day life of the Akamba in their conversations.

  31. *Nde*[23]   *ngoò*

      No   heart/anger

      "He does not get angry easily." Literally, "he has no anger"

A common domestic saying that captures this is:

  32. *Musyai*   *nde*   *ngoò*

      Parent   no   anger

      "A parent does not get angry easily." Literally, "a parent has no anger"

---

    22. The Akamba differentiate polysemous words by intonation. The difference between *ngoo* "heart" and *ngoò* "anger" is that of intonation. The challenge with the Kĩkamba language is that it is a tonal language but the orthography has no tonal markings.

    23. "nd-" is the stem for the personal pronoun for negation. The suffix marks the number, in this case it is the 3rd person singular.

33. *e. ngoò   yĩ   vakuvĩ*
3sg. Anger   is   near
"He is easily angered." Literally, "his anger is near"

34. *e. ngoò   mbingĩ*
3sg.anger   much
"He gets very angry (when provoked)." Literally, "he has much anger"

35. *e. ngoò   nthũku*
3sg. Anger   bad
"He has a bad anger." Literally, "he has a bad heart"

36. *e.ngoò   ya   nyamũ*
3sg- anger   of   animal/wild animal
"He has an extraordinary anger." Literally, "his heart is of an animal"

These expressions are the common ones and the word *ngoò* features in all of them. Importantly, these expressions are not only mentioned in *ngoò* "anger" contexts, but in all other contexts where Ego is angry regardless of which Kĩkamba anger word is in focus. These expressions which cut across all other anger words among the Akamba inform the position that *ngoò* "anger" is a foundational expression of anger among the Akamba. The following expressions that are used to ask the hurting Ego to control his anger confirm this position.

37. *Kũnanga   ngoò*
Kũna.nga
Pat- (repeatedly)   anger
"Relent in your anger." Literally, "pat repeatedly your heart"

38. *Ololosya   ngoò*
Soften   anger
"Relent in your anger." Literally, "soften your heart"

39. *Tũnganga   ngoò*
Tũnga.nga

Return back (repeatedly) anger

"Relent in your anger." Literally, "return back repeatedly your heart"

40. *Melya*   *ngoò*   *isu*[24]
Swallow   anger   those

"Relent in your anger." Literally, "swallow those hearts"

When Ego is unable to control his *anger*, the result is an act of retribution. This act of retribution is regarded as showing Ego's heart.

41. *kwonania*   *ngoò*
kũ.ona.ni.a
INF-show-3sg.FV   anger
To show   anger

"Act of retribution out of anger." Literally, "to show your heart"

An Ego experiencing *ngoò* "anger" does not say that he is "showing" *anger*. However, the person to whom *ngoò* "anger" is expressed against will normally warn Ego against showing *ngoò* "anger." When Ego speaks about his anger, normally the pronounced statement will have an ellipsis as explained in the following example:

42. *nĩngũkwonia*
nĩ.nkũ.kũ.ona.i.a
FOC.1sg.show.PERF.FV
"I will show (you)"

In this phrase, the speaker does not explicitly state what it is that he will show. However, there is another phrase which is equally common and is pertinent in understanding what is it that Ego would show the aggravating party. This phrase is:

43. *nũũmbona*
nĩ.ũ.mb.ona
FOC-1sg-see
"You will see me"

---

24. The demonstrative "those" always accompanies this expression. This use of the demonstrative presents *ngoo*-anger as though it is something visible.

According to this phrase, an angry person is one who explains himself. Therefore, the phrase in example 42 has an ellipsis of "self." Looking at this phrase in the context of kwonania ngoo "to show Ego's heart," it is plausible to conclude that the word ngoo "heart" is used as a synecdoche of a part for the whole referring to the whole person.

The data collected also suggest that *ngoò* "anger" is conceptualized depending on age and body size. Children have "small" anger while grown-ups have "big" anger. The following sayings demonstrate this. First is an example of a parent speaking to her child:

> 44. ndūkambonie   tūkolo   tu
> ndū.kamb.ona.ni.e   tūkolo   tu
> NEG.show.me.FV   small angers   DEM
> Don't show me   small angers   those
> "Don't act from your anger." Literally, "don't show me those small hearts"

The second example is a conversation of two grown-ups. When a grown-up X angers Ego, Ego would sarcastically say:

> 45. ndūkandetee   makolo   asu
> ndūka.nde.ete.e   ma.kolo
> NEG-bring-FV   much anger   DEM
> Don't bring me   much anger   those
> "Don't act from your *anger*." Literally, "don't bring me that disgusting anger"

These examples, 44 and 45, show that both the young and the grown-ups have the potential of getting angry. It is therefore necessary to consider how this *ngoò* "anger" emotion is acquired.

4.4.2 *Ngoò* "Anger": The Source

Everyone among the Akamba has the potential of experiencing *ngoò* "anger" but the difference is its intensity. The Kamba people believe that the intensity of *ngoò* "anger" temperaments are acquired either from the genes of the parents or from naming of a newborn child. My informants said that if the parents of a child are known to be people who get very angry or are slow in getting angry, the same character trait would be passed on to their children genetically. Among the Akamba, parents refer to their children as *'nthakame yakwa* "my blood" and this necessitates the thinking that they have a lot in common with their children besides the physical looks. This way, *ngoò* "anger" is an innate temperament.

In contrast, the *ngoò* "anger" temperament is also believed to be acquired through the naming of children. Normally the naming of children is done by using the name of a relative who is either old or deceased. Some Akamba believe that a child will acquire to a large extent the character of the person he/she is named after. Therefore, if the parents of a newborn child have low anger temperaments but they give their child the name of a relative who has a bad temperament, that child will acquire the *ngoò* "anger" temperament of the person he/she is named after. This mode of acquiring a *ngoò* "anger" temperament through naming is considered more powerful than the first one and supersedes it. In this way, *ngoò* "anger" is an acquired temperament.

According to the modes of acquiring a *ngoò* "anger" temperament described above, it is fair to conclude that there is no one among the Akamba who does not get angry. The difference is the intensity of that anger. With this information, the difference is in how long the *ngoò* "anger" emotion lasts. Determining how long the *ngoò* "anger" emotion lasts can be ascertained by analyzing whether it is an event condition or a state condition. The following section will ascertain how the Akamba differentiate the *ngoò* "anger" event condition from the *ngoò* "anger" state condition.

4.4.3 Event and State

In Kĩkamba, all the emotions are associated with the verbs *ĩw'a* "feel," *likwa* "be entered" or *ena* "owns." The verbs *kwĩw'a* "to feel" and *kũlikwa* "to be entered" are used to denote an event condition that has just happened while *ena* "she/he has" is used to denote a state condition. All the examples given above in section 4.4 have *ĩw'a* "feel" and denote an event condition. It is the same case with the example on *likwa* "entered" in example 17 and 18.

As for the state condition, a prefix *ena* "she/he has" is used. To demonstrate this, I will use a story as told by Mwikali Kieti and Peter Coughlin.[25] The story is about two boys who were on a journey and were warned by their grandmother not to eat anything on the way. However, one of them ate

---

25. Kieti and Coughlin, *Kamba Oral Literature*, 53.

something and his feet changed and became wood. The boy who did not eat was disturbed by this. The story says:

> 46. kavĩsĩ   ku   yu   weethĩa   kena   kĩthikiii   kiingĩ   vyu
> kavĩsĩ   ku   yu   we.ĩthĩa   ke.ena   kĩthikiii   ki.ingĩ   vyu
> boy   that   now   3sg.happen   3sg-has   disturbance   3sg.a lot   very
> Now, it happened that the boy had a lot of disturbance.

"The boy was very disturbed." Literally, "the boy was the owner of disturbance."

By using either *kwĩw'a*-feel or *ena*-owner, a listener is able to tell whether the event has lasted a short or a long period, though it is hard to precisely determine the length or shortness of the event. Here are some examples that illustrate this further:

> 47. kwĩw'a ngoò
> kũ.ĩw'a ngoò
> INF.feel anger
> to.feel anger, to be angered (event)
> Ego is getting/becoming angry.

> 48. ena ngoò
> ena ngoò
> "she/he has" of anger, angered (state)
> Ego is angry.

> 49. kwĩw'a muyo
> kũ.ĩw'a muyo
> INF.feel happy
> "To feel happy, to be happy (event)"
> Ego is experiencing happiness.

> 50. ena muyo
> "she/he has" of happy, happy (state)
> Ego is happy.

The Akamba differentiate between a person who is experiencing an emotion, regardless of whether it is an event or state, and one who has the potential to experience that emotion. The verb *ena* "she/he has" is used in reference to a person who is already in a state condition, *ĩw'a* "feel" and *likwa* "entered" is used in an event condition and the prefix -e- is used to denote a person who has the potential to experience emotion. This potential is inferred from the context since the same prefix -e- is also a 3cs (common singular) maker. For example, one can say:

> 51. Ego *enangoò*
> Ego *ena ngoò*
> Ego owns angry
> "Ego is angry." Literally, "she/he has" a heart

This statement means Ego is now angry. In contrast:

> 52. Ego *engoò*
> Ego *e ngoò*
> Ego 3cs anger
> "Ego has the potential of getting angry." Literally, "Ego has anger"

According to this analysis, the Akamba differentiate an event condition from a state condition by the use of different verbs. For a person who is prone to a certain emotion, they use the prefix -e-. When the Akamba experience *ngoò* "anger," regardless of whether it is an event or a state condition, they display similar physiological effects.

4.4.4 Somatic Phenomenology

Some of the somatic phenomena in Akamba emotion of anger are similar to those observed in the BHS. These include; trembling which is equivalent to רָגַז, foaming of the mouth which is similar to קֶצֶף (according to Zacharias Kotzé as discussed in chapter 1 section 1.5.2, but this research has a different conclusion) and heavy breathing similar to אָנַף (אַף) or רוּחַ in the contexts where this is used to mean hot air from the nostrils. Sometimes אַף (אָנַף) is used to mean hot nose or hot face in which case it would be a different somatic phenomenon.

However, there are other physiological effects that are different from the BHS. These are: darkening of the face, bulging of the blood vessels, walking with a bent head, staggering and inability to talk. Although these are the main effects that can be observed, the Akamba have internal physiological effects that are not displayed but they talk about them. These are *ũũ* "bitterness," *kŭlalakwa* "to be irritated," *kŭtangwa* "to be choked" and *kwĩwa makindi* "feeling of a lump in the throat."

These physiological effects, both internal and external, are primarily caused by the following antecedent conditions.

4.4.5 Antecedent Conditions

The antecedent conditions that make a Mŭkamba experience *ngoò* "anger" can be classified into two categories: *kĩvŭthya* "disrespect" and *naĩ* "bad mood." Ego places the focus for the *kĩvŭthya* "disrespect" on the offender while the focus for the *naĩ* "bad mood" is on the offense. When Ego is provoked, Ego will either wonder why the offender is disrespecting him/her by doing this, or focus on the offense which made him/her have a bad mood. Although there are a myriad of specific offenses that would make Ego experience *ngoò* "anger," they can all be summarized in these two categories mentioned above. In the following section, the two categories are explained further.

4.4.5.1 Kĩvŭthya "Disrespect"

Disrespect is likened to belittling and the common saying is that of *kŭndwikĩthya kana*, "making me a child." Where disrespect is perceived, when a person offends another, the offended person generally retorts by asking the offender why he is disrespecting him. When a senior person in the society is angered by a junior person, the outright assumption is that the junior is disrespecting the senior. Similarly, when the junior is hurt by the senior, his/her conclusion is that the senior is taking the liberty of hurting him/her out of disrespect. *Kĩvŭthya* "disrespect" has the focus on the offender and not the offense.

A basic scenario provided by one of my informants illustrates this: "I left the house in the morning and instructed my house help to wash my clothes. I came in the evening and found that she had not done so. Among the clothes she was to wash, was my favorite dress that I wanted to put on the following day. That was *kĩvŭthya* 'disrespect' and I felt *ngoò nthŭkŭ* 'bad anger.'"[26] Other than disrespect, the other cause for *ngoò* "anger" is *naĩ* "bad mood."

---

26. Janet Muthoka, personal communication, 13 April 2012.

4.4.5.2 Naĩ "Bad Mood"

The word *naĩ* is polysemous. It is used to mean "sin, sickness or having a bad feeling." *Naĩ* is an antecedent condition for *ngoò* in the sense of being anything that would make Ego have a bad mood. Usually the focus is on the offense and not the offender. A basic scenario from one of my informants that illustrates this is as follows: "One day I received a call from my friend who had loaned my younger brother some money, and which my brother had not refunded as planned. So, I called my brother who promised to pay it back in two days. After the two days, my brother failed to honor his commitment and my friend felt *naĩ*. He later called me in *ngoò mbĩngĩ* to explain that my brother did not pay him back his money."[27]

4.4.6 Affective Phenomenon of *Ngoò* "Anger"

The Akamba classify emotional feelings as either good or bad. This classification takes place at both the individual and social level. *Ngoò* "anger," which is the focus of this chapter, is appraised at both an individual and social level as a good and a bad expression. The details of how each is perceived are analyzed below.

4.4.7 Self-appraisal

At an individual level, Akamba treasure their *ngoò* "anger." Having *ngoò* "anger" is valued as strength while lack of it is weakness. Therefore, demonstrating Ego's *ngoò* "anger" is a good thing, which builds one's self-esteem while the inabilities to show how much *ngoò* "anger" you have is a bad thing. This demonstration is at a physiological level but not at the level of retribution.

Men and women alike boastfully talk of how they feel when they experience *ngoò* "anger." The ability of Ego to experience *ngoò* "anger" earns Ego *kĩkĩo* "respect." When people know that Ego easily experiences *ngoò* "anger," they will avoid provoking Ego to anger. If they provoke Ego by mistake, they will be quick to apologize and make peace with him/her. This kind of treatment amounts to *kĩkĩo* "respect."

People who don't have visible physiological effects of *ngoò* "anger" are viewed as weak. The Kĩkamba verbal expression is: *maina ũũme* "they lack manhood." The word "manhood" is a euphemism that refers to the testicles.

---

27. Moses Mutua, personal communication, 23 April 2012.

Even women talk of their "manhood" as an idiom implying that they are worth the respect accorded men. People who have no visible physiological effects of *ngoò* "anger" or who do not have the courage to talk about their *ngoò* "anger" are normally scorned and disrespected. Children who want to earn respect from their peers fake the physiological effects of anger to scare their peers and in return be respected.

4.4.8 Social Appraisal

Although experiencing *ngoò* "anger" is individually valued as a good thing, socially the act of becoming violent at the slightest provocation is considered a bad thing. When Ego controls his/her *ngoò* "anger," which is socially valued, it is a good thing.

The attitude of being violent at the slightest provocation is likened to being a *kĩvĩsĩ* "uncircumcised boy." This is motivated by the attitude of *ivĩsĩ* "uncircumcised boys" who always provoke each other and fight a lot. Although the *ivĩsĩ* "uncircumcised boys" are not bad, their actions are perceived as done out of immaturity. Hence, a person who is unable to control their anger is likened to an uncircumcised boy.

On the other hand, people who control their anger are likened to *atumĩa* "elders." Although the name *mũtumĩa* "elder" normally refers to a person who is old, it is also given to young people who have won the respect of the community. Therefore, depending on whether Ego is able to manage his/her anger or not, that will determine whether Ego will be disrespected by being called *kĩvĩsĩ*-uncircumcised boy, or respected and earn the name *mũtumĩa* "elder."

4.4.9 *Ngoò* "Anger" as an Inferred Emotion

Ngoò "anger" is an inferred emotion, especially from what the Akamba call *kũtukya ũthyũ* "darkening of face." From the information I got from my informants, *kũtukya ũthyũ* "darkening of face" is similar to frowning. Although grief also has this somatic phenomenon, *ngoò* "anger" is the common inference.

Depending on the context, *ngoò* "anger" is also inferred from the way an elderly man clears his throat. In general, elderly people among the Akamba constantly clear their throats when angered. This is closely related with the somatic phenomenon of being choked when Ego experiences *ngoò* "anger." The experience of being choked is believed to be an act of ancestors who want to ensure that Ego does not speak in anger. The words of an elderly man or woman may amount to a curse and that is why being choked is a common somatic phenomenon among the elderly in the Akamba community. However, this does not mean that the other age categories are not choked. The case of the elderly was singled out as a unique one in this case.

Verbally, *ngoò* "anger" is inferred from *kũng'athia* "to be stiff." The word *kũngathia* itself does not mean anger. Unlike a frowning face which can mean that either Ego is angry or grieved, there is no other emotion inferred from *kũng'athia*. For example, if Ego is angry, X will ask him:

53. *Ko   wa ng'athia?*
    QUE   1sg.become.stiff (from anger)?
    "Are you angry?" Literally, "have you become stiff from anger?"

The lexical meaning of *ng'athia* is best understood when looked at from, first, the behavior of a little beetle known n a*ĩng'athũ*. This is a beetle which stiffens and becomes motionless when threatened.[28] Its nan a*ĩng'athũ* was coined from that behavior. Second, *ng'athia* can be understood from the Kĩkamba word for epilepsy. Epilepsy is an attack that throws the victim to the ground and makes Ego stiff. Suffering from epilepsy is known as *kũng'athũka* "a disease which makes one stiff." From these examples, the root is noticeable -*ng'ath*-; the rest are prefixes and suffixes.

The usage of this term does not necessarily m'an that EIo is visibly stiff. It is used even when Ego is composed, but it implies that Ego is angry to a point of being stiff. Some of the phrases commonly used are:

54. *Nĩ   -wa-   ng'athia*
    FOC-   2sg-   stiffen
    "He has stiffened"

When this term is used in the context of one who is angry; Ego may not visibly be stiff from anger as in the case of an epileptic victim or a beetle.

Another common phrase is when X is asking Ego, who is not angry, not to *ng'athia* "be angry." Assuming X has made a promise to Ego and X cannot keep it, X will talk to Ego and beseech him/her not to get angry.

55. *Ndũ.ka.ng'athie   mbũ.mĩĩ.sye*

---

28. This is its defense mechanism against danger.

> Don't.2sg.stiffen   be.patient.with me
> "Do not become angry, be patient with me"

In this case, the Ego is not yet angry but is in a situation where he/she can become angry. The speaker would therefore use *ndūkang'athie* to beseech the person not to give in to anger although he/she is rightfully entitled to.

4.5 Classification of Kīkamba Anger Words

From the Akamba folk theory described above, all the different anger words fit within a unified corpus that can be classified into three categories: anger in reference to the ngoo "heart" where the emotion occurs, anger in reference to different physiological effects experienced by the Ego and anger in reference to different specific forms of anger. For comparative purposes, קצף is a close equivalent of *ngoò* "retributive anger." Section 4.4 above in this chapter has focused on *ngoo* which is the basis for understanding *ngoò*.

The difference between *ngoo* and *ngoò* is that of intonation. *Ngoò* is pronounced with a slightly higher-pitched tone than *ngoo*, perhaps in some regions of Ūkambanī. While Kīkamba has a developed orthography, intonation markers that mark low tone or high tone are missing in the school textbooks[29] and also in most of the existing literature in Kīkamba, including the Kīkamba dictionary.

In most of the polysemous lexical items in Kīkamba, the difference in their meaning is accomplished by either intonation or the use of phrases. Concerning *ngoo*, the differences in its various meanings: anger, heart, nausea and desire is usually differentiated by use of both phrases and intonation. The data for *ngoo* has demonstrated how different phrases distinguish *ngoò* when it is for anger. One of the characteristics of *ngoò* is its retributive qualities.

The phrase "retributive anger" is used to mean anger which would lead Ego to hurt the self, the other, or property in retribution. Normally, *ngoò* is not the anger that Ego would experience at the slightest provocation. Because of its nature – experienced after numerous warnings – it is usually associated with people in authority over their juniors. Therefore, *ngoò* is never provoked by an inanimate object such as a car that breaks down often, or the wind that blows away your grains in the threshing floor. Mostly people and animals

---

29. Kīkamba is taught in the lower primary from nursery to standard three.

would provoke the Akamba to *ngoò* "anger." For example, an insult from a person would make Ego experience *ngoò* "anger." A cow that breaks away from the cowshed and feeds on the crops would provoke Ego to experience *ngoò* "anger."

When Ego is provoked by a human being, mostly the provoking individual would be a person with whom Ego has a relationship. This could be children to parent, subject to master, employee to employer, students to teacher, and civilians to government official or villagers to elder. The research confirmed that a stranger rarely provokes Ego to *ngoò* "retributive anger" since they have no relationship. If Ego experienced *ngoò* having not warned the provocative individual, with whom they have a relationship, then Ego is perceived as evil.

However, this domain has some exceptions. The experience of *ngoò* by government officials over civilians, teacher to students, or elder to villagers is motivated by the oversight role vested in those in authority. In such cases, an activity may provoke Ego to *ngoò* directly without a warning or in scenarios where such warning was not feasible. The following basic scenario illustrates this. A village elder at *Aĩmi ma Kĩlũngũ* (*Kĩlũngũ* Farmers) ranch was notified of the invasion of the village at night by the neighboring Maasai community who made away with herds of cattle, sheep and goats. The elder *eew'a ngoò* "felt angry" and ordered a pursuit. In this scenario, although the elder was not directly affected and there was no prior warning, he was justified to *kwĩw'a ngoò* "feel angry" because of his oversight role.

With this brief review about *ngoò* "retributive anger," the following section is a diagram that illustrates what the anger concept is like among the Akamba.

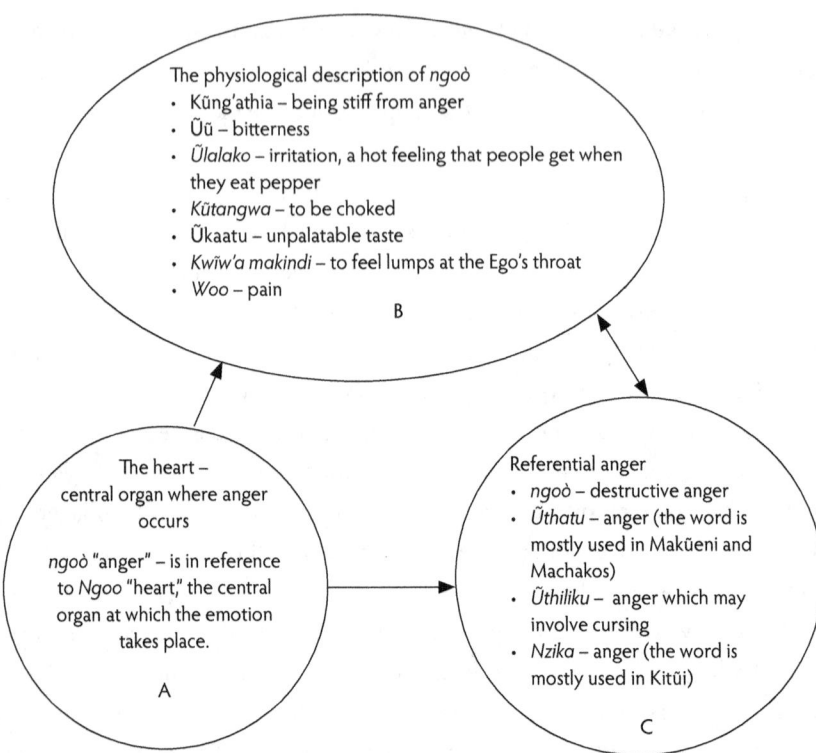

Chart 8

The occurrence of the emotion at the heart is the basis for the physiological effects in category B and the specific references to the different forms of anger in category C. In the expressions, Ego can go back and forth in describing a specific kind of anger in category C and the physiological effects in category B, hence the double pointed arrow.

4.6 The BHS Lexical Equivalent of *Ngoò* "Anger"

The investigation of the *ngoò* "anger" folk theory discussed in section 4.5 above forms the backdrop for the cross-cultural comparison of *ngoò* and קצף. As mentioned in section 4.5, *ngoò* is experienced within the context of human relationships. The Ego is deemed evil if he/she experiences *ngoò* without giving a warning, but if Ego gives warning first, then Ego is justified in experiencing *ngoò*. Usually, *ngoò* is retributive. Therefore, the קצף contexts evoke the *ngoò* frame.

4.7 *Ngoò* Frame: Relationship-retribution

This section shows how the mention of *ngoò* evokes the relationship and retribution frame, and proposes that when *ngoò* is mentioned, the hearer will retrieve from the memory that this is caused by a person who has a form of relationship with Ego and that Ego has acted or intends to act. In this frame, *ngoò* is the profile while relationship-retribution is the domain. The table below illustrates this frame.

Table 4

Profile element	frame
ngoò	Parent-child
	Teacher-pupil
	Master-servant[30]
	Government official-civilian
	Elder-villager
	Husband-wife

This chapter so far has explained how *ngoò* frame fits within the Akamba folk theory. That review is the background for the comparative study of the קצף and *ngoò* frame. The questions, as proposed by Richard Shweder and Jonathan Haidt, form the basis of the comparative study of *ngoò* and קצף. The questions are: Are they alike or different in their antecedent conditions? Are they alike or different in their perception as abstract objects? Are they alike or different in their association with people in leadership roles? Are they alike or different in their intention or implementation of retribution? Are they alike or different in their frames? Are they alike or different to be regarded as close equivalents? Are they alike or different in their categorization as either good or bad emotions?

This study is not just a comparison of two lexical items. The specific investigation of each of the two lexical items and the comparative analysis is useful for exegesis and understanding of the biblical text. This is demonstrated in chapter 5. In that chapter, the different facets of קצף are highlighted and established as to how they have been overlooked in the Kĩkamba Bible.

---

30. "Servant" refers to someone who is hired and paid for his or her services. The Akamba have not had and do not have slaves.

4.8 Distinctiveness of *Ngoò*

In addition to the discussion in Section 4.4 concerning the *ngoò* folk theory, the following section examines the distinctive features of *ngoò*, which are not shared by any other Kĩkamba word that refers to anger.

4.8.1 *Ngoò* Is an Abstract Object

Although the details on *ngoò* – that imply that it is an abstract object – are given in section 4.4 in examples 37 to 40, the same examples are replicated here for illustrative purposes.

    56. Kũnanga   ngoò
    Kũna.nga
    Pat.(repeatedly)   anger
    "Relent in your *anger*." Literally, "pat your anger repeatedly"

This phrase portrays *ngoò* as if it is a tangible object that one can pat.

    57. *Ololosya*   ngoò
    Soften   anger
    "Relent in your *anger*." Literally, "soften your anger"

In this phrase, *ngoò* is figuratively depicted as if it is a hard substance that should be softened.

    58. *Tũnganga*   ngoò
    Tũnga.nga
    Return a bit   anger
    "Relent in your *anger*." Literally, "return back repeatedly your anger"

This phrase figuratively describes *ngoò* as if it is an object that one can hold and carry. It also suggests that *ngoò* has a known locality to which it should be taken back once it departs from it.

    59. *Melya*   ngoò   isu[31]
    Swallow   angers those
    "Swallow those angers"

---

    31. The demonstrative "those" always accompanies this expression. This use of the demonstrative presents ngoo-anger as though it is something visible and countable.

All these examples imply that *ngoò* is something tangible. Example 56 implies that someone can pat, example 57 implies that *ngoò* is a hard substance that can be softened, example 58 implies that *ngoò* is something that has left its usual place and can be put back, and example 59 implies that *ngoò* is like food or drink that can be swallowed. In addition to being abstract objects, since *ngoò* is closely related to *ngoo* "heart" – which is the central organ where the emotion occurs – *ngoò* is expressed as if it is coming out of inside of Ego. With this understanding, example 56, pat anger, is sometimes accompanied by actual patting at the back of the Ego as if pressing the *ngoò* back. Example 58 is an urge to put back the anger into its usual place – inside of the Ego. The swallowing of anger as given in example 59 is not conceptualized as something external that Ego is swallowing but something that is coming from inside of Ego and which Ego needs to recover.

4.8.2 The Usage of *Ngoò* Presupposes Intended Retribution

With regard to *ngoò*, its usage suggests intended retribution. The examination of the *ngoò* phrases supports this claim as it is clarified below. In addition, other *ngoo* phrases – expressing other emotions – also demonstrate that the phrases are accompanied by an action or the intention of it. Below is a consideration of other *ngoo* phrases (for other emotions other than anger) in support of this claim. Later, *ngoò* phrases are considered.

    60. *Kwĩkya ngoo*
    Kũ.ĩkya ngoo
    To.throw heart

The literal translation of this phrase is "throw heart (away)." Mũtĩsya translates this as "to become disgusted and lose interest."[32] This phrase connotes giving up and the accompanying action is that of withdrawal from that which the person was pursuing.

    61. *Kwĩsũva ngoo*
    Kũ.ĩsũva ngoo
    To.entreat heart

This phrase literally means "to treat your heart nicely." The word *ĩsuva* has the idea of politely being persuasive. It is therefore used idiomatically

---

32. Mutĩsya, *Kĩkamba Proverbs and Idioms*, 107.

to mean "to entertain yourself occasionally – to give yourself a treat." The accompanying or the intended action is that of treating oneself usually by celebrating over a meal or going out on holiday. In this phrase, *ngoo* is used as a synecdoche of the part for the whole, meaning the whole person.

> 62. *Kwimbwa nĩ ngoo*
> *Kũ.imb.wa   nĩ   ngoo*
> To.swell.PASS   by   heart
> Literally, it means "to be swollen by the heart"

Mainly this phrase is used in relation to nausea. Mũtĩsya highlights its proper translation as "to be overcome by nausea."[33] The action accompanied by this usage is that of throwing up.

> 63. *Ngoo yĩsaa   kĩla   ĩ.kw.enda*[34]
> The heart eats   what   it.to.desire
> The literal translation of this phrase is "the heart eats what it desires"

This is another synecdoche of the part for the whole; *ngoo* is used to mean the entire person. This metonymic usage is captured by Mũtĩsya who translates the phrase as, "If that is what he really want[sic], then let him proceed with it."[35] The accompanying action is that Ego does that which he desires and there is no turning back.

The examples in 60 to 63 support the argument in examples 56 to 59 showing that an action is intended or accompanies the particular usage. Similarly, the phrases used to describe *ngoò* suggest an intended action – retribution. The four examples in 56 to 59 are also used to illustrate how revenge is prevented. It is believed that if Ego does not control his/her *ngoò* by patting it, pressing it back, softening it and swallowing it, then out of the influence of the *ngoò* Ego will avenge. In addition to those examples, others that support the intention of retribution are as follows.

> 64. *Kwĩw'a ngoo/ngoò*
> *Kũ.ĩw'a ngoo/ngoò*
> To.feel nausea/anger

---

33. Mutĩsya, 107.
34. The word *ĩkwenda* was initially *ĩkũenda*.
35. Mutĩsya, *Kĩkamba Proverbs and Idioms*, 111.

This phrase literally means "to feel nauseated/anger"

Depending on the intonation, it means Ego is being nauseated or is angry. Mūtisya translates the phrase as "to be provoked to action/to be overcome by nausea." The example given below is mainly used in the contexts where the Ego is a person who either is a child or is small in stature or junior in status.

65. ndŭkambonie	tŭkolo	tu
ndŭ.kamb.ona.ni.e	tŭkolo	tu
NEG.2sg.show.me.FV	small.angers	DEM
Do not show me	small.angers	those

"Do not act from your anger." Literally, "don't show me those small angers/hearts"

A person who is acting out of *ngoò* is one who is "showing anger." This phrase is used in contexts where the Ego is already doing something because she/he is angry. While example 65 is for either children or people of small stature or junior in status, the following one is for grown-ups – usually big bodied people.

66. ndŭkandetee	makolo	asu
ndŭka.nde.ete.e	ma.kolo	
NEG-bring-FV	big.anger	DEM
Don't bring me	big.anger	those

"Don't act from your *anger*." Literally, "don't bring me that big (nasty) anger/heart"

Examples 65 and 66 are pleas for Ego to reconsider his/her intended action. Section 4.8.2, therefore, demonstrates that *ngoò* has an intention of retribution.

4.8.3 *Ngoò* Is Associated with Leaders

Below are examples that illustrate how *ngoò*'s usage is related to leaders or persons with specific roles.

67. *Mŭingi wa ĭsoma   nde.ngoò*
The guide of an emaciated (animal) does not have.anger
"The shepherd, one who guides an emaciated animal of his herd, does not get angry (easily)"

68. *Mŭsyai nde ngoò*
Parent not anger
"A parent does not get angry (easily)"

The examples given in 67 and 68 have a direct application to people who have an oversight role: a shepherd has an oversight role over the cattle while the parent has an oversight role over the children. The implied message is that of patience by the Ego. The shepherd is urged to be patient with his/her emaciated animal(s) since when the rains come there will be plenty of pasture and the animal will regain its strength. Concerning the parent, the urge is to be patient with erring children since with time they will hopefully grow up and change.

Although the examples given in 67 and 68 apply directly to people who have an oversight role, they are also used for the general public. They are intended to persuade people to be responsible in the way they act out of anger, when angry. Therefore, an expression of anger by any individual would be guided by the advice. Anyone in the community who fails to heed the proffered advice can be described by the following phrases.

69. *E.ngoò nthŭku*
She/He has anger bad (She/He has a bad heart)
"Ego has bad anger"

This is used to describe Ego who is very violent when angered. Mainly it means that Ego is less thoughtful of his/her actions – Ego acts without thinking – or takes pride in being violent. Such a person is also branded as having:

70. *E.ngoò ya nyamŭ*
She/he has anger of an animal (wild)
"Ego has a (wild) animal's anger"

This is a comparison of Ego and a wild animal in their action. While example 69 is for one who is less thoughtful, example 70 is for one who is thoughtless – Ego's actions are like those of a wild animal that does not have a conscience or cannot show mercy. Although there are a few people who would take pride in being violent since it makes them less provoked, the majority would retreat from being violent since the community appraises this behavior as foolishness and as an act that is equal to being an animal.

The Akamba community appraises the whole situation of the emotion, and the *ngoò* phrases have a specific application to the people who have oversight roles.

This chapter has so far looked at the Akamba folk theory of anger. The data analyzed has ascertained that *ngoò* is an intonation of *ngoo* "heart," the central organ where anger is believed to take place. The details explained on *ngoò* form the basis for its comparison with קצף, as explained in the following chapter.

CHAPTER 5

Frames of קצף and *Ngoò*: The Differences, Similarities and How Some Facets of the קצף Frame are Represented in the Kĩkamba Bible

This chapter offers a comparison of קצף and *ngoò* and ascertains that they are close equivalents. As mentioned in chapter 4, this study benefits both the learned and the lay people. While the learned – who can read and interact with both Hebrew and Kĩkamba – can interrogate the two lexical items, the lay people (in this case the Akamba) have the context of קצף in the 1974 Kĩkamba Bible edition, which, when they read it or it is read to them, evokes the *ngoò* frame. This research is, therefore, a study that benefits both the scholar and the laypeople. Since the examples given later are from both the BHS and the Kĩkamba Bible, it is fitting to give a brief history of the Kĩkamba Bible.

5.1 A Brief History of the Kĩkamba Bible

The first Kĩkamba Bible translation was the product of a process which was begun by Johann Ludwig Krapf in 1850 and ended in 1956, taking 106 years to complete. There are two reasons given as to why it took so long to translate: first, the translation "was prematurely terminated when Krapf gave up his ministry among the Kamba."[1] Second, it is suspected that part of the work

---

1. Wanjohi, "Scripture Translations in Kenya," 28.

done before had to be repeated because of "the haphazard and superficial way in which the whole enterprise was executed."[2] Most of the translators, in addition to Krapf, who were involved in the translation process were: "J. Hoffmann, H. Pfitzinger, Ernest Brutzer . . . George W. Rhoad, Nellie Rhoad, Hattie Newman, C. F. Johnston, H. S. Nixon, Rose W. Horton, L. E. Davies, Emma Farnsworth, Clara Guilding and Frances Johnson."[3] The only Akamba recorded who joined the committee as informants were Aaron Kasyoki and Jeremiah Kyeva. Although it is hard to establish the exact number of nationals who were involved, it appears that they were few, as Aloo Mojola noted. Mojola recorded that the first translation "was a result of much interest, cooperation and collaboration on the part of the missionaries. It is unfortunate that the input of native speakers was kept at a minimum."[4] In reference to the finished translation, Mojola adds that the "problems of unnaturalness, lack of clarity or even ungrammaticality, in this translation, are due to the literal approach adopted by the translators but also reflects the translators' linguistic competence as non-native."[5] It seems that the above nationals Aaron Kasyoki and Jeremiah Kyeva may have been involved in the first days of translation, when they were young. This assumption is based on the comments of Douglas Waruta who reported on the completion of the Gospel of John as follows: "Mr. Rhoad, with the assistance of one of the earliest Kamba nationals (whom the writer personally interviewed at his own home in Kangundo) by the name of Aaron Kasyoki continued with success to translate the Gospel of John."[6] This gospel was published in 1915.[7] One of my informants specifically talked about Kasyoki and identified him as the father of one of our current Kenyan politicians, Honorable Charity Kaluki Ngilu, the governor of Kītui County.[8]

This translation was revised in 1974, in the hope of offering a better translation. Waruta, writing in 1975, noted the following: "The revision of the Kamba Bible has since been completed by Mr. and Mrs. Normal Johnson, assisted by

---

2. Mojola, *God Speaks*, 16.
3. Mojola, 17.
4. Mojola, *God Speaks*, 17.
5. Mojola, 18.
6. Wanjohi, *Scripture Translations in Kenya*, 29–30.
7. Mojola, *God Speaks*, 17.
8. Dr. Nathan Nzyoka Joshua, the Biblical Studies Head of Department at Africa International University.

nationals. This latest revision should provide the Kamba people with a satisfactory translation of the Scriptures when it is finally published."[9] However, the grammatical challenges still abound, as it is evident in this research. Currently there are two more Kĩkamba Bibles: The New Testament Kĩkamba Bible by John Mbiti, which was completed and launched in December 2014, and a revised complete Kĩkamba Bible launched in April 2012. The revised complete Bible has been received with resistance by some church members and pastors, since most people feel it is paraphrased and does not give the Scripture the required force.[10] Others use the two translations for comparison when they are studying. One of my informants, Professor Samuel Ngewa, thinks that all these translations will co-exist just the same way we have many English translations.[11] Currently, the widely used translation is the 1974 edition, and it is the one used for this research.

In the effort to justify the claim that קצף and *ngoò* are close equivalents and that some facets of קצף are overlooked in the Kĩkamba Bible, this chapter employs two sections: the comparative analysis of קצף and *ngoò*, and the analysis of the קצף frame in the Kĩkamba translation. A third section is added with discussions on the value of cross-cultural study in biblical studies. As a preliminary step, the first section of this chapter examines the similarities and differences between the קצף and *ngoò* frames, which form the background for the biblical analysis that follows. A comparative examination of the similarities and the differences between קצף and *ngoò* show that these two concepts are different. They are different in the manner in which they are expressed and in the experiencesIwhich they refer, such as good or bad emotions. Also, they are different because they cover different domains. But they are the same in that they do profile similar elements. For example, they have similar antecedent conditions, are perceived as abstract objects, are associated with people in leadership roles and they are used with an intention and/or implementation of retribution. Their similarities, which far outweigh the differences – not in numerical strength but in significance to the two frames – stand as evidence that they are close equivalents. To begin with, the

---

9. Wanjohi, "Scripture Translations in Kenya," 31.

10. This is what Pastor Chris Mwalw'a said. He was the master of ceremonies during the launch of this edition.

11. Professor Samuel Ngewa is a New Testament Professor at Africa International University.

following section is on the comparative analysis of קצף and *ngoò*, beginning with the differences between their frames.

5.2 Differences of the קצף and *Ngoò* Frames

There are three main differences between קצף and *ngoò*. First, the difference between קצף and *ngoò* is how the emotion is experienced. The verb used by the Akamba is *ĩw'a* "feel" when they verbally express their emotions. For example,

> 71. Nĩ.ĩw'a *ngoò*
> I.feel anger
> "I am angry"

The use of *ĩw'a* in the sense of "feel anger" has no close equivalent in the BHS. This proves that קצף and *ngoò* are different in the way they were experienced. Although Jean Harkins and Anna Wierzbicka propose "feel" as one of the universal concepts that are useful for comparison of emotions, "feel" does not apply in the BHS.[12]

The second difference is categorizing the emotions as either good or bad in the two cultures. According to the data analysis in chapter 4, section 4.3, examples 17 and 18, bad emotions are perceived as external objects which enter Ego. Good emotions on the other hand are experienced from within and are usually associated with the word *ĩw'a*. On this basis, *ngoò* is a good emotion although it can have bad effects. The קצף is not explicitly categorized as either a good or bad emotion. As it is explained in this research, each culture has its own uniqueness, and the researcher has to identify what concepts are similar for comparison.

The third difference is their frames, at the domain levels. The קצף frame clearly identifies the source, the trajector, the trajectory and the landmark. On the other hand, the *ngoò* relationship-retribution frame is traced through the five-point logic and identifies different levels the injury (emotional injury) is "carried" before Ego gets *ngoò*. Through these levels, it is demonstrated in chapter 4 that *ngoò* "anger" is an intonation of *ngoo* "heart" which is the central organ where the emotion occurs. The available BHS data is limited

---

12. Wierzbicka and Harkins, "Introduction," 9.

to revealing the process through which an emotional injury goes to make Ego experience קצף. In addition, the BHS data does not explicitly state the specific body organ that is associated with the experience of קצף. However, *ngoò* and קצף show that these differences are at the domain level but display similar frame elements, as is explained later in this chapter. As mentioned in chapter 2, each frame has its domain and the profiled elements. The domains are the backgrounded information while the profiled elements are the specific features of the frame that are explicitly stated. While *ngoò* and קצף differ at their domain levels, their profiled elements are similar in significant ways as analyzed below.

5.3 Similarities of the קצף and *Ngoò* Frames

The *ngoò* frame is similar to the קצף frame in four areas: Both *ngoò* and קצף are perceived as abstract objects, both have similar antecedent conditions,[13] both are emotions with intended retribution, and both emotions are associated with people in leadership or with specific responsibilities.[14] These four distinctions and the close association of the two emotions make them close equivalents, which is the basis for their comparative study in this research. The four categories are analyzed in detail below.

5.3.1 Both קצף and *Ngoò* Are Abstract Objects

Both the BHS and the Kīkamba Bible have different words that refer to anger. While most of these words are Ego narratives, *ngoò* and קצף have peculiar properties, one being that they are perceived by the narrators as abstract objects. The phrase "Ego narrative" is used here to mean the description of what the Ego – the angered party – is experiencing and/or is expressing the anger emotion without giving details of the situation that provoked the

---

13. This category, the antecedent conditions, will not be analyzed separately like the other three. Since it is interwoven into the other three, it is discussed in the context of the other three.

14. The use of "specific responsibility" refers to an expectation of Ego to behave in a specific way. Although Ego may not be acting in a leadership capacity, there is an expectation that she/he upholds a certain standard while performing the task at hand. Furthermore, the emotion being associated with people in leadership also brings the aspect of relationship – קצף is not associated with stranger(s) but people who had an existing relationship when the Ego is a person.

emotion. The first subsection is on the Kīkamba data – *ngoò* is an abstract object – and is summarized as follows.

The idea of an abstract object is embedded in the utterances that suggest that both *ngoò* and קצף are abstract objects which could leave the Ego. The utterances, discussed in the preceding chapters 3 and 4, describe these abstract objects as if they are visible and tangible. These are features that are not shared by other words that carry the meaning of anger in both the BHS and the Kīkamba language. Other than *ngoò* and קצף being abstract objects, both have an intention of retribution.

5.3.2 Both *Ngoò* and קצף Have Intended Retribution

The subsection on *ngoò*, examining how it is used and how retribution is intended, is supported by the utterances in which *ngoò* is used and supported by other passages that have a different intonation of *ngoo*. The subsection on קצף that supports this claim is demonstrated by the contexts in which קצף occurs and explains that retribution was either intended or effected. In addition to *ngoò* and קצף having an intended retribution, both are associated with people in leadership or who have specific roles.

5.3.3 Both *Ngoò* and קצף Are Associated with People in Authority or Who Have Specific Roles

The specific sections in chapter 3 and 4 on the distinctive features of both *ngoò* and קצף demonstrated that they have a specific reference to people in leadership and/or have specific leadership roles. Although this does not mean that people outside this scope cannot experience *ngoò* and קצף, the utterances of the two emotions *ngoò* and קצף are specifically associated with people in leadership.

So this far this chapter has explained that *ngoò* and קצף have significant similarities which make them close equivalents. The following section examines how קצף as a lexical item and the קצף frame is represented in the Kīkamba Bible.

5.4 The קצף Frame Representation in the Kīkamba Bible

The examination of how the קצף frame is represented in the Kīkamba Bible explains that, first, *ngoò* is not used in the Kīkamba Bible as a translation for קצף. Second, there is no consistency in the different lexical items that are used in place of קצף, and third, the קצף frame is partially represented in the Kīkamba Bible: some passages have adopted the קצף frame while others have used terms that are similar to *ngoò* frame – implying the concept of this frame is something that was at the back of their minds but not employed fully in the translation.

The words that are mainly used in the Kīkamba Bible referring to anger are *ūthatu* "anger" (noun) and its verbal forms; *ūthiliku* "anger" and its verbal forms; and *woo* "pain, anger" and its verbal forms. An additional word, *ūū* "unpalatable taste," is also used although it does not occur in passages that have קצף. The following section examines how קצף is translated in the Kīkamba Bible. As it is explained, the translation of קצף in the Kīkamba Bible is marked by two significant characteristics: inconsistency in the use of a single Kīkamba word and the partial adoption of the קצף frame. These two categories are analyzed under the consideration of, first, the קָצַף verbal forms and second, the קֶצֶף noun forms.

5.4.1 The Translation of קָצַף Verbal Forms in the Kīkamba Bible

The lexical item קצף has been translated in the Kīkamba Bible into three different verbs: *kūthīliku, kūthata, kwīw'a woo* and *ūū* as illustrated below. The Kīkamba translations are taken from the Kīkamba Bible but modified for the sake of the interlinear translation. Where a modification is done, an explanation is given in the footnote explaining how the modified word grammatically occurs in the Kīkamba Bible. The examples given are in the set of three and the other references are mentioned but not discussed. Concerning *woo*, only two examples are given since it occurs only twice in the prophetic books.

5.4.1.1 Kūthilīka

- Exod 16:20 וַיִּקְצֹף עֲלֵהֶם מֹשֶׁה and Moses was angry against them

Na	Mose	a.ma.thilīka.īla[15]	mūno
And	Moses	he.them.angry. PERF	very

    "And Moses was very angry against them"

Kĩkamba has five past tenses which are distinguished by tone and the final vowel as explained in chapter 4 examples 2, 3, 4 and 5. In the Kĩkamba translation, *amathilīkĩla*, whose infinitive root form is *kūthilīka*, is in the immediate past. This immediate past tense fits within the context since the Israelites had just provoked Moses to קצף. The Kĩkamba Bible has *mūno* "very" which is not in the BHS reference. An observation to note is that קצף is translated as *kūthilīka*. A second example in which קֶצֶף is translated as *kūthilīka* is as follows:

- 1 Sam 29:4 וַיִּקְצְפוּ עָלָיו שָׂרֵי פְלִשְׁתִּים and the chiefs of Philistines were angry against him

    Ĩndĩ a.nene me   mbee ũsumbĩnĩ ma Avilisiti ma.mũ.thilīka.īla[16]
    Now they.big were head kingdom.in of Philistine they.him.angry. PERF
    "Now the heads of the kingdom of the Philistines became angry against him"

The addition of the word *ũsumbĩnĩ* "in kingdom" is added to make clear to the Akamba readers that the Philistine chiefs were part of the Philistine kingdom. The BHS does not have a word for kingdom in the text. This is a translation tendency aimed at helping the reader understand the text with less mental processing. It is assumed, therefore, that the translation of קֶצֶף as *kūthilīka* is consciously chosen to communicate the intended meaning from the source language. The last example is from Isaiah 47:6.

---

15. This word occurs in the Kĩkamba Bible as *amathilīkĩla*. It is modified here for the purposes of the interlinear. The root is *thilīk*. The suffix *īla* is a perfect marker and the a identifies the immediate past. It therefore means that God has been angry with them in the immediate past. This description is true of the third example below.

16. The word in the Kĩkamba interlinear translation is *mamũthilīkĩla*.

- Isa 47:6 קָצַ֥פְתִּי עַל־עַמִּ֖י I was angry against my people

Nī.na.thilīka.īle[17]	andū	makwa
Against.I.angry.PERF	people	of me

"I became angry against my people"

The Kīkamba word of קָצַף *nīnathilīkīle* fits within the remote past tense. The context in this verse is a reference to the life of bondage that the Israelites suffered after they angered God. Since the BHS perfect, קָצַ֥פְתִּי "I was angry," does not communicate the past tense of the action, the context is the cardinal guide to determine when this action occurred. The setting guides the understanding that it happened many years ago, therefore, the translation of קָצַ֥פְתִּי as *nīnathilīkīle*, in the remote past tense, is proper. The same translation technique applied in determining which past tense in which to place קָצַ֥פְתִּי is also used in the translation of קָצַף as *kūthilīka*.

In the three examples given above, the Kīkamba word translated in the place of קצף is *kūthilīka*. Other passages where *kūthilīka* and its cognates are used are in Genesis 40:2; 41:10; Numbers 16:22; 31:14; Deuteronomy 1:34; 9:19; Esther 1:12; 2:21; Isaiah 54:9; 57:16–17; 64:5, 9; Jeremiah 37:15; Lamentations 5:22 and Zechariah 8:14. Other than *kūthilīka*, קצף is also translated as *kūthata* as explained in the following section.

5.4.1.2 Kūthata

- Lev 10:6 וְעַ֥ל כָּל־הָעֵדָ֖ה יִקְצֹ֑ף and he will be angry against all the congregation

Na	kana	nda.ka.thata.i.e[18]	ūmbano	wʼonthe
That	Neg(sg).angry.PERF.FV		gathering	all

"He will not be angry against the whole gathering"

The context of this verse is the advice given by Moses to Aaron and his remaining two sons against having unkempt hair and wearing torn clothes. The

---

17. This word occurs as *nīnathilīkīle* in the Kīkamba translation; it is modified in this example for the purposes of the interlinear. As discussed in chapter 4, and as it is recommended in chapter 6, Kīkamba is a tonal language but the current grammar lacks the tonal markings. As for the word *nīnathilīkīle*, the final vowel should be *ê* but it is not marked. This final vowel explains this is a remote past, as opposed to the a final vowel which marks immediate past.

18. This example has two verbs which occur in the Kīkamba translation as *mūikakwʼe* and *ndakathatīe*, respectively.

advice is that if they kept unkempt hair and wore torn clothes, God would be קָצַף against the whole gathering of the Israelites. In the Kīkamba translation, יִקְצֹף is negated as *ndakathatīe* "he does not get angry" although it is not negated in the BHS. The negation of this verb is coherent with the preceding phrase in which the advice is negated: do not have unkempt hair and do not wear torn clothes. Therefore, the negation of יִקְצֹף in the Kīkamba translation is a necessary adjustment to limit the chances of misreading the phrase. The verb *ndakathatīe* is in the immediate future tense, which is supported by the context since it implies that as soon as Aaron and his sons disobeyed, then God would be angry with them. This carefulness also necessitated translation of יִקְצֹף as *kūthata*, which is a different lexical item from *kūthilīka* as used in the examples given in the preceding section. Another passage where קָצַף is translated as *kūthata* is Joshua 22:18.

- Josh 22:18 אֶל־כָּל־עֲדַת יִשְׂרָאֵל יִקְצֹף he will be angry with all the congregation of Israel

    Aka.thata.ī.a[19]   Ibano   wʼonthe   wa   Isilaeli
    He.angry.FUT.FV   gathering   all   of   Israel
    "He will be angry against all the gathering of Israel"

In this passage Joshua is warning the tribes of Reuben, Gad and the half tribe of Manasseh against apostasy. If they turn to other gods, then God will be קָצַף "angry" with them immediately – implied by the use of "if they rebel today tomorrow God would have קצף 'angry' with them." Just as in example 4 above, *akathatīa* is in the immediate future tense and its root is "*that*," the translation that is given for קָצַף. The rest of the Kīkamba traIion *ūmbano wʼonthe wa Isilaeli* "all the gathering of Israel" is a direct translation of כָּל־עֲדַת יִשְׂרָאֵל, capturing the construct form of כָּל־ "all of" which in KīkaIs translated as *wʼonthe wa*. With this attention to details, קָצַף is translated as *kūthata*. The last example to be considered is in 2 Kings 13:19.

---

19. In the Kīkamba translation, this verb appears as *akathatīa*.

- 2 Kgs 13:19 וַיִּקְצֹף עָלָיו אִישׁ הָאֱלֹהִים and the man of God was angry with him

Na	ũ	mũndũ	wa	Ngai	amũ.thata.i.a[20]
And	he	person	of	God	him.angry.PERF.FV

    "And the man (person) of God became angry against him"

This passage is about Elisha being angry against Joash, the king of Israel, because he did not hit the ground with the arrows many times (at least five or six times) as Elisha had hoped. One of the features in Kĩkamba translations that will become apparent later in this chapter is that, הָאֱלֹהִים is translated as *Ngai* – as in the 2 Kings 13:19 – while יְהוָה is translated as *Yeova*. The different examples show consistency in this translation which is unlike קָצַף which is as *kũthata* in 2 Kings 13:19.

In all the three examples given above, the Kĩkamba translation for קָצַף is *kũthata* and its cognates. Other verses in the Kĩkamba translation where קָצַף is translated as *kũthata* are Leviticus 10:16; Deuteronomy 9:7–8, 22; 2 Kings 5:11; Psalm 106:32; and Ecclesiastes 5:6.

Thus far, the data considered explains that *kũthilĩka* and *kũthata* are Kĩkamba translations for קָצַף. The third and the last Kĩkamba translation for קָצַף is *kwĩw'a*[21] *woo* "to feel anger." Unlike *kũthilĩka* and *kũthata*, *woo* is always accompanied by *kwĩw'a* "to feel" and in its verbal form it occurs only twice as a translation for קָצַף.

5.4.1.3 Kwĩw'a woo

- Zech 1:2 קָצַף יְהוָה עַל־אֲבוֹתֵיכֶם קָצֶף the Lord was very angry against your forefathers

Yeova	nĩwew'ĩthiw'e[22]	woo	nĩ	aa.ĩthe	menyu
YHWH	he.was.made.feel.PERF.FV	anger (pain)	by	many.father	yours

    "God was made to feel anger (pain) by your fathers"

The verb *nĩwew'ĩthiw'e* "he was made to feel" is in the remote past tense. Since Zechariah is referring to an event that took place years back, translating this

---

20. In the Kĩkamba translation, this verb appears as *amathatĩa*.
21. The word *kwĩw'a* is a contraction of *kũĩw'a* which means "to feel."
22. In the Kĩkamba translation, this verb appears as *nĩwew'ĩthiw'e*.

verb in the remote past tense is fitting. The ordinary translation of forefathers is *aaũmae* "grandfathers," but the translation given above is *aaĩthe* "fathers" which is a direct translation of אֲבוֹתֵיכֶם "your fathers." It is also important to note that יְהוָה is translated as *Yeova* and not *Ngai*. These two examples show a careful attention to the context and also the vocabulary used. It is the same attention given to the translation of קָצַף as *kwĩw'a woo*. The second example is in Zechariah 1:15.

- Zech 1:15: אֲנִי קָצַפְתִּי מְּעָט וְהֵמָּה עָזְרוּ לְרָעָה I was angered a little and they helped quicken[23] their affliction

  Ne.e.w'ĩ.ĩthĩw'e   woo   o vanini, na ma.kalaata[24] *thĩna   wũke*
  I.PRG.FOC.feel anger just.little and they.hurry suffering to.come
  I was made angry, just a little and (by so doing) they hurried suffering to come

This passage concerns the nations that had enslaved the Israelites. The verb *neewĩthĩw'e* "I was continuously made to feel" is a continuous remote past tense, signifying the amount of time that had lapsed between the writing of this prophecy and the time when the slavery took place. The BHS verb עָזְרוּ "they helped" is omitted in the Kĩkamba translation and replaced with *makalaata* "they hurried." In the English translation, the supply of "quicken" makes "they helped" redundant. Having the same verbs together in the Kĩkamba translation would equally be unnecessary repetition. Instead, the addition of *wũke* "to come" complements *makalaata* "they hurried" in that, these nations have hurried suffering to come their way. These grammatical adjustments in the Kĩkamba translation make it natural and sensible. However, this verse has *kwĩw'a woo* as a translation for קָצַף.

The examples given above demonstrate that the Kĩkamba Bible translates the קצף lexical item as *kũthilĩka* and its cognates, *kũthata* and its cognates, and *kwĩw'a woo*. There is no identifiable pattern that demonstrates the reason the translators chose different lexical items in the receptor language to represent one lexical item in the source language. What is clear, however, is

---

23. This verse is discussed three times in this section. Each time it is referenced, a different item is in focus and it would be confusing to discuss all the elements in focus within a single reference.

24. In the Kĩkamba translation, these verbs appear as *neew'ĩthĩw'e* and *makalaata*, respectively.

the translators' effort to accommodate different words that carry the meaning of anger in their translation. Since the available literature reveals no research done to date on the Akamba folk theory of *ngoò*, it is assumed that a lack of prior research on the subject made the translation process harder.

While section 5.4.1 has considered the translation of the קָצַף verbal form in the Kĩkamba Bible, the following section analyzes the translation of קֶצֶף noun forms in the Kĩkamba Bible.

5.4.2 The Translation of קֶצֶף Noun Forms in the Kĩkamba Bible

The same words, *kũthilĩka* and its cognates, *kũthata* and its cognates, and *kwĩw'a woo*, that are translated in the קָצַף verbal forms are also used in the קֶצֶף noun forms. The examples given below illustrate this. As is done with the קָצַף verbal forms, the following section gives three examples and others with the same translation are mentioned without discussion. However, in the sections where it is not possible to allocate examples from each of the aforementioned categories, it is stated so in that particular section.

5.4.2.1 Ũthilĩku

The first word considered in this section for a translation for קֶצֶף is *ũthilĩku*. The following examples demonstrate this.

- Num 17:11[16:46] כִּי־יָצָא הַקֶּצֶף מִלִּפְנֵי יְהוָה Because anger has come out from the face (presence) of the Lord.[25]

Nũndũ	ũthilĩku	nĩw.umĩ.ete	kwa	Yeova
Because	anger	it.come.PRG	from	God

  "Because anger is coming from God"

The Kĩkamba translation takes מִלִּפְנֵי יְהוָה "from the face of God" as a synecdoche of a part representing the whole. Therefore, it rightfully says anger came from God. The context of this verse is about the rebellion of the Israelites against Moses and Aaron. In this verse, קֶצֶף is translated as *ũthilĩku*. The next example is from 2 Chronicles 32:26.

---

25. This verse is referenced and discussed twice in this chapter because the focus is different each time it is referenced. Discussing all the elements in one reference would result in a lack of coherence in the argument.

- 2 Chr 32:26 וְלֹא־בָא עֲלֵיהֶם קֶצֶף יְהוָה בִּימֵי יְחִזְקִיָּהוּ and the anger of the Lord did not come out on them in the days of Hezekiah.

    Kwondũ wa ũu   ũthilĩku wa Yeova   nd.wa.a.mo.ũka.ĩ.a
    mĩthenya ya Esekia
    Because of that   anger of God   not.it.CONT.them.come.PTSd.FV
    days of Hezekiah

    "Because of that (Hezekiah's humility), the anger of the God did not come on them in the days of Hezekiah"

The context of this verse is about Hezekiah who repented of his pride; hence God's קֶצֶף did not come upon the Israelites. The Kĩkamba translation has every single word in the BHS translated. Just as in the 9th reference, קֶצֶף is translated as *ũthilĩku*.

- Isa 54:8 בְּשֶׁצֶף קֶצֶף הִסְתַּרְתִּי פָנַי רֶגַע מִמֵּךְ In great anger I hid my face from you for a moment or very angrily I hid my face from you for a moment

    Yila kũthilika   kũ.usua,i.e   nĩ.na.kũ.vith.a.ie   ũthyũ
    wa.kwa   kavinda kanini
    When anger   to.fill.PERF.FV I.do.to.hide.PERF.FV face   of.me
    time   little

    "When the anger was filled I hid my face for a short time"

The Kĩkamba translation of this verse implies that a unique challenge was encountered in the translation process. First, the verb בְּשֶׁצֶף "in flood" which is figurative language, meaning "in great," is translated in Kĩkamba as *kusũa* "to be full" which does not capture the entire sense of a flood. Perhaps this is due to the lack of a word for flood in Kĩkamba. Ũkamba land is mainly semiarid and hardly gets any floods. Second, the noun קֶצֶף is translated as a verb *kũthilika* "to be angry" and not a noun. This is clearly an effort to offer a natural translation in the receptor language while at the same time remaining faithful to the source language. The Kĩkamba word *kũthilika* is a verbal form for *ũthilĩku*, which is translated here for קֶצֶף. Other passages where קֶצֶף is translated as *ũthilĩku* are Numbers 1:53; 18:5; 1 Chronicles 27:24; 2 Chronicles 19:2, 10; 24:18; 29:8; 32:25–26; Esther 1:18; Psalm 38:1; Psalm102:10; Ecclesiastes 5:17; Isaiah 54:8; Jeremiah 10:10; 50:13; and Zechariah 7:12.

5.4.2.2 Ūthatu

Other than *ūthilīku*, the other word translated for קֶצֶף is *ūthatu*. The examples given below illustrate this.

- Josh 22:20 וְעַל־כָּל־עֲדַת יִשְׂרָאֵל הָיָה קָצֶף and on all the congregation of Israel the anger came?

    Na ūthatu wa yeova Ialūka.ī.la   ūmbano   wònthe
    wa Isilaeli?
    And anger of God   it.fall.PERF. `   congregation   all
    of Israel
    "And the anger of God fell on all the congregation of Israel"

This verse, in the BHS, does not have the name for God, which is supplied in the Kīkamba translation *Yeova*. According to the context, it is clear that the Ego of קֶצֶף is God. Since, so far, the Kīkamba translation is using two names for God: *Yeova* and *Ngai*, it is of importance to determine what led to the choosing of *Yeova* and not *Ngai* in this verse. The influence here is assumed to be verse 19 that uses *Yeova* for God.

This verse also presents a unique translation of הָיָה which is translated as *wavalūka* "fell," meaning God's קֶצֶף fell on the Israelites. The Kīkamba translation is in harmony with the earlier discussion that since the קצף frame has a vertical relationship, then translating the verb הָיָה "fall" is appropriate. In other passages as is explained later in this chapter, הָיָה is translated as *wooka* "came," meaning God's קֶצֶף came on the landmark. These two words: "to fall on" and "to come on," do not necessarily have the same sense. In addition, the sense of falling is associated with קֶצֶף in the BHS but is not used with *ngóó*. This notwithstanding, the inclusion of *Yeova* depicts the effort put in to give a translation that was less ambiguous – not to leave the readers guessing who the Ego of קֶצֶף is. The translation of הָיָה as *wavalūka* is presumably aimed at highlighting the penalty that accompanied God's קֶצֶף, in that, it was so fatal it did not just come on them but fell on them. Factoring in this careful interpretation and translation process, קֶצֶף is translated as *ūthatu*. The next example is from 2 Kings 3:27.

- 2 Kgs 3:27 וַיְהִי קֶצֶף־גָּדוֹל עַל־יִשְׂרָאֵל and great anger came on Israel
    Na kwaī ūthatu mūnene iūlū wa Isilaeli
    And there was anger great on top of the Israel

"And there was great anger on Israel"

In this verse, קֶצֶף is accompanied by the adjective גָּדוֹל "great" to mean great anger. This phrase קֶצֶף־גָּדוֹל is translated as *ūthatu mūnene* "great anger" which is a faithful translation of the phrase in the BHS, although *ūthatu mwingĩ* "much anger" is more natural in Kĩkamba. It is understandable that translators were faced with a myriad of challenges and they had to make a decision – in this case it was to give a direct translation. This decision meant קֶצֶף is translated as *ūthatu*. The third example is from Isaiah 60:10.

- Isa 60:10 כִּי בְקִצְפִּי הִכִּיתִיךָ Because in anger I struck you

Nũndũ	nĩ.nakũ.kũna.i.e	nĩ	mũthatu
Because	I.you.struck.PERF.FV	from	anger

    "Because I struck you in anger"

This verse is a reference to the exile experience the Israelites had as a result of God's קֶצֶף. The Kĩkamba translation captures the simultaneous occurrence of striking and anger, that is, God struck them while angry. In this verse, קֶצֶף is translated as *ūthatu*. Other passages where קֶצֶף is translated as *ūthatu* are Joshua 9:20; 22:20; 2 Kings 3:27; Psalm 102:10; Isaiah 34:2; 60:10; Jeremiah 21:5; and Jeremiah 32:37. In addition to *ūthilĩku* and *ūthatu*, the other Kĩkamba word translated for קֶצֶף is *woo*.

5.4.2.3 Woo

Unlike *ūthilĩku* and *ūthatu*, *woo* is used only three times as a translation for קֶצֶף. The three references are cited and analyzed below. It first occurs in Deuteronomy 29:27[28]. The verse number in the brackets represents the verse number in the English translations while the other one represents the verse number in the BHS.

- Deut 29:27[28] וַיִּתְּשֵׁם יְהוָה מֵעַל אַדְמָתָם בְּאַף וּבְחֵמָה וּבְקֶצֶף גָּדוֹל וַיַּשְׁלִכֵם אֶל־אֶרֶץ אַחֶרֶת כַּיּוֹם הַזֶּה׃ And the Lord uprooted them from their land in anger (reddening of face), in anger (internal irritation), and בְקֶצֶף

"in great anger" (abstract object), and cast them out into another land, until this day

Na Yeova a.ma.kũa   nthĩ   yoo   e na ũthatu, na ũthilĩku, na woo mwingĩ,
And God he.them.chase   land   their   with anger and anger and pain(anger) much

Na   a.me.kya   nthĩ   ĩngĩ, o ũndũ   kũilyĩ   ũmũnthĩ.
and   he.them.throw   land   another just   it is   today

"and the Lord uprooted them out of their land in reddening of face, in internal irritation and great anger and he threw them to another land just as it is today"

This verse has three different words: אף, חמה and קצף, which carry the meaning of anger. These words are taken in this research to be used for emphasis since they are hendiatris. The Kĩkamba translation does not factor in the use of emphasis, but instead translates אף, חמה and קצף individually, that is, *ũthatu, na ũthilĩku, na woo mwingĩ*. Notice, the two words – *ũthatu* and *ũthilĩku* – that are used for קצף in the examples given above are now used for אף and חמה.[26] Maintaining the three words is a decision of remaining faithful to the source text. The same faithfulness is evident in the way the symbolic language of uprooting and casting – which is a plant metaphor – is still maintained in the Kĩkamba translation. This decision of remaining faithful to the source text must have been at play when considering *woo* as a translation for קֶצֶף. A similar set of the above words with a corresponding translation in the Kĩkamba Bible is in Jeremiah 21:5.

- Jer 21:5 וְנִלְחַמְתִּי אֲנִי אִתְּכֶם בְּיָד נְטוּיָה וּבִזְרוֹעַ חֲזָקָה וּבְאַף וּבְחֵמָה וּבְקֶצֶף גָּדוֹל: And I myself will fight against you with an outstretched

---

26. This is not the only reference where *ũthatu* and *ũthilĩku* are translations for אף and חמה. In fact, both *ũthatu* and *ũthilĩku* are used interchangeably mainly in anger contexts regardless of the word in the BHS used.

hand and mighty arm, in of anger (reddening of face), in of anger (internal irritation), and in of great קֶצֶף anger (abstract object).

Nakwa mweene ngo.kita nenyu na kw'oko kū.tambūūku na kw'oko kwī

Me myself will.fight with.you with hand being.outstretched and hand that

vinya, nī na ūthatu, na ūthilīku, na woo mwingī

is strong with anger, and anger, and pain (anger) much

"I, myself, will fight against you with outstretched hand, a hand that is strong, in reddening of face, in internal irritation and in great anger"

Just as in Deuteronomy 29:28, this verse has three different words – אַף, חמה and קצף – which occur in that sequence and refer to anger. Just as in the preceding verse, these three are translated in Kīkamba as *ūthatu, na ūthilīku, na woo mwingī*, respectively. Apart from the translation of these words, the interlinear translation provides a direct translation of the BHS into the Kīkamba translation, a sign of remaining faithful to the source text. In this verse, just as in the preceding one, the translation for קֶצֶף is *woo*. The last example in which קֶצֶף is translated as *woo* is Zechariah 1:15.

- Zech 1:15a וְקֶצֶף גָּדוֹל אֲנִי קֹצֵף עַל־הַגּוֹיִם I was greatly angry against the nations.

Na nī.ngw.īw'īth.wa woo mūno nī mbaī ila ithūmūīte.

And I am.to.feel.PASS pain (anger) very by tribe those resting.

"I am made angry by the resting tribes"

In this verse קֶצֶף is translated as *woo*.

All the examples in section 5.4.2 show that the Kīkamba Bible uses three different lexical items for the קֶצֶף noun forms. A similar pattern is observed in the קצף verbal forms. The examples given also show a deliberate effort to remain faithful to the source text while translating in the Kīkamba way. The examples given also show consistency in patterns that were clear. For example, first, there is consistency in the way *ūthatu, ūthilīku* and *woo* are translated for אַף, חמה and קצף respectively. Second, there is consistency in the translation of *Yeova* for יְהוָה and *Ngai* for אֱלֹהִים. The inconsistencies, therefore, of translating קצף into three different words imply that it was an unclear concept. Further evidence that this concept wasn't clear is explained in the way the קצף frame is partially imported into the Kĩkamba Bible.

5.4.3 The קצף Frame Is Partially Imported into the Kĩkamba Bible

Sections 5.4.1 and 5.4.2 have looked at how קצף as a lexical item has been translated in the Kĩkamba Bible. In this section, I examine how the קצף frame is treated in the Kĩkamba Bible. The data analyzed below explains that the קצף frame is partially imported in some passages in the Kĩkamba translation and that it is overlooked in other passages in favor of the *ngoò* frame. This swap of the two frames in the different passages analyzed further enhances the claim in this research that קצף and *ngoò* are close equivalents.

5.4.3.1 Partial Import of the קצף Frame

The way the קצף lexical units are translated in the Kĩkamba Bible show a partial import of the קצף frame. This import is seen when the קֶצֶף accompanying verbs and prepositions are considered. The קצף frame is featured by two sets of verbs: those showing the trajector's departure from Ego and those showing the trajectory. The trajector follows an abstract trajectory identified by the verb היה and rests on the landmark, identified by the על preposition. This frame is replicated in some passages in the Kĩkamba Bible – hence the partial import. The first examples given below show the departure of קֶצֶף from the Ego.

- Num 17:11[16:46] כִּי־יָצָא הַקֶּצֶף מִלִּפְנֵי יְהוָה Because anger has come out from the face (presence) of the Lord
  Nũndũ ũthĩlĩku nĩwumĩte kwa Yeova.
  Because anger it.come from Jehovah
  "Because anger has come from God"

The context of this verse is God's anger. The verb יָצָא which can be translated as come out, come forth, go out or go forth has the idea of exiting. Therefore, its use in this verse has the idea of קֶצֶף having already exited from God – Ego. This same idea is replicated in the Kĩkamba translation: *ũthĩlĩku nĩwumĩte kwa Yeova* "anger is coming from God." The other passage that illustrates קֶצֶף exiting from Ego is 2 Chronicles 32:26.

- 2 Chr 32:26 וְלֹא־בָא עֲלֵיהֶם קֶצֶף יְהוָה בִּימֵי יְחִזְקִיָּהוּ and the anger of the Lord did not come out on them in the days of Hezekiah.[27]
  kwondū wa ūu ūthilīku wa Yeova ndwa.a.mo.kīa
  Because of that anger of Jehovah did not.them.come
  "Because of that (the repentance of Hezekiah) the anger of God
      did not come on them"

In this passage, Hezekiah repented of his sins and God's קֶצֶף did not come on him. The use of the verb בָּא connotes "coming out" or "entering" depending on the perspective of the speaker as earlier discussed in chapter 3, section 3.1.1.1. The Kīkamba translation replicates this same idea in that *ūthilīku wa Yeova ndwaamokīa* "the anger of God did not come on them."

Examples 18 and 19 show how קֶצֶף was exiting from Ego. The following examples demonstrate the קֶצֶף trajectory, which is marked by the use of היה "to come/fall."

- 1 Chr 27:24 וַיְהִי בָזֹאת קֶצֶף עַל־יִשְׂרָאֵל in this (the numbering of Israelites) anger came/fell on all Israel.
  Na kwondū wa ūndū ūsu ūthilīku wa.mo.kīe Isilaeli
  And because of thing that anger. them.come to Israel
  "Because of that thing[28] the anger came on Israel"

The context of this verse is that of the census of the Israelites by David, through Joab son of Zeruiah. David ordered the counting against the instructions of God, but the counting was not completed. As a result of this unauthorized counting, God's קֶצֶף came/fell on them. The Kīkamba word translation for the verb היה and the preposition עַל is *wamokīe* "it came to them." The *ngoò* frame does not have this trajectory of היה "come." Therefore, this is an import of the קצף frame. This import is supported by examples 11–19 in section 3.1.1.1 of chapter 3 which identify anger as the trajector that comes on the landmark. There is no indication in chapter 4 in the discussion of the Akamba folk theory of anger that explains that anger has an identified trajectory. Another example that supports the import of the קצף frame is 2 Chronicles 19:10.

---

27. This verse has different elements in focus, and is referenced and discussed twice in this chapter.

28. The context is the numbering of the Israelites by Joab, son of Zeruiah. God was against the numbering of the Israelites and that is why he was angry when it was done.

- 2 Chr 19:10 וְהָיָה־קֶצֶף עֲלֵיכֶם וְעַל־אֲחֵיכֶם and anger came/fell on you and on your brothers

  Na kwondũ wa ũu ũthilĩku wĩ.mũ.kĩa   ĩnyw'ĩ
  And because of that anger it.you.will come   you
  Because of that (sin), anger will come on you.

This passage is about the warning that Jehoshaphat gave the Levites and the priests concerning their ministry. He admonished them to warn the Israelites against sinning against God so that God's קֶצֶף does not come on them – both the Levites and priests, and the Israelites. The verb היה is translated, as *wĩmũkĩe* "will come on you." This is yet another example of import of the קצף frame. The last example given is from Zechariah 7:12.

- Zech 7:12 וַיְהִי קֶצֶף גָּדוֹל מֵאֵת יְהוָה צְבָאוֹת and great anger came/fell from the Lord of hosts.

  Nĩkwaumie   ũthilĩku   mũnene   kwa Yeova wa nguthu.
  There.came   anger   great   from Jehovah of hosts
  "Great anger came from the Lord of hosts"

The context of this passage is that of rebellion against God. God through Zechariah had warned the Israelites against the injustices characterized by failure to show mercy and compassion to one another; oppressing the poor, fatherless or foreigners and scheming evil against each other (vv. 8–10). As a result, God's קֶצֶף came/fell on them. The *waw*-consecutive form of היה is translated as *nĩkwaumie* "there came." It is interesting to note that, in this verse, the Kĩkamba translation forsakes the Kĩkamba word order: subject-verb-object, and adopts the BHS's word order: Verb-subject-object. The Kĩkamba interlinear given confirms this adaption. It is not just the word order that is adopted, but also the קצף frame where the trajectory of קֶצֶף is identified by the use of the היה verb and the same is translated in the Kĩkamba Bible.

Other passages where verb היה – identifying the trajectory of קֶצֶף – is used in the BHS and adopted in the Kĩkamba Bible are Numbers 16:46[27:11]; Joshua 22:20; 1 Chronicles 27:24; 2 Chronicles 19:10; 24:18; 32:26. Other than the היה verb, the other lexical item, which explains an import of קצף frame, is the Kĩkamba translation of the preposition עַל.

5.4.3.2 The Preposition עַל

The use of the preposition עַל identifies the landmark – patient – of קֶצֶף. The following examples illustrate how the preposition עַל is adopted in the Kīkamba translation as part of the קצף frame. The first example given is from Numbers 1:53.

- Num 1:53 וְהַלְוִיִּם יַחֲנוּ סָבִיב לְמִשְׁכַּן הָעֵדֻת וְלֹא־יִהְיֶה קֶצֶף עַל־עֲדַת בְּנֵי יִשְׂרָאֵל and the Levites shall pitch around the tabernacle of testimony that anger will not come/fall on the congregation of the children of Israel.

    Indī Alivai makambae maeema moo mathyūlūlūkīte   wīkalo
    ǿ Levites them.pitch tents thiers them.sorounding dwelling
        wa   ūkūsī,
        of   testimony
    nī kana vai.ke.thīwe ūthilīku īūlū wa ūmbano wa ana ma Isilaeli.
    so that not.be.found anger on top of gathering of sons of Israel
    "And the Levites should be pitching their tents surrounding the dwelling of testimony so that there may not be anger on the gathering of the sons of Israel"

The phrase in the BHS which says וְלֹא־יִהְיֶה קֶצֶף עַל־עֲדַת בְּנֵי יִשְׂרָאֵל which is literally translated as "not be anger on the congregation of the sons of Israel," is translated literally the same way in the Kīkamba Bible with the exact word order. It says, *vaikethīwe ūthilīku īūlū wa ūmbano wa ana ma Isilaeli*. The idea of קֶצֶף coming on the congregation of Israel is maintained, thereby adopting *īulu* "on" for עַל. The second example is taken from 2 Chronicles 19:2.

- 2 Chr 19:2 וּבָזֹאת קֶצֶף עָלֶיךָ מִלִּפְנֵי יְהוָה and by this anger from God is on you.
    Nūndū wa ūndū ūū ūthiliku wī īūlū waku kuma kwa Yeova
    "Because of thing this anger is on top of you from Jehovah."

In the English translation of the BHS, the phrase מִלִּפְנֵי יְהוָה "from the face of God" is understood as a metonymy of the part for the whole meaning "from God." This same understanding is replicated in the Kīkamba translation in which the word "face" is omitted. The phrase וּבָזֹאת קֶצֶף עָלֶיךָ "by this anger is on you" is translated in that exact form: *nūndū wa ūndū ūū ūthiliku wī* iūlū waku, which in turn is the adoption of קצף frame. The final illustrative example given is from 2 Chronicles 29:8.

- 2 Chr 29:8 וַיְהִי קֶצֶף יְהוָה עַל־יְהוּדָה וִירוּשָׁלָם and God's anger came/fell on Judah and Jerusalem
  kwondū wa ūu ūthilīku wa Yeova waī iūlū wa Yuta na Yerusaleme
  "because of that anger of Jehovah was on top of Judah and Jerusalem"

The context of this passage is about Hezekiah warning the Levites and the priests against sinning. He reminded them how God's קֶצֶף came/fell on Judah and Jerusalem when they sinned against God. The עַל preposition "on" is translated as iūlū "on," meaning that God's קֶצֶף came/fell on Judah and Jerusalem. The mention of Judah and Jerusalem are metaphors meaning the divided kingdom – southern and northern kingdoms, respectively. Other passages where the preposition עַל is used in the BHS and adopted in the Kīkamba translation are on Numbers 1:53; 18:5; Joshua 9:20; 2 Kings 3:27; 2 Chronicles 19:2; and 2 Chronicles 29:8; 32:25.

Section 5.4.3.2 has explained how the קצף frame has been imported in some passages in the Kīkamba translation. The following section explains other passages where elements that imply a conscious awareness of the *ngóò* frame are used instead of the elements of the קצף frame. These occurrences, as explained below, highlight how the קצף frame is partially adopted in the Kīkamba translation.

5.4.3.3 Use of the Ngoò Frame Instead of the קצף Frame

The purpose of this section is to demonstrate the way the Kīkamba translation used elements that are associated with the *ngóò* frame. In so doing, the translators avoided importing the elements of the קצף frame. The first example is from Ecclesiastes 5:16[17] in which the preposition *e na* "with" is supplied since it does not match any Hebrew word.

- Eccl 5:16[17]: גַּם כָּל־יָמָיו בַּחֹשֶׁךְ יֹאכֵל וְכָעַס הַרְבֵּה וְחָלְיוֹ וָקָצֶף
  All his days also he eats in darkness, and will have much sorrow, sickness and anger/frustration.
  O na mīthenya yake yonthe aīaa kīvindunī, na nūthīnaw'a mūno, na e na ūwau na ūthilīku

Even days his all eats darkness.in, and he.sorrow. PASS a lot and
  with sickness and anger
"He eats in darkness in all his days and he is made more
  sorrowful in sickness and anger"

The word "with" has to be supplied in this verse for it to make grammatical sense. In the Kĩkamba translation, the word *e na* "she/he has" is supplied. This word is commonly used with *ngóó* and carries the sense of ownership – that is to say, the owner of *ngóó*. See examples 48, 50 and 51 in Section 4.4.3 of chapter 4.

Here is an example where a verb has to be supplied and the chosen one is that which is in tandem with the *ngóó* frame and not קצף frame as explained in immediate example above. Another example that has a need for the supply of the verb *e na* "with" is in Isaiah 34:2.

- Isa 34:2 כִּי קֶצֶף לַיהוָה עַל־כָּל־הַגּוֹיִם because the anger of the Lord is on all the nations
  nũndũ Yeova e na ũthatu kwa mbaĩ syonthe
  Because Jehovah has anger to tribes all
  "Because the Lord is angry against all the nations"

This phrase has no verb, which has to be supplied. The Kĩkamba translation supplies *e na* "he has" which functions as a "to be" verb, and which complements the *ngóó* frame.

The following section gives examples from verses that have the preposition בְּ and shows that the preposition was translated in a manner to reflect the *ngóó* frame. The first example is from Deuteronomy 29: 27[28].

- Deut 29:27[28] וַיִּתְּשֵׁם יְהוָה מֵעַל אַדְמָתָם בְּאַף וּבְחֵמָה וּבְקֶצֶף גָּדוֹל וַיַּשְׁלִכֵם אֶל־אֶרֶץ אַחֶרֶת כַּיּוֹם הַזֶּה: And the Lord rooted them out of their land in anger (reddening of face), in anger (internal irritation), and בְּקֶצֶף "in great anger" (abstract object), and cast them out into another land, until this day

  Na   Yeova amakua   nthĩ yoo   e na ũthatu, na ũthilĩku, na
  And Jehovah he.them.root land theirs with anger, and anger, and
       woo
       pain

mwingĩ, na amekya nthĩ ĩngĩ, o ũndũ kũilyĩ ũmũnthĩ.
Much and he.them.throw land other just as it is today
"And God uprooted them from their land in great anger and threw them to another land just as it is today"

This verse has three BHS words that refer to anger: וּבְקֶצֶף, וּבְחֵמָה and וּבְאַף, and all of them have the בְּ preposition. This preposition is translated as *e na* in the Kĩkamba Bible.

- Jer 21:5 וְנִלְחַמְתִּי אֲנִי אִתְּכֶם בְּיָד נְטוּיָה וּבִזְרוֹעַ חֲזָקָה וּבְאַף וּבְחֵמָה וּבְקֶצֶף גָּדוֹל: And I myself will fight against you with an outstretched hand and mighty arm, in of anger (reddening of face), in of anger (internal irritation), and in of great קֶצֶף anger (abstract object).

Nakwa mweene ngokita nenyu na kw'oko
I personally will.fight with you with hand
kũtambũũku na kw'oko kwi
outstretched and hand with

vinya, nĩ na ũthatu, na ũthilĩku, na woo mwingĩ
strength with anger and anger and anger much
"I will personally fight you with an outstretched strong arm with great anger"

In this verse, the three words that refer to various components of anger, וּבְאַף, וּבְחֵמָה and וּבְקֶצֶף, have the preposition בְּ fixed to the verbs. The equivalent of the preposition בְּ in Kĩkamba verbs is *nĩ* as explained in these verbs: *ũthatunĩ, na ũthilikunĩ, na woonĩ mwingĩ*. This is unlike examples 26 and 28 above where the three verbs occur in the same order. In example 26, the preposition בְּ is captured by the use of *e na* "he.having" while in example 28, it is captured by the use of *ni na* "I.with." The *e na* "she/he has" and *ni na* "I.have"[29] both represent the *ngoò* frame as explained in chapter 4 section 4.4.1. Both verbs also have an idea of Ego owning something. They are rightfully used although the use of *nĩ* suffix to represent the preposition בְּ is the natural way of putting it in Kĩkamba. Some of the other passages where

---

29. The *e na* "he.with" and *ni na* "I.with" can also mean "he.has" and "I.have," respectively.

the preposition בְּ is represented by *nī* suffix in the Kīkamba Bible are given below. For illustrative purposes, only two examples are given.

- Psalm 38:1 יְהוָה אַל־בְּקֶצְפְּךָ תוֹכִיחֵנִי O Lord, do not rebuke me in your anger.

  Ndŭ.kangan'ye   ūthilīku.nī   waku
  Do not.rebuke   anger.in   yours
  "Do not rebuke me in your anger"

The verb בְּקֶצְפְּךָ "in your anger" is translated as *ūthilīku.nī waku* "anger in yours – in your anger." It is noted that the preposition בְּ is used as a suffix in the Kīkamba translation. The second example that explains the suffixing of the preposition בְּ is in Jeremiah 32:37.

- Jer 32:37 הִדַּחְתִּים שָׁם בְּאַפִּי וּבַחֲמָתִי וּבְקֶצֶף גָּדוֹל I was caused to banish them in my anger (reddening of face), in my anger (internal irritation) and in great anger (abstract object).

  Vala namalŭngīlīilye ūthatu.nī wakwa, na   kuthilīka.nī kwakwa,
  when I.them.banished anger.in   mine,   and anger.in   mine
          na woonī   wakwa   mwīngī
          and anger.in   mine   a lot
  "When in my great anger I banished them."

The word *wakwa* "of me" is repeated three times in example 31 given above. When used with the words that refer to anger, it means "in my anger" and has the same idea as *nī na* "I.have anger." Therefore, the use of *wakwa* "of me" complements the use of *e na* "she/he.has" in the *ngoò* frame.

This category has explained that the Kīkamba translation adopted the *ngoò* frame instead of the קצף frame. Comparing this category and the section on the import of the קצף frame, this research demonstrates an overlap of the two in the passages where קצף occurs. This scenario, therefore, supports the argument of this research that some facets of the קצף frame are overlooked in the Kīkamba translation. While the examples in 30 and 31 have explained the idea of *e na* in the Kīkamba translations, the following example shows the use of *īwa* "feel" in contexts of anger. As mentioned in chapter 4 and at the beginning of this chapter, *īwa* "feel" is associated with good emotions – *ngóó* is one of them – among the Akamba but קֶצֶף is not used with the verbs of "feel."

- Zech 1:15a וְקֶצֶף גָּדוֹל אֲנִי קֹצֵף עַל־הַגּוֹיִם I am greatly angry against the nations.

Na	nĩngwĩw'ĩthwa	woo	mũno	nĩ	mbaĩ	ila
And	I.being made.to feel.PASS	anger	very	by	tribes	that
	ithũmũĩte.					
	are.resting					

"And I am made very angry by the tribes which are feeling secure (resting)"

The only verb in this phrase is the active qal participle קֹצֵף which is replaced with the *nĩngwĩw'ĩthwa* "I am made to feel" in the Kĩkamba translation. The Kĩkamba translation is not only a replacement of the different verb, it is also a change in the voice of the verb from a participle to an indicative in the passive voice meaning, "I am made to feel *woo* angry." The use of *ĩw'a* "feel" in anger contexts in Kĩkamba is very common and the same applies for *ngoò*: *nĩ ĩw'a ngoò* "I feel angry – I am angry." This is an example where the verb's form and its voice in the BHS are changed to accommodate the natural way of expression in the receptor's language.

The data analyzed so far, some passages adopting the קֶצֶף frame and others adopting the use of the *ngoò* frame, explain a conscious effort to remain faithful to the source text and also an effort to present a dynamic natural translation in the receptor language. It is the belief of the author of this research that if a research on the comparative study of the emotion of anger in the BHS and the folk theory of anger among the Akamba existed at the time of the Kĩkamba translation, the discrepancies noted would not have occurred or, if the translators had a good knowledge of Hebrew and applied it consistently in translation, the differences would have been avoided.

As a way of further demonstrating that the effort to accommodate as many words referring to anger is at play in the Kĩkamba translation, the following section explains an additional Kĩkamba word, *woo*, that is used in the Kĩkamba Bible although not in the translation of קֶצֶף. It is also explained that there is no consistency in its representation of the BHS lexical item under consideration, and a similar observation is made concerning the קֶצֶף translation.

5.5 Extra Words for Anger in Kĩkamba

The purpose of this section is to highlight all the anger words that are used in the Kĩkamba Bible, demonstrate the inconsistencies in the Kĩkamba translation and show that the translators were conscious of the different words that could be accommodated in different contexts as used in the BHS. This conscious effort validates the value of the Akamba folk theory of anger and explains the importance of this study. Three references are given below for illustrative purposes, which have the phrase מָרַת נֶפֶשׁ "bitterness of soul" – which is an idiom for anger in the BHS.

The first reference is in Judges 18:25. This verse reads, "The Danites answered, don't argue with us, or some of the men may get angry and attack you, and you and your family will lose your lives" (NIV). The phrase translated as "men may get angry" is אֲנָשִׁים מָרֵי נֶפֶשׁ which literally means, "men of bitterness of soul." This phrase is translated in the Kĩkamba Bible as simply *ũthatu* "anger."

The second reference considered here is 1 Samuel 1:10. It reads: "In her deep anguish Hannah prayed to the LORD, weeping bitterly." The phrase translated as "in her deep anguish" is וְהִיא מָרַת נֶפֶשׁ which is literally translated as "and she in bitterness of soul." In Kĩkamba, it is written as *ũũ mũnene an goo* "great bitterness of the heart."

The third reference is from 2 Samuel 17:8: "you know your father and his men; they are fighters, and are as fierce as a wild bear robbed of her cubs. Besides, your father is an experienced fighter, he will not spend the night with the troops." The phrase translated here as "are as fierce as a wild bear" is וּמָרֵי נֶפֶשׁ הֵמָּה כְּדֹב, which is literally translated as "they are bitter ones of soul as bear." In Kĩkamba, it is written as *mena woo ililikanoni syoo* "they have anger in their minds."

These three references show that the idiom מָרֵי נֶפֶשׁ "bitterness of soul" is translated in the Kĩkamba Bible into three different anger words *ũthatu*, *ũũ* and *woo*, respectively. While *ũthatu* and *woo* have already been mentioned in the earlier references, *ũũ* is the fourth Kĩkamba word with a sense of anger to be used in the Kĩkamba Bible. This clearly demonstrates the effort made to accommodate as many words in the receptor language as possible, that would be close equivalents to the source language. This effort is a hint that a study on the Akamba folk theory of anger is necessary for Akamba exegetes. In addition, this research adds value to the Kĩkamba exegetical process by demonstrating that *ngoò* and קֶצֶף are close equivalents. Therefore, the inclusion of *ngoò* in the future Kīkamba Bible revision should be considered.

Another observation made from the examples given above is יְהוָה, translated as *Yeova* while אֱלֹהִים is translated as *Ngai*. This is a deliberate move to accommodate Kīkamba lexical items, which are considered close equivalents to the matching BHS ones.

5.6 The Value of Cross-Cultural Study in Biblical Studies

Although the examples given so far in this chapter appear to show a translation oversight, they instead demonstrate a greater task of exegesis – translation work is an exegetical process. This research largely explains the need for cross-cultural studies in biblical studies. A translated Bible is one that is carrying a message imbedded in one culture and making it intelligible in another. A cross-cultural study, therefore, is helpful in that "1) It removes the basic barrier to communication, language. 2) It provides unrestricted access to God's message for the Christian community without dependence on the continual presence of a human communicator. 3) It can provide a contextualized message that is understood in the culture."[30] The third point, as highlighted by Robert Litteral, particularly underscores the need for a comparative cross-cultural study as elaborated in this research. The translation of *ngoò* for קֶצֶף is one way of providing a contextualized message that is understood by the community. The need for sensitivity in making the message relevant to the receptor is further emphasized by Charles Kraft who said, "the receiver has the final say over what the results will be. It thus behooves us to learn as much as we can about what is going on at the receptor's end when we attempt to communicate."[31] The proposed strategy of learning as much as possible concerning the receptor language is partly addressed by cross-cultural study.

---

30. Litteral, *Community Partnership*, 30.
31. Kraft, *Communication Theory*, 67.

CHAPTER 6

Conclusion and Recommendations

This chapter offers a conclusion of the findings and recommendations in this research. The conclusion has the thesis statement restated and gives a summary of each chapter. The recommendations double up as areas for further research.

6.1 Conclusion

This work is a research on the cross-cultural study of קֶצֶף "anger" in the BHS and *ngoò* "anger" in Kīkamba. The value for this research is detailed based on chapter 1. The main argument is as follows: A cross-cultural conceptual study of the emotion of קֶצֶף reveals how קֶצֶף was conceptualized in the ancient Hebrew culture, and its comparative study with the folk theory of the emotion of *ngoò* shows that concept of *ngoò* would have been the best rendering for the Hebrew concept קֶצֶף in the Kīkamba Bible. In advancing this argument, three goals are met: First, this research has explained the conceptualization of קֶצֶף in the ancient Hebrew culture. In particular, this research has demonstrated how קֶצֶף functions within the קֶצֶף frame which was explained in detail in chapter 3. This frame is supported by the use of קֶצֶף as subject accompanied by the verbs הָיָה, יָצָא and בּוֹא. Second, it has employed a cross-cultural study of קֶצֶף and *ngoò*, and demonstrated the variance in their conceptual facets, and third, it has demonstrated the value of cross-cultural study in biblical studies.

In chapter 1, the author highlighted the need for the study of emotions. In addition, he has exemplified the value for cross-cultural study of emotions. This chapter notes the gap in knowledge that is not sufficiently addressed by previous scholarship. Key attention is given to the use of cognitive linguistics theories, since the present data is analyzed through a combination of methods in the cognitive linguistics field. The reviewed theories are the prototypical anger and the conceptual metaphor theories. The noted gap is met by the use of the complementary approach of several theories, which are proposed in chapter 2.

Chapter 2 has the complementary approach of the three theories: frame semantics, the symbolic approach and Fessler's six-point logic. Frame semantics theory is an invention of Charles Fillmore, the symbolic approach was developed by Richard Shweder and Jonathan Haidt, and Fessler's six-point logic was developed by Daniel M. T. Fessler. The overview of these theories' development is helpful to both the researcher and reader in the data analysis which follows. In addition to the overview of the theories, the terminologies used in chapters 3, 4, 5 and 6 are defined in this chapter too.

Chapter 3 is an analysis of the BHS data. This chapter explained how קצף fits within a frame that is very different from the other BHS words that have anger senses. Of importance is taking note of how קצף changes meaning with the change of stem. Also, the meaning of קצף changes depending on whether the emotion is projected against an object or not.

Chapter 4 is an analysis of the Kīkamba data. The data analyzed describes the Akamba folk theory of anger with a focus on *ngoò* since it is the closest equivalent to קצף. This lexical item, *ngoò*, is not used in the Kīkamba Bible. These findings do not fault the translators. Rather, these findings affirm the need for a cross-cultural study of concepts. In addition, the findings in this chapter are helpful for consideration during the future revision of the Kīkamba Bible.

Chapter 5 is the analysis of the differences and the similarities of the קצף and *ngoò* frames, and how the *ngoò* frame complements the קצף frame in exegesis. This chapter has ascertained the use of different words in Kīkamba for קצף, with no clear noticeable pattern. The assumption is that the translators did not use the BHS text – considering the Kīkamba is over one hundred years old – for consistency in the choice of the correct lexical item. However, the different words used demonstrate the translators' attempt to accommodate the Kīkamba words that were possible equivalents to the BHS text.

In summary, the findings have established that the קצף is a close equivalent of *ngoò* in Kīkamba and that the *ngoò* relationship-retribution frame complements the קצף frame in Scripture. The Kīkamba data demonstrate that the lexical item, *ngoò*, is not in the Kĩkamba Bible. In light of the findings analyzed in this research, a number of recommendations can be made.

6.2 Recommendations

The findings in this research necessitate five recommendations: more cross-cultural study of Scripture, consistency in the Kĩkamba translation, improvement of the Kĩkamba orthography, development of the lexicography and development of Kĩkamba learning materials using frame semantics theory.

6.2.1 Cross-Cultural Study of Scripture

The findings of this research are the product of a cross-cultural approach to the study of Scripture. This approach is also known as cross-cultural dialogue. Since cultures are different, it should not be assumed that the meaning of a particular lexical item is universal and therefore should be imported into the receptor language. Although some facets may be similar, not every single component of the concept is the same and, hence, the need for cross-cultural study.

6.2.2 Consistency in the Kĩkamba Translation

The examination of the קצף translation in chapter 5 demonstrates inconsistencies in two areas. First, there are inconsistencies in the adoption of the קצף frame. Second, there are difficulties in choosing a Kĩkamba lexical item that is close to קצף. Concerning the קצף frame, the analyzed data also explains that the *ngoò* frame complements the קצף frame. This research recommends either total adoption of the קצף frame or a total shift to the *ngoò* frame, but not a mixture of both.

The data discussed in the earlier chapters also show inconsistencies in the translation of the specific Kĩkamba lexical item that was considered a close equivalent to קצף. This research has explained that *ngoò* which is the closest equivalent of קצף is not used in the Kĩkamba Bible. In light of these findings, this research recommends the inclusion of *ngoò* in the future revision of the Kĩkamba Bible.

6.2.3 Improvement of Kĩkamba Orthography

While Kĩkamba has a developed orthography, the *ngoò* analysis has explained that Kĩkamba is a tonal and unmarked language. The difference between *ngoò* and *ngoo* is that of intonation. There are more examples (20 to 23) in section 4.2 of chapter 4 that illustrate how tonal marking differentiate meaning of words that have the same letters. This research proposes inclusion of tonal markings.

6.2.4 Development of Kĩkamba Lexicography

The benefits of a lexicon developed from frame semantics perspective is addressed in chapter 2 and demonstrate deficiencies of the existing lexicons. The development of a Kĩkamba lexicon would be an invaluable reference for Bible scholars, pastors and the general public, which should aid in understanding Scripture better.

Bibliography

Alexander, Joseph A. *Commentary on the Prophecies of Isaiah*. Grand Rapids: Zondervan, 1978.

Allen, Leslie C. *Jeremiah: A Commentary*. 1st ed. Old Testament Library. Louisville: Westminster John Knox Press, 2008.

Ap-Thomas, D. R. *A Primer of Old Testament Text Criticism*. 2nd ed. Facet Books Biblical Series 14. Philadelphia: Fortress, 1965.

Arnold, Bill T., and John H. Choi. *A Guide to Biblical Hebrew Syntax*. Cambridge: Cambridge University Press, 2003.

Atkins, Beryl T. "Analysing the Verbs of Seeing a Frame Semantics Approach to Corpus Lexicography." In *Proceedings of the Twentieth Meeting of the Berkelely Linguistics Society*, edited by Johnson Chris, 42–56. Berkeley: Berkeley Linguistics Society, 1994.

———. "The Role of the Example in a Frame Semantics Dictionary." In *Essays in Semantics and Pragmatics: In Honor of Charles J. Fillmore*, edited by Masayoshi Shibatani and Sandra A. Thompson, 25–42. Pragmatics & Beyond 32. Amsterdam: J. Benjamins, 1995.

Atkins, Beryl T., and Charles J. Fillmore. "Starting Where the Dictionaries Stop: The Challenges of Corpus Lexicography." In *Computational Approaches to the Lexicon*, edited by Antonio Zampolli, 349–98. Oxford: Oxford University Press, 1994.

Baldwin, Joyce G. Haggai, Zechariah, Malachi: An Introduction and Commentary. London: Tyndale, 1972.

Batten, Loring W. A Critical and Exegetical Commentary on the Books of Ezra and Nehemiah. ICC. Edinburgh: T.&T. Clark, 1972.

Bergen, Robert D. *1, 2 Samuel*. NAC 7. Nashville: Broadman & Holman, 1996.

Bergman, Nava. *The Cambridge Biblical Hebrew Workbook: Introductory Level*. Cambridge: Cambridge University Press, 2005.

Berlin, Adele. *The Dynamics of Biblical Parallelism*. Indiana: Indiana University Press, 1985.

Berlyn, Patricia J. "The Wrath of Moab." *Jewish Bible Quarterly* 30, no. 4 (2002): 216–26.

Biblia Hebraica Stuttgartensia. Edited by K. Elliger and W. Rudolph. 5th ed. Stuttgart: Deutsche Bibelgesellschaft, 1997.

Bright, John. *Jeremiah*. AB 21. New York: Doubleday, 1981.

Brown, Francis, Samuel R. Driver, and Charles A. Briggs, eds. *The Brown-Driver-Briggs Hebrew and English Lexicon*. Reprinted from the 1906 edition. Oxford: Clarendon, 1996.

Brown, Lesley, ed. *The Shorter Oxford English Dictionary on Historical Principles*. Vol. 2. 2 vols. 3rd ed. Oxford: Clarendon Press, 1973.

Bullinger, Ethelbert William. *Figures of Speech Used in the Bible: Explained and Illustrated*. Grand Rapids: Baker Book House, 1968.

Calvin, John, and John Owen. *Commentaries on the Book of the Prophet Jeremiah and the Lamentations*. Vol. 1. 5 vols. Calvin's Commentaries. Grand Rapids: Wm. B. Eerdmans, 1948.

Cathy, Cogen, ed. "An Alternative to Checklist Theories of Meaning." *Essays in Semantics and Pragmatics: In Honor of Charles J. Fillmore*. Berkeley: Berkeley Linguistics Society, 1975.

Charles, Bridges. *An Exposition of the Book of Ecclesiastes*. Geneva Series Commentary 6. London: The Banner of Truth Trust, 1960.

Chisholm, Robert B. *From Exegesis to Exposition: A Practical Guide to Using Biblical Hebrew*. Grand Rapids: Baker Books, 1998.

Clifford, Richard J. *Proverbs: A Commentary*. 1st ed. Old Testament Library. Louisville: Westminster John Knox, 1999.

Clines, David J. A., ed. "אַף (אנף)." *The Dictionary of Classical Hebrew*. Sheffield: Sheffield Academic, 1993.

———, ed. "אֲשֶׁר." *The Dictionary of Classical Hebrew*. Sheffield: Sheffield Academic, 1993.

———, ed. "בוֹא." *The Dictionary of Classical Hebrew*. Sheffield: Sheffield Academic, 1996.

———, ed. "זור." *The Dictionary of Classical Hebrew*. Sheffield: Sheffield Academic, 1996.

———, ed. "זעם." *The Dictionary of Classical Hebrew*. Sheffield: Sheffield Academic, 1996.

———, ed. "זעף." *The Dictionary of Classical Hebrew*. Sheffield: Sheffield Academic, 1996.

———, ed. "חמה." *The Dictionary of Classical Hebrew*. Sheffield: Sheffield Academic, 1996.

———, ed. "חרה." *The Dictionary of Classical Hebrew*. Sheffield: Sheffield Academic, 1996.

———, ed. "יצא." *The Dictionary of Classical Hebrew*. Sheffield: Sheffield Academic, 1998.

———, ed. "כעס." *The Dictionary of Classical Hebrew*. Sheffield: Sheffield Academic, 1998.

———, ed. "מלא." *The Dictionary of Classical Hebrew*. Sheffield: Sheffield Academic, 2001.

———, ed. "מן." *The Dictionary of Classical Hebrew*. Sheffield: Sheffield Academic, 2001.

———, ed. "עבר." *The Dictionary of Classical Hebrew*. Sheffield: Sheffield Academic, 2007.

———, ed. "עִם." *The Dictionary of Classical Hebrew*. Sheffield: Sheffield Academic, 2007.

———, ed. "קנא." *The Dictionary of Classical Hebrew*. Sheffield: Sheffield Academic, 1993.

———, ed. "קצף." *The Dictionary of Classical Hebrew*. Sheffield: Sheffield Academic, 1993.

———, ed. "רגז." *The Dictionary of Classical Hebrew*. Sheffield: Sheffield Academic, 1993.

———, ed. "רוח." *The Dictionary of Classical Hebrew*. Sheffield: Sheffield Academic, 1993.

Cogan, Mordechai, and Hayim Tadmor. *1 Kings: A New Translation*. 1st ed. AB 11. New York: Doubleday, 1988.

Cohen, Harold R. *Biblical Hapax Legomena in the Light of Akkadian and Ugaritic*. Edited by Howard C. Kee and Douglas A. Knight. Society of Biblical Literature Dissertation Series 37. Montana: Scholars, 1978.

Cohn, Robert L. *2 Kings*. Edited by David W. Cotter, Jerome T. Walsh, and Chris Franke. Berit Olam. Minnesota: Liturgical, 2000.

Cole, R. Dennis. *Numbers*. NAC 3B. Nashville: Broadman & Holman, 2000.

Collins, Terence. "The Physiology of Tears in the Old Testament." *Catholic Biblical Quarterly* 33 (1970): 185–97.

Conrad, Edgar W. *Zechariah*. New Biblical Commentary. Sheffield: Sheffield Academic Press, 1999.

Conti, Marco and Thomas C. Oden, eds. *1–2 Kings, 1–2 Chronicles, Ezra, Nehemiah, Esther*. Ancient Christian Commentary on Scripture: Old Testament, 5. Downers Grove: InterVarsity, 2008.

Croft, William, and D. A. Cruse. *Cognitive Linguistics*. Cambridge Textbooks in Linguistics. Cambridge: Cambridge University Press, 2004.

Curtis, Edward L., and Albert Alonzo Madsen. *A Critical and Exegetical Commentary on the Book of Chronicles*. ICC. Edinburgh: T&T Clark, 1910.

Daviau, P. M. Michèle, and Margreet Steiner. "A Moabite Sanctuary at Khirbat Al-Mudayna." *Bulletin of the American Schools of Oriental Research* 320 (2000): 1–21.

Davies, Gordon F. *Ezra and Nehemiah*. Edited by Jerome T. Walsh, David W. Cotter, and Chris Franke. Berit Olam. Collegeville: Liturgical, 1999.

Day, Linda M. *Esther*. Abingdon Old Testament Commentaries. Nashville: Abingdon, 2005.

Durham, John I. *Exodus*. WBC 3. Waco: Word Books, 1987.

Farrar, F. W. *The Expositor's Bible: The Second Book of Kings*. London: Hodder & Stoughton, 1894.

Fessler, Daniel M. T. "Toward an Understanding of the Universality of Second Order Emotions." In *Biocultural Approaches to the Emotions*, edited by Alexander Laban Hinton, 75–116. Cambridge: Cambridge University Press, 1999.

Fillmore, Charles J. "An Alternative to Checklist Theories of Meaning." *Proceedings of the Annual Meeting of the Berkeley Linguistics Society*. Berkeley: Berkeley Linguistics Society, 1975.

———. "Frame Semantics." In *Linguistics in the Morning Calm: Selected Papers from the SICOL-1981*, edited by Linguistic Society of Korea, 111–38. Seoul: Hanshin, 1981.

———. "Frame Semantics and the Nature of Language." In *Annals of the New York Academy of Sciences*, 20–32. New York: New York Academy of Sciences., 1976.

———. "Scenes-and-Frames Semantics." In *Linguistic Structures Processing*, edited by Antonio Zampolli, 55–81. Fundamental Studies in Computer Science, 5. Amsterdam: North-Holland, 1977.

———. "The Case for Case." In *Linguistic Universals*, edited by R. Harms and E. Bach, 1–88. New York: Holt Rinehart and Winston, 1968.

Fillmore, Charles J., and Beryl T. Atkins. "Towards a Frame-Based Organization of the Lexicon: The Semantics of Risk and Its Neighbors." In *Frames, Fields, and Contrasts: New Essays in Semantic and Lexical Organization*, edited by Adrienne Lehrer and Eva Feder Kittay, 75–102. Hillsdale: Lawrence Erlbaum, 1992.

Fillmore, Charles J., and Collin F. Baker. "A Frames Approach to Semantic Analysis." In *The Oxford Handbook of Linguistics Analysis*, edited by Bernd Heine and Heiko Narrog, 313–39. Oxford: Oxford University Press, 2010.

Fox, Nili Sacher. "Clapping Hands as a Gesture of Anguish and Anger in Mesopotamia and in Israel." *Journal of Ancient Near Eastern Society* 23 (1995): 49–60.

Fretheim, Terence E. "Yahweh." In *New International Dictionary of Old Testament Theology & Exegesis*, edited by Willem VanGemeren, 1295–300. Vol. 4. 5 vols. Grand Rapids: Zondervan, 1997.

Fuller, Robert C. "Spirituality in the Flesh: The Role of Discrete Emotions in Religious Life." *Journal of the American Academy of Religion* 75, no.1 (2007): 25–51.
Garrett, Duane A. *Hosea, Joel*. NAC. 19A. Nashville.: Broadman & Holman, 1997.
Gesenius, Wilhelm. *Gesenius' Hebrew Grammar*. Edited by E. Kautzsch and A. E. Cowley. 2nd ed. Oxford: Clarendon, 1910.
Gibson, John C. L. *Davidson's Introductory Hebrew Grammar: Syntax*. 4th ed. Edinburgh: T&T Clark, 1994.
Gray, George Buchanan. *A Critical and Exegetical Commentary on Numbers*. International Critical Commentary. Edinburgh: T&T Clark, 1976.
———. A Critical and Exegetical Commentary on the Book of Isaiah. Vol. 1. 3 vols. ICC. Edinburgh: T&T Clark, 1912.
Guthrie, Malcolm. *The Classification of the Bantu Languages*. London: Dawsons of Pall Mall, 1967.
Hanks, Patrick, ed. *Collins Dictionary of the English Language*. London: Collins, 1984.
Hawk, Lewis Daniel. *Joshua*. Berit Olam. Minnesota: Liturgical, 2000.
Hayes, John H., and Stuart A. Irvine. *Isaiah, the Eighth Century Prophet: His Times & His Preaching*. Nashville: Abingdon, 1987.
Howard, David M. *Joshua*. NAC 5. Nashville: Broadman & Holman, 1998.
Irwin, Nato, and Tim Meadowcroft. *The Book of Daniel*. Asia Bible Commentary Series. Singapore: Asia Theological Association, 2004.
Johnson, Gordon H. "מששׁ." In *New International Dictionary of Old Testament Theology and Exegesis,* edited by Willem A. VanGemeren, 1145–1147. Vol. 2. 5 vols. Michigan: Zondervan, 1997.
Johnstone, William. *1 and 2 Chronicles*. Journal for the Study of the Old Testament Supplement Series 253 & 254. Sheffield: Sheffield Academic Press, 1997.
Joüon, Paul S. J., and Takamitsu Muraoka. *A Grammar of Biblical Hebrew*. Subsidia Biblica 27. Rome: Pontifical Biblical Institute, 2006.
Kieti, Mwikali, and Peter Coughlin. Barking, You'll Be Eaten!: The Wisdom of Kamba Oral Literature. Nairobi: Phoenix, 1990.
Kintsch, Walter. *Comprehension: A Paradigm for Cognition*. Cambridge: Cambridge University Press, 1998.
Köhler, Ludwig, and Walter Baumgartner. *The Hebrew and Aramaic Lexicon of the Old Testament*. 2 Volumes. Study Edition. Leiden: Brill, 2002.
Koole, Jan L. *Isaiah III*. Vol. 2. 2 vols. Historical Commentary of the Old Testament. Leuven: Peeters, 1998.
Koptak, Paul E. *Proverbs: From Biblical Text . . . to Contemporary Life*. New International Version Application Commentary. Grand Rapids: Zondervan Grand Rapids, 2003.

Koteskey, Ronald L. "Toward the Development of a Christian Psychology: Emotion." *Journal of Psychology and Theology* 8, no. 4 (1980): 303–13.

Kotzé, Zacharias. "A Cognitive Linguistic Methodology for the Study of Metaphor in the Hebrew Bible." *Journal of Northwest Semitic Languages* 31, no. 1 (2005): 107–17.

———. "The Conceptualisation of Anger in the Hebrew Bible." PhD diss., University of Stellenbosch, 2004.

———. "Humoral Theory as Motivation for Anger Metaphors in the Hebrew Bible." *South African Linguistics and Applied Language Studies* 23, no. 2 (2005): 205–9.

Kövecses, Zoltán. "Anger: Its Language, Conceptualization, and Physiology in the Light of Cross-Cultural Evidence." In *Language and the Cognitive Construal of the World*, edited by John R. Taylor and Robert E. MacLaury, 181–196. Trends in Linguistics 82. Berlin: Walter de Gruyter, 1995.

Kövecses, Zoltán. "The Concept of Anger: Universal or Culture Specific?" *Publication of Medline* (2000): 159–70.

Kraft, Charles H. *Communication Theory for Christian Witness*. Rev. ed. New York: Orbis Books, 1991.

Kruger, Paul A. "A Cognitive Interpretation of the Emotion of Anger in the Hebrew Bible." *Journal of Northwest Semitic Languages* 26, no. 1 (2000): 181–93.

Laney, J. Carl. *Zechariah*. Everyman's Bible Commentary. Chicago: Moody, 1984.

Latvus, Kari. *God, Anger and Ideology: The Anger of God in Joshua and Judges in Relation to Deuteronomy and the Priestly Writings*. Journal for the Study of the Old Testament Supplement Series 279. Sheffield: Sheffield Academic Press, 1998.

Lee, Nancy C. The Singers of Lamentations: Cities Under Siege, from Ur to Jerusalem to Sarajevo. Bible Interpretation Series 60. Leiden: Brill, 2002.

Levenson, Jon Douglas. *Esther: A Commentary*. London: Westminster John Knox, 1997.

Levine, Baruch A. Numbers 1–20: A New Translation with Introduction and Commentary. 1st ed. AB 4. New York: Doubleday, 1993.

Litteral, Robert Lee. *Community Partnership in Communications for Ministry*. Illinois: Billy Graham Center, 1988.

Lutz, Catherine. Unnatural Emotions: Everyday Sentiments on a Micronesian Atoll & Their Challenge to Western Theory. Chicago: University of Chicago Press, 1988.

Mays, James Luther. *Hosea: A Commentary*. Old Testament Library. London: SCM, 1969.

Mbiti, John. *Akamba Stories*. Oxford: Oxford University Press, 1983.

Mbivilia. Nairobi: The Bible Society of Kenya, 1974.

McKane, William. *A Critical and Exegetical Commentary on Jeremiah*. Vol. I. 25 vols. ICC. Edinburgh: T&T Clark, 1986.

Merriam, Sharan B., ed. "Introduction to Qualitative Research." *Qualitative Research in Practice: Examples for Discussion and Analysis*. San Francisco: Jossey-Bass, 2002.

Merrill, Eugene H. *Deuteronomy*. NAC 4. Nashville: Broadman & Holman, 1994.

Mertens, Donna M. Research and Evaluation in Education and Psychology: Integrating Diversity with Quantitative, Qualitative, and Mixed Methods. 2nd ed. Thousand Oaks: Sage, 2005.

Meyers, Carol L., and Eric M. Meyers. *Haggai, Zechariah 1–8: A New Translation with Introduction and Commentary*. 1st ed. AB 25B. New York: Doubleday, 1987.

Minsky, Marvin. "A Framework for Representing Knowledge." In *The Psychology of Computer Vision*, edited by Patrick Henry Winston, 211–80. McGraw-Hill Computer Science. New York: McGraw-Hill, 1975.

Mojola, Aloo Osotsi. God Speaks in Our Own Languages: Bible Translation in East Africa, 1844–1998: A General Survey. Nairobi: Bible Society of Kenya, 1999.

Montgomery, James A. *A Critical and Exegetical Commentary: The Book of Kings*. Edited by Henry Snyder Gehman. ICC. Edinburgh: T&T Clark, 1967.

Murphy, Roland E. *Proverbs*. WBC. 22. Nashville: T. Nelson Publishers, 1998.

Mūtīsya, Roy M. *Kikamba Proverbs and Idioms*. Nairobi: Roma Publishers, 2002.

Mūtīsya, Roy M. and Simon Ndūnda. *Kīkamba-English Dictionary*. Nairobi: Roma, 2003.

Paton, Lewis Bayles. A Critical and Exegetical Commentary on the Book of Esther. ICC. Edinburgh: T&T Clark, 1976.

Perry, T. Anthony. *Dialogues with Kohelet: The Book of Ecclesiastes: Translation and Commentary*. Pennslyvania: Pennsylvania State University Press, 1993.

Petruck, Miriam R. L. "Frame Semantics." In *The Handbook of Pragmatics*, edited by Jef Verschueren, Jan-Ola Östman, and Jan Blommaert, 1–13. Amsterdam: J. Benjamins, 1996.

———. "Frame Semantics and the Lexicon: Nouns and Verbs in the Body Frame." In *Essays in Semantics and Pragmatics: In Honor of Charles J. Fillmore*, edited by Masayoshi Shibatani and Sandra A. Thompson, 279–300. Pragmatics & Beyond 32. Amsterdam: J. Benjamins, 1995.

Procter, Paul, ed. *Cambridge International Dictionary of English*. Cambridge: Cambridge University Press, 1995.

Reiterer, F. V. Salzburg. "קצף." In *Theological Dictionary of the Old Testament*, edited by G. Johannes Botterweck, Helmer Ringgren, and Heinz-Josef Fabry. Vol. 13. 13 vols. Grand Rapids: Eerdmans, 2004.

Renkema, Johan. *Lamentations*. Historical Commentary of the Old Testament. Leuven: Peeters, 1998.

Rogland, Max. "'Striking a Hand' (TQ' KP) in Biblical Hebrew." *Vetus Testamentum* 51, no. 1 (2001): 107–9.

Rooker, Mark F. *Leviticus*. NAC 3A. Nashville: Broadman & Holman, 2000.

Ross, Allen P. *Introducing Biblical Hebrew*. Michigan: Baker Academic, 2001.

Schlimm, Matthew Richard. "From Fratricide to Forgiveness: The Ethics of Anger in Genesis." PhD diss., Duke University, 2008.

Segal, Eliezer. "Human Anger and Divine Intervention in Esther." *Prooftexts* 9, no. 3 (1989): 247–56.

Seow, Choon-Leong. *A Grammar for Biblical Hebrew*. Nashville: Abingdon, 1995.

Shimasaki, Katsuomi. Focus Structure in Biblical Hebrew: A Study of Word Order and Information Structure. Bethesda: CDL, 2002.

Shweder, Richard A., and Jonathan Haidt. "Cultural Psychology of Emotions: Ancient and New." In *Why Do Men Barbecue?: Recipes for Cultural Psychology*, edited by Richard A. Shweder, 133–67. Harvard: Harvard University Press, 2003.

Smelik, Klaas A. D. "The Literary Structure of King Mesha's Inscription." *Journal for the Study of the Old Testament* 15, no. 46 (1990): 21–30.

Smith, Ralph L. *Micah–Malachi*. WBC 32. Waco: Word Books, 1984.

Stuart, Douglas K. *Hosea–Jonah*. WBC 31. Waco: Word Books, 1987.

Struthers, Gale B. "קצף." In *The New International Dictionary of Old Testament Theology and Exegesis*, 962–63. Vol. 2. 5 vols. Grand Rapids: Zondervan, 1996.

Taylor, John R. *Cognitive Grammar*. Oxford: Oxford University Press, 2002.

———. Linguistic Categorization: Prototypes in Linguistic Theory. London: Oxford University Press, 1989.

Taylor, John R., and Robert E. MacLaury. "Language and the Cognitive Construal of the World." In *The Oxford Handbook of Cognitive Linguistics*, edited by Dirk Geeraerts and Hubert Cuyckens, 51–79. Oxford: Oxford University Press, 2010.

Van der Merwe, Christo H. J., Jackie A. Naudé, and Jan H. Kroeze. *A Biblical Hebrew Reference Grammar*. Edited by Stanley E. Porter and Richard S. Hess. Sheffield: Sheffield Academic, 1999.

Vorwahl, Heinrich. *Die Gebärdensprache im Alten Testament*. Berlin: Emil Ebering, 1932.

Waltke, Bruce K., and Michael Patrick O'Connor. *An Introduction to Biblical Hebrew Syntax*. 9th ed. Winona Lake: Eisenbrauns, 1990.

Wanjohi, Douglas Waruta. "Scripture Translations in Kenya." University of Nairobi, 1975. http://uonlibrary.uonbi.ac.ke/content/scripture-translations-kenya (accessed on 29 July 2016).

Wardlaw, Terrance Randall. Conceptualizing Words for "God" within the Pentateuch: A Cognitive-Semantic Investigation in Literary Context. Library of Hebrew Bible/Old Testament Studies 495. Edinburgh: T&T Clark, 2008.

Wendland, Ernst R. *Analyzing the Psalms: With Exercises for Bible Students and Translators*. 2nd ed. Dallas: Summer Institute of Linguistics, 2002.
Westermann, Claus. *Genesis 37–50*. Translated by John J. Scullion. Minneapolis: Augsburg, 1986.
Whorf, Benjamin Lee. Language, Thought, and Reality: Selected Writings of Benjamin Lee Whorf. Edited by John B. Carroll. New York: MIT, 1956.
Wierzbicka, Anna. "Everyday Conceptions of Emotion: A Semantic Perspective." In *Everyday Conceptions of Emotion: An Introduction to the Psychology, Anthropology, and Linguistics of Emotion*, edited by James A. Russell, José-Miguel Fernández-Dols, Antony S. R. Manstead, and J. C. Wellenkamp, 17–47. North Atlantic Treaty Organization-Advanced Studies Institute 81. Dordrecht: Kluwer Academic, 1995.
Wierzbicka, Anna, and Jean Harkins. "Introduction." In *Emotions in Crosslinguistic Perspective*, edited by Jean Harkins and Anna Wierzbicka, 1–35. Berlin: Walter de Gruyter, 2001.
Wildberger, Hans. *Isaiah 1–12*. Translated by Thomas H. Trapp. Continental Commentary. Minneapolis: Fortress Press, 1991.
Wiseman, Donald J. *1 and 2 Kings: An Introduction and Commentary*. Tyndale Old Testament Commentary 9. England: Inter-Varsity, 1994.
Woolf, Henry Bosley, and Noah Webster. *Webster's New Collegiate Dictionary*. 2nd ed. Springfield, MA: G&C Merriam, 1977.
Young, Edward J. *The Book of Isaiah*. Edited by K. R. Harrison. Michigan: Eerdmans, 1972.

Langham Literature, with its publishing work, is a ministry of Langham Partnership.

Langham Partnership is a global fellowship working in pursuit of the vision God entrusted to its founder John Stott –

> *to facilitate the growth of the church in maturity and Christ-likeness through raising the standards of biblical preaching and teaching.*

Our vision is to see churches in the Majority World equipped for mission and growing to maturity in Christ through the ministry of pastors and leaders who believe, teach and live by the word of God.

Our mission is to strengthen the ministry of the word of God through:
- nurturing national movements for biblical preaching
- fostering the creation and distribution of evangelical literature
- enhancing evangelical theological education

especially in countries where churches are under-resourced.

Our ministry

Langham Preaching partners with national leaders to nurture indigenous biblical preaching movements for pastors and lay preachers all around the world. With the support of a team of trainers from many countries, a multi-level programme of seminars provides practical training, and is followed by a programme for training local facilitators. Local preachers' groups and national and regional networks ensure continuity and ongoing development, seeking to build vigorous movements committed to Bible exposition.

Langham Literature provides Majority World preachers, scholars and seminary libraries with evangelical books and electronic resources through publishing and distribution, grants and discounts. The programme also fosters the creation of indigenous evangelical books in many languages, through writer's grants, strengthening local evangelical publishing houses, and investment in major regional literature projects, such as one volume Bible commentaries like the *Africa Bible Commentary* and the *South Asia Bible Commentary*.

Langham Scholars provides financial support for evangelical doctoral students from the Majority World so that, when they return home, they may train pastors and other Christian leaders with sound, biblical and theological teaching. This programme equips those who equip others. Langham Scholars also works in partnership with Majority World seminaries in strengthening evangelical theological education. A growing number of Langham Scholars study in high quality doctoral programmes in the Majority World itself. As well as teaching the next generation of pastors, graduated Langham Scholars exercise significant influence through their writing and leadership.

To learn more about Langham Partnership and the work we do visit **langham.org**